These Are Our Horizons

NEW EDITION

By
Sister M. Perpetua, R.S.M., M.A.
Mary Synon, LL.D., and
Katherine Rankin

GINN AND COMPANY

BOSTON · NEW YORK · CHICAGO · ATLANTA
DALLAS · PALO ALTO · TORONTO · LONDON

Acknowledgments

Grateful acknowledgment is made to the following authors, publishers, and other holders of copyright for permission to use copyrighted materials.

Brandt & Brandt for "Walter Reed," from *A Book of Americans*, Rinehart & Company, Inc. Copyright © 1933 by Rosemary and Stephen Vincent Benét.

Dodd, Mead & Company for "Ten Miles High," from *With Wings as Eagles*, by William Rose Benét. Copyright © 1940 by Dodd, Mead & Company, Inc.

Doubleday & Company, Inc., for "Citizen of the World," from *Trees and Other Poems*, by Joyce Kilmer. Copyright 1914 by Aline Kilmer. Reprinted by permission of Doubleday & Co., Inc.

E. P. Dutton & Co., Inc., for "Heritage," from the book *I Sing the Pioneer* by Arthur Guiterman. Copyright, 1926, by E. P. Dutton & Co., Inc.; renewal, 1954, by Mrs. Vida Linda Guiterman. Reprinted by permission of the publishers.

Henry Holt and Company, Inc., for "The Runaway," from *New Hampshire*, by Robert Frost. Copyright, 1923, by Henry Holt and Company, Inc.; copyright, 1951, by Robert Frost. By permission of the publishers.

J. B. Lippincott Company for "To the Little House," from *Songs for a Little House*, by Christopher Morley. Copyright 1917, 1946, by Christopher Morley. Published by J. B. Lippincott Company.

The Macmillan Company for "On a Night of Snow," from *Night and the Cat*, by Elizabeth Coatsworth; "Gates," from *Selected Poems*, by Sister M. Madeleva, C.S.C.; The Macmillan Company, The Society of Authors, and Dr. John Masefield, O.M., for "West Wind," from *Collected Poems*, by John Masefield.

Random House, Inc., for "The Trail Breakers," from *Trappers and Traders of the Far West*, by James Daugherty. Copyright 1952 by James Daugherty.

Benziger Brothers for "The Lights of Worcester Town," by Rev. Michael Earls, S.J.

The Catholic World for "I Am America," by Richard J. Geehern.

Chicago Province of the Society of Jesus for "Boscobel," by Rev. James J. Daly, S.J.

Ginn and Company for "Saint of France," by Joseph Auslander.

Good Housekeeping for "The Legend of Befana," by Phyllis McGinley.

Herbert Jenkins Ltd., for "The Homecoming of the Sheep," from *The Complete Poems of Francis Ledwidge*.

Junior Red Cross Journal and Eric P. Kelly for the story, "Lead Not Forth, O Little Shepherd."

National Council of Catholic Men, the National Broadcasting Company, and the author for "North Atlantic Testament," by Timothy J. Mulvey, O.M.I., and to Mrs. Mary Washington for material used in the introduction to the selection.

Sheed and Ward, Inc., for "Weather," by Martha Elizabeth Ahrens from *Beginnings*, copyright 1956, Sheed and Ward, Inc., New York.

The Torch and the author for "My Dad and the Rosary," by Sister Louis Bertrand, O.P.

The University Press, Notre Dame, Indiana, for "Our Lady Passes," from *The Collected Poems of C. L. O'Donnell* (copyright 1942).

Dorothy Pryor Armel for "A Letter to Mary," by Louis and Laura Pryor.

Citizens Fidelity Bank and Trust Company, trustee of the estate of Cale Young Rice, for "The Mystic," by Cale Young Rice.

Mildred H. Crew for "Marda's Masterpiece," from *Saturday's Children*, by Helen Coale Crew.

Newman Levy for his poem "I Wonder What Became of Rand-McNally."

Rev. John G. McGee for "High Flight," by Flight Officer John Gillespie McGee, Jr.

Rev. Albert R. O'Hara and Rev. Gerard Sloyan, S.T.L., for material in "Letters Home."

Marion Plew Ruckel for "Abraham Lincoln," by Mildred Plew Merryman.

Richard Sullivan for his story, "Things Past," originally printed in *The Bengalese*, published by Holy Cross Missions.

Nancy Byrd Turner for her poem "Courage Has a Crimson Coat."

Burke Walsh for his article "The Vatican and the Nations."

Mary Fabyan Windeatt for her poem "Project."

The pictures in this book are by Merrill Bent, Cheslie D'Andrea, Bruce Howson, Will Huntington, Charles Kerins, C. A. Murphy, Dale Nichols, Walter Richards, Harve Stein, Earle Winslow, Cleveland Woodward.

Faith and Freedom

NIHIL OBSTAT: JAMES J. KORTENDICK, M.A., S.T.B., *Censor Deputatus*

IMPRIMATUR: ✝ PATRICK A. O'BOYLE, D.D., *Archbishop of Washington*
Washington, November 2, 1959

<table>
COMMISSION ON   THE CATHOLIC

AMERICAN   UNIVERSITY

CITIZENSHIP   OF AMERICA
</table>

Rt. Rev. Msgr. William J. McDonald, *President of the Commission*

Rt. Rev. Msgr. Joseph A. Gorham, *Director*

Mary Synon, LL.D., *Editorial Consultant*

Sister Mary Lenore, O.P., *Curriculum Consultant*

Published for The Catholic University of America Press

Washington, D. C.

Contents

1. Your Land and My Land

THIS is our land:
Here God's abundance follows springtime rain
and hillsides blossom with the planted grain;
here wheat fields turn from green to paling gold
and sheep come home at evening to the fold.
Here are our cities, built on burning plains,
built in the snows, and built beneath the rains,
built upon highlands and on desert sands,
built with the hopeful hearts and struggling hands
of many people. Here we can see God's majesty in all
His miracles, from dawn to evenfall,
and know His coming by His greeting sign,
as once upon the roads of Palestine.

These are our homes:
a mansion on a hill above the sea,
a houseboat rocking, rocking endlessly,
a penthouse looking down on city lamps,
a trailer wandering through crowded camps,
a spreading rancho on a mountain trail,
a tumbling hovel near the city jail;
some rich, some poor, but every one a place
where youth may learn, through God's all-loving grace,
the love of others. Here, in bright
sunlight and in shadows dim,
we come in lifted spirit close to Him
(Brother to all who suffer want and woe),
Who dwelt in Nazareth long years ago.

9

These are our neighbors:
the people in the houses on our square,
the men and women, boys and girls we meet
in friendliness that beams a greeting smile
as we pass one another on the street;
the postman, and the doctor, and the nurse,
the blind man whom we lead down to the store,
the woman in the house across the way,
who helps us often; and the man next door,
who burns his candles on the Feast of Lights
and treats my father like an older brother.
Neighbors and friends, we know that we should keep
the Word of God in loving one another.

This is our hope:
for people in the town we call our own,
for crowds who surge to work before the light
breaks on the street in dismal overtone,
for men who lift their planes up to the sky,
for girls who greet tomorrow with a song,
for those who nurse the sick when death is nigh,
for nameless ones who move in surging throng.
Some rich, some poor, some happily between
the two; we travel, brother linked with brother.
This is our hope: with Word of God as guide
let us remember we must "Love ye one another."

Not Always Blind

I. THE BANDAGE HOLDS

At the front of the Criminal Court Building stands a statue of Justice, a stone woman whose eyes are tightly bandaged and whose hand holds a wavering scale. It is, people say, a symbol of the fairness of justice. There are some, however, who declare that even the statue sometimes lifts the stone bandage and takes a look at what is going on before her.

One man who says this is Judge Jonathan Lacey of the Criminal Court. Judge Lacey insists that there was a day when the statue showed almost wild excitement. If you do not believe him, he tells you the story of his friend, Judge William Harrison, and Lanny Baker.

On a day almost at the end of the spring term of court—Judge Lacey says—Judge Harrison looked down from the bench at Lanny Baker, and Lanny Baker looked up at Judge Harrison; and over the railing between the judge's bench and the prisoner's table stretched a distance far wider than the architects of the courtroom had measured.

Even in the premature heat of an early June afternoon Judge Harrison looked cool, calm, serene, like the gentleman he was, conscious of the dignity of his position, aware of his obligations of office, a good judge and a good citizen.

Lanny Baker, wizened, shabby, and more than a little furtive, also looked what he was, a lawbreaker who had been caught in a mean dishonesty. In his eyes gleamed the terror of the trapped. His thin shoulders sagged under a worn coat. His weak mouth twisted as the assistant district attorney spoke to the judge.

"We want a continuance of this case, Your Honor," the attorney said. "Our principal witness, the victim of this man's dishonesty, is in the hospital. He can't appear for three weeks."

Judge Harrison looked at the calendar upon his desk. "Three weeks from today is the twenty-fifth of June," he said. "Court adjourns for the summer vacation on June twenty-first."

"Then the case will have to go over to the fall term of court," the assistant district attorney said placidly; but from his post in the big chair on the judicial bench the judge saw the trapped look in Lanny Baker's eyes deepen into desperation.

"Are you sure the witness cannot appear before the twenty-first?" the judge asked.

"Certain," said the attorney readily.

"Where's this man's counsel?" Judge Harrison asked.

"He had none of his own," the assistant said, "and so Webster was assigned to defend him; but Webster has another case in Judge Lacey's court today and couldn't come here."

"Is this man out on bail?" the judge inquired.

"No, Your Honor. He couldn't raise bail. Do you want to set trial for the first week in October?"

The judge ignored the question. He spoke directly to Lanny Baker. "How long have you been in jail?" he asked the prisoner.

"Five months," Baker said.

"In the county jail?"

"Yes, Your Honor."

"Why the delay?" the judge asked the lawyer.

"Crowded court calendar, Your Honor," he answered. "As you know, there aren't judges enough to hear these cases as they come along. Would October eighth be all right for the hearing?"

"That's four months away," said Judge Harrison. "He's been in jail five months already. That seems a long time to wait for trial."

The assistant district attorney shrugged his shoulders. "There's nothing we can do about it, Your Honor," he said.

"I suppose not," the judge said, a little wearily. Then, seeing again the tragic despair of Lanny Baker's gaze, he added: "But let's not decide this today. Let's take it up again on Friday morning."

"Yes, Your Honor," said the lawyer reluctantly. Into the prisoner's eyes flashed a gleam of hope, which vanished quickly when an officer stepped forward to lead him back to jail.

The routine of justice went on through the morning. The assistant district attorney asked for other continuances, all in cases where prisoners were out on bail. Defense attorneys sought continuances, too. The fall calendar of the court piled up like logs whirling downstream.

"I'll need a long vacation to meet this jam on my return," Judge Harrison told himself.

It was only while he lunched later at the City Club with old Judge Lacey that he remembered Lanny Baker.

"Going up to the island?" Judge Lacey asked.

"Of course," Judge Harrison replied. "Can you imagine my family wanting to go anywhere else?"

"Don't blame them," said the older man. "Lovely place, the island. No motorcars. No crowds. No jail. Peace. Quiet. Beauty."

"Why don't you visit us there, Jonathan?"

"No." The older judge shook his head. "I have promised myself to finish my book this summer."

"That will be pleasant, too."

"Yes, but not like the island. How long have you been going there, William?"

"All my lifetime. My grandfather built the log cabin, which is one of the wings now. My father enlarged the house. I've done nothing to it, but it manages to take care of Clem and Nancy and their friends, as well as of ours. I think that, all through the rest of the year, we look forward to going there in June."

"I begin to believe you took the judgeship, William, to be sure of the long vacation," Judge Lacey said.

"How about yourself and the book you're writing?"

They both laughed, but William Harrison was the first to grow serious. "There's another side to these long vacations, Jonathan," he said. "I had a case before me this morning which troubled me. A poor fellow has been five months in the county jail, awaiting trial. The district attorney's office came into court with a request for continuance because its principal witness is ill. If I grant the request, as I should do in justice, it will put off the trial until the fall term of court. That means the man must stay in jail four months longer—while I am up on the island."

"Pretty tough," said Judge Lacey. "We really need twice as many judges as we have for these hearings. No one ever catches up with the court calendar."

"I suppose not," Harrison said. "Have you ever gone through the jail, Jonathan?" he asked the older man.

"No," said Judge Lacey. His tone held a note of surprise. "Have you?"

"No," said Judge Harrison.

The thought of the difference between the county jail and the big log house on a northern island stayed with him as he walked back to the Criminal Court Building. How many prisoners, he wondered, were waiting in jail because of the lack of judges to hear their cases? Under what conditions were they being held? "I must get the evidence," he suddenly decided.

Through the hot afternoon, while flies buzzed between his bench and the dusty windows of the courtroom, Judge Harrison heard cases diligently, deciding each point with his usual quiet fairness, and apparently thinking only of the groups before him at the bar of justice. All through the hours, however, he kept seeing, intermittently, the misery in Lanny Baker's eyes as he had gone with the officer back to the jail. As soon as he had risen from the bench, the judge turned to the bailiff. "Isn't there a passageway from the court building to the county jail?" he asked him.

"Why, yes, Your Honor. There's a bridge—they call it the Bridge of Sighs—between this building and the jail. You don't want to go over there, Your Honor? I can bring over here anyone you want to see."

"I want to see the jail, Ferris. You can't very well bring that over here to me."

"No, Your Honor. Don't you want me to go with you?"

"No," said the judge. "I'm going alone."

"It'll be pretty hot over there at this time in the afternoon," the bailiff said.

"That's just what I've been thinking," said the judge.

II. The Bandage Moves a Little

It was hot, almost unbearably hot, in the corridors of the jail. Even above the odor of disinfectant arose rancid smells which, for a

14

moment, appalled Judge Harrison. Moans, shouts, and cries sounded on his ears.

"Is it always like this?" he asked the warden.

"Oh, no," the warden said. "We have silence most of the time. They have to let off steam, though,"— he waved toward the tiers of cells around and above them,—"once in a while. Want to see someone in particular, Judge?"

"No," said Judge Harrison. "No one in particular. I have been wondering, however, what this place is like in summer."

"Well, this is a rehearsal for it." The warden mopped his brow. "But this is nothing to what it will be in July and August. You see, we get the sun nearly all day on these unshaded windows. That would heat any building up over a hundred if the temperature outside went to ninety-five—and it does pretty often."

"And there's no relief possible?"

"What can anyone expect? Air-conditioning?"

"No," said the judge. The close sultriness of the place pressed down upon him until he gasped for breath. "This is, of course, a penal institution. Men who commit crimes against the law must be tried and punished for their offenses. Nevertheless—" he broke off sharply. "Is the place very crowded?"

"Too crowded," said the warden. "It'll be like this, or worse, all summer."

"Why?" the judge asked, although he felt that already he knew the answer.

"Court vacation," the warden said casually. "All of them here who can't get bail will have to wait for trial until the fall term of court. All who will be brought in will be waiting trial, too. It's always been that way," he hurried to add.

"Does it always have to be that way?" Judge Harrison asked.

"You know the answer to that better than I do, Judge," the other man said. "It's up to the committee of the judges of the criminal court to decide the length of summer vacations for the courts."

"Are you here all summer?"

"I certainly am," said the warden. "This is the worst season of the year for discipline. I wouldn't be farther than a mile away from this place during the summer."

Slowly they went from block to block of the many cells. Curious eyes, some of them hostile, others pleading, gazed out at them.

"Are they all waiting for trial?" the judge asked.

"Most of them. A few have been sentenced and are waiting to be transferred to the state prison."

"Have many of them been here long?"

"Four months, five months, six months."

"And if their trials are not held during the next few weeks, they'll be here four months, five months, six months longer?"

"That's it, Judge. Anything else you'd like to see?"

"Nothing," Judge Harrison said.

He came out into the city street with a deep sigh of relief. The late afternoon wind, hot though it was, seemed clean and fresh after the foul air of the jail. He felt miserably soiled, desperately in need of a bath and clean linen, after his brief visit to the institution so closely associated with his work. "And I was there less than thirty minutes," he told himself. "Thirty minutes," he said aloud, and he thought of the men waiting months for his return from the island.

At home, in the big apartment which looked out on the city whose streets were far from the island three hundred miles to the north, the judge hurried to bathe and change into cooler, cleaner clothes. He could not, however, rid himself of the thought of the jail quite as easily. All through dinner he spoke so seldom that his wife and Clem and Nancy watched him a little uneasily. As they rose with him to leave the room, he spoke in what Clem called his "bench voice," a tone which reminded them of his judicial position. "I want to talk to all of you," he said, and led them into the library.

"Can you speed it, Father?" Clem asked. "I'm secretary of the Confraternity meeting in the parish hall tonight. It begins at eight, and I don't want to be late."

"I won't keep you long," the judge said.

He sank down in his red-leather armchair, but did not light his usual cigar. He turned a paper-cutter

over and over as he spoke. "I have to make a decision which concerns all of you," he said slowly. "That is why I think that you should hear the evidence in the case."

"What is it, William?" his wife asked anxiously. "Are you ill?"

"No," he said. He smiled at the worry in her voice, but the smile faded as he went on. "I believe that I should not take a vacation this summer," he said. "If I were the only one affected by this belief, I would not bring you into helping me with the decision. But I'm not. The three of you are going to be affected almost as much as I am. Do you want to go up to the island without me?"

"No," his wife promptly said. "You know I wouldn't think of leaving you if you're going to stay here." She looked then at Clem and Nancy. Clem was bent forward, frowning at his father. Nancy was tossing back her hair in a gesture which her mother knew meant disappointment and displeasure. "If you and I can't go, William," his wife hurried to say, "perhaps Marcia and Robert could take their children and stay up there with Clem and Nancy."

"I don't want to stay up on the island with a crowd of little children," Nancy said sullenly.

"If Mother and you don't go," Clem said evenly, but his father caught the regret in his voice, "I don't want to go. I can find plenty to do here in town."

"Well, I can't," Nancy said. "The island would be heavenly—but not with Aunt Marcia. Why can't you go this summer, Father? You've always gone other years."

"Yes," said the judge. "I've always gone other years. I'm afraid, Nancy, I've been as blind as the stone woman they carved for the courthouse and call Justice. Her eyes are bandaged, you know. I'm afraid that my own eyes have been bandaged."

"What happened today?" his wife asked.

"Nothing much. I happened to see what a long vacation for the judge of the criminal court means to the unbailed defendants waiting for their trials. Months of misery in the county jail while I'm up on the island, enjoying myself."

"But there are other judges," Clem protested.

"Yes, but I'm the one responsible for myself."

"Do you mean," Nancy asked indignantly, "that you'll hear cases all summer even if no other judges stay in town?"

"I'll hear cases if I'm permitted. The committee of the criminal court will have to decide that. I hope that it will let me, and that when the other judges see the situation from the point of view of the men held in the jail, some of them will be glad to keep their courts open through the summer."

"Perhaps," Nancy said, "the committee will refuse to let you do this."

"I'll have to see what the members will decide."

"Then, perhaps, after all, we can go to the island."

"I wouldn't count on it, Nancy," her mother said. "Your father was a good special pleader before he became a judge."

"I've got to go to the meeting now," Clem said. From the doorway he looked back at his father. "I think you're pretty grand," he said huskily, then dived out into the hall. "I'll be home early," he shouted.

"It's going to be hard for me," Nancy declared, "because I've already asked Mary Kirby and Sylvia MacDonald to come up to the island in August. You said I might, Mother."

"You can have them there if your Aunt Marcia takes the house," her mother said.

"O Mother, how could we have any fun with those little children there all the time?"

"I seem to remember that your father and I had a pretty good time while some little children were there."

"You're unreasonable," Nancy said. "Neither of you is being fair. Why should you think of some old prisoners in the jail rather than of your own children?"

A heavy shadow fell over Judge Harrison's face, but his wife spoke as if their daughter had raised no question. "Didn't you plan to go over to Sylvia's house tonight? You'd better start now if you're going to be home by ten o'clock."

"All right," Nancy said.

Her father sighed as she left the library, but her mother smiled. "Don't take her too hard, William," she said. "You never can tell how Nancy is going to respond to a family decision, nor what she's likely to do after she's made her first speeches. Don't worry about our staying in town, either. We'll have plenty of good company. About a million other people will be staying, too."

"I know. I'm afraid, though, that I made this decision without taking Clem and Nancy into consideration."

"You can't take anyone else into consideration, my dear," his wife said. "This is for you to decide as you think best."

"I'm afraid it has become just that," said the judge.

"Then all you can do is go forward."

"Even if I march alone?" He

smiled at her as he reached for his usual cigar.

"Even if you march alone," she said.

III. The Bandage Is Lifted

The committee of the criminal court had seven members present when Judge Mason opened the meeting. The session, as usual, promised to be placid. The heat still hung over the city. The sun beat against the walls of the court building so that, in spite of their drawn Venetian blinds, the judicial chambers were uncomfortably warm. Under Judge Mason's easy guidance the meeting was speeding toward a hasty end when Judge Harrison rose.

"The chair recognizes the judge from Section C," Judge Mason said amiably. "That is your section, isn't it, Harrison?"

"That's my section," Judge Harrison said, "but this isn't a section matter. It is one which concerns all the judges of the criminal court." Then, as the chairman waved him permission to proceed, he outlined the situation. "There are nearly five hundred prisoners in the jail who will have to stay there until the fall term of court unless there is someone willing—there is no obligation in this—to hear cases throughout the summer."

"Give up our vacations?" Judge Blackwell leaped to his feet, breaking up the order of the proceedings by his vehemence. "What are you thinking of, Harrison? The judges of the county criminal court have always had these vacations."

"I know we have had them," Judge Harrison said, "and there is no reason why any one of us should give up a vacation now unless he feels as I do. Some of you have already made plans for work which is important to our profession. My suggestion is for myself alone. To carry it out, however, I need the vote of this committee."

"I'm afraid you won't get it," Judge Blackwell said, "for anything so absurd, so ridiculous."

Absurd. Ridiculous. Two other judges, Davis and Sloan, repeated the words. Sloan expanded them. Davis emphasized them more strongly. The others, Jonathan Lacey and old Judge Eubank, said nothing.

Judge Harrison spoke again. "I seem to be in a minority," he said, "but that is just where I expected to be. I am afraid, gentlemen, that you have not clearly realized just what I am proposing. I am not asking that all judges of the criminal court remain to hear cases through the summer. I ask only for permission from this committee for myself and anyone else who wishes to do the same thing to hold court continuously from June 21 to October 4. That is the question. I'm putting it in the form of a motion, and I so move."

"I want to talk on that motion." Judge Lacey rose, a little heavily. "I wish it had been mine. I have been on the bench sixteen years longer than William Harrison. I should have been the one to see this condition that he has shown us. I should have been the one to propose a remedy for it. Well, it's not too late to say that I'm with him a hundred per cent. If this committee gives permission to him, I ask that it give permission to me."

"I also wish to speak on the motion." Judge Eubank, the oldest of them all, both in years and term of service, had to clutch the chair before him to steady himself as he rose; but his voice was firm as he spoke. "Gentlemen," he said, in his dignified, old-fashioned manner, "I have always had a deep pride in my profession, both as a lawyer and as a judge. I have always thought that I served my community with a strong sense of responsibility. I have never seen, until this hour, how I might do more than my duty. Judge Harrison has done me a great favor. He has shown me my obligation to certain of my fellow citizens, those unfortunate ones who have broken the laws we

are sworn to uphold. It is not our right to coddle them, or to give them anything but justice. It is our duty, however, to see that they are given this justice without undue delay. I see now that I have injured a great many wretched people, men who are, in a sense, wards of the state, since they are in the custody of the state. There is nothing I can do now to undo the past. I can, however, see that I no longer fail in charity. I therefore ask that I may be permitted by the committee to serve throughout the summer."

"That's all fine," Judge Blackwell said, "for you men who don't care whether or not you stay or go away. But I have made certain

plans which I can't change now. I have undertaken a lecture course at the Far River Institute."

"I am not asking you to give up your vacation," Judge Harrison said. "I am only asking you to let me give up mine."

"But what real good will it do?" Judge Blackwell persisted.

His voice lifted as Judge Lacey slipped a note to Harrison. The note read: "We have three votes. Sloan and Davis will vote with Blackwell. Mason will cast the deciding vote. Watch him." Judge Harrison grinned as he slipped the paper into his pocket. Even in the heat of argument, Jonathan Lacey never forgot to count the possible votes. He glanced at Judge Mason; but the chairman was looking blandly noncommittal.

"I wonder how it will go?" Judge Harrison thought.

"And, after all, why is this our obligation?" Judge Blackwell was ending.

"I'll tell you why it is," Judge Harrison was on his feet in a flash of time. "Everyone of us knows that he is, by the grace of God, favored beyond millions of his fellows. We are not better men than they are. We have no superior minds which thousands of men could not have had by the same kind of training. We are merely men in higher positions than most

men. These positions may give us what we call rights, but these rights certainly put responsibilities on us. We owe the state we serve the best that is in us to give. We owe every prisoner who comes before us full justice. That means more than what goes to the jury for consideration and even more than decisions. It means seeing these prisoners as human beings possessed of rights which God gives to them, as well as to us. One of these rights is the right to a fair trial. That certainly means trial without undue delay. That's all I'm asking for them."

"You are doing more than that, Harrison," old Judge Eubank said solemnly. "You are restoring a fine tradition to the American bench. Thank you for this restoration."

"It's not as much as that, Judge Eubank," the younger man said. "It's nothing but a decent deal for the poor fellows in the jail. I imagine I'm selfish in asking it. I know I shan't be able to sleep well, even up on the island, unless I've done everything in my power to have these prisoners brought to trial as soon as possible. That's all."

"Ready for the vote?" Judge Mason asked, his voice still indifferent.

Jonathan Lacey nodded to Harrison. "Ready," said Harrison.

"All those in favor," Judge Mason began.

Eubank and Lacey and Harrison stood up. "Aye," they said.

"All those opposed," said Judge Mason.

Blackwell and Sloan and Davis rose. "Nay," they almost shouted.

"The chair will cast the deciding vote," said Judge Mason. He did not look at any of the six men before him. "The chair votes aye," he said. "The ayes have it."

"It is understood, is it not," Judge Harrison asked, "that this commits to the work only those who have voted aye?"

"That is my understanding," said Judge Mason.

"I wish to state," said Judge Davis stiffly, "that I will take an assignment to hold court during the summer. I have voted against it, but the majority has outvoted me. I will therefore do my part."

"So will I," said Judge Sloan. "I can't refuse to go along with what the rest of you consider a public service. I don't want to stay in town through spells of heat like this—but what can I do in the face of your decision?"

"That leaves Judge Blackwell," said Jonathan Lacey. "He is, of course, free to go to the Far River Institute."

"I must go," Blackwell flung out his hands. "I made this arrangement months ago. I cannot change it now." Impatiently he turned to

Judge Mason. "Why did you vote with Harrison?" he asked the chairman.

"Why?" Judge Mason repeated. "It was like this. I wasn't very much concerned, either way, until he spoke about not being able to sleep nights for thinking of the prisoners in the jail. I have insomnia, very badly. I dread adding new problems to those I already have which keep me awake."

Jonathan Lacey moved around to put his hand on Judge Mason's shoulder. "You're a humbug," he said. "You know you're just as softhearted as Harrison. You try to hide it, but once in a while it shows through the bark."

"Nonsense," said Judge Mason. "Nonsense." But he smiled at Judge Lacey. "Will you help me with the assignments, Jonathan?" he asked.

At dinner that night Nancy was the first to mention summer plans. "Do you know what I'd like to do this summer?" she asked; and her father waited, a little angrily, for her to return to her protests against staying in the city. "I'd like to go with Sylvia MacDonald," she went on, "out into the country districts to teach religion in the summer schools. You know it's a perfectly wonderful work," she declared with enthusiasm. "There are Sisters in charge of each school, but there are not enough Sisters to teach all the children. That is why they are enrolling college and high-school girls to help in the teaching. Sylvia's father and mother know all about it, and they are letting Sylvia go. Can't I go with her? We'll be perfectly safe," she hurried to add. "The Sisters look after each group of girls. Don't you think it's won-der-ful?"

"Yes," her mother said, "I do." Her look at her husband told him that she believed their daughter quite as wonderful as the cause she was championing. "When does the work begin?"

"Three days after school closes."

"That's a pretty short vacation," her father said.

"It's longer than yours, isn't it?" she questioned. "O Father, I must do this! Here you'll be working all summer at something you don't need to do, and Mother will be here with you, and Clem's going to take on a class for Mexican boys out on the South Shore. I must do something. I can't be left out of everything."

"All right," her father said.

She kissed him hastily but gratefully, as she went off with Clem.

"It's a snowball," Mrs. Harrison said. "You start a little one rolling downhill, and before it gets to the bottom it's a huge mass."

"It's always like that," the judge

23

said; "and it's so easy to make the first little ball that you wonder why more people aren't making them."

"It's not so easy," his wife said. "You were in misery yesterday, I seem to remember."

"I'm happy today."

"What of next year—and the year afterward?" she went on. "These cases will be piling up, year after year. Judges have many obligations, like teaching and writing, which they can meet only by summer work. Vacations don't always mean leisure."

"I know," Judge Harrison said. "Blackwell has some right in hold-ing out against the rest of us. The only solution, I think, will be to have more judges in the criminal court. But until that time comes, I feel it is my personal duty to keep on hearing cases through the summer. Of course the fact that a few men are doing this doesn't mean very much, but—"

"You can't tell how much it means," his wife said. "No one who does a deed beyond and above the call of duty ever knows how far his action may influence the lives of others."

"You make me sound heroic," the judge laughed.

"Aren't you?" she asked.

The stone figure of Justice at the front of the Criminal Court Build-ing still wears the bandage over her eyes as she balances the scales in her hand. However, Judge Jonathan Lacey says that she lifted the bandage for a moment and winked at him as he went in to hear the first case of the new summer term of the court. The lady in stone is, he says, not always as blind as people think her. She knows, he declares, when the men who have taken their oaths to uphold her are doing their duty to other men; and he told Judge Mason that the bandaged figure waved the scales in triumphant tribute on the blistering hot June day when Judge Harrison heard the case of Lanny Baker.

Remembering Facts

Some of the information given in the following statements is correct, some is incorrect, and some is not told in the story. Write on your paper, beside the number of each statement, C if it is correct; I if it is incorrect; NT if the information is not told.

_____ 1. Judge Harrison was a dignified gentleman, aware of the duties of his office as judge.

_____ 2. Lanny Baker was accused of shoplifting.

_____ 3. Conditions in the county jail were very bad.

_____ 4. Baker's case had not been heard before because of a crowded court calendar.

_____ 5. Mrs. Harrison was appalled that her husband had not thought of his family in making the decision to forego his vacation.

_____ 6. It had been a custom of the Harrisons to spend their entire summer on a northern island.

_____ 7. It was up to the committee of judges of the Criminal Court to decide the length of summer vacation for the court.

_____ 8. Judge Eubank presided at the meeting and cast the deciding vote.

_____ 9. Although Judge Blackwell could not hold court that summer, he accepted assignments in the years that followed.

_____ 10. Nancy decided to spend her summer teaching religion in the country.

_____ 11. This story took place in the early twentieth century.

_____ 12. Eventually all the judges were convinced that it was their duty to hold court during the summer months.

MARTHA ELIZABETH AHRENS

Weather

RAIN on the pavement
And a brisk wind blowing,
Of clouds there are plenty
Green shoots are showing—
Just the very kind of day
To walk the roads to Far Away.

Sun shining through the leaves
And a soft wind singing,
White clouds in a blue sky
And sea birds crying—
Just the very kind of day
To walk the roads to Far Away.

Snow softly falling down,
The gray trees hover
Faint and ghostly through the flakes.
The creek's frozen over—
Just the very kind of day
To walk the roads to Far Away.

Sleet striking on the panes,
Gales shrieking round the house,
Black clouds streak the sky—
This is no day for man or mouse.
O! It's not the time and it's not the day
To walk the roads to Far Away.

A Ride in the Country[1]

WHEN DAD DECIDED he wanted to take his twelve children for an outing in the car, he'd whistle assembly, and then ask, "How many want to go for a ride?"

The question needed no answer, for when Dad rode, everybody rode. So we'd all say we thought a ride would be fine.

Actually, this would be pretty close to the truth. Although Dad's driving was fraught with peril, there was a strange fascination in its brushes with death and its dramatic, traffic-stopping scenes. It was the sort of thing that you wouldn't have started yourself, but wouldn't have wanted to miss. It was standing up in a roller coaster. It was going up on the stage when the magician called for volunteers. It was a back somersault off the high diving board.

A drive, too, meant a chance to be with Dad and Mother. If you were lucky, even to sit with them on the front seat. There were so many of us and so few of them that we never could see as much of them as we wanted. Every hour or so, we'd change places so as to give someone else a turn in the front seat with them.

Dad would tell us to get ready while he brought the car around to the front of the house. He made it sound easy—as if it never entered his head that *Foolish Carriage*, as he called his first automobile, might not *want* to come around front. Dad was a perpetual optimist, confident that brains someday would triumph over inanimate steel; bolstered in the belief that he entered the fray with clean hands and a pure heart.

While groans, fiendish gurglings, and backfires were emitting from the barn, the house itself would be organized confusion, as the family carried out its preparations in accordance with prearranged plans. It was like a newspaper on election night; general staff headquarters on D-Day minus one.

Getting ready meant scrubbed hands and face, shined shoes, clean clothes, combed hair. It wasn't advisable to be late, if and when Dad finally came rolling up to the door.

[1]From *Cheaper by the Dozen*, by Frank B. Gilbreth, Jr., and Ernestine Gilbreth Carey. Copyright, 1948, by Frank B. Gilbreth, Jr., and Ernestine Gilbreth Carey. Thomas Y. Crowell Company, New York.

And it wasn't advisable to be dirty, because he'd inspect us all.

Besides getting himself ready, each older child was responsible for one of the younger ones. Anne was in charge of Dan, Ernestine in charge of Jack, and Mart in charge of Bob. This applied not only to rides in the car but all the time. The older sister was supposed to help her particular charge get dressed in the morning, to see that he made his bed, to put clean clothes on when he needed them, to see that he was washed and that he appeared on time for meals, and to see that his process charts were duly initialed.

Anne, as the oldest, also was responsible for the deportment and general appearance of the whole group. Mother, of course, watched out for the baby, Jane. The intermediate children, Frank, Bill, Lill, and Fred, were considered old enough to look out for themselves, but not old enough to look after anyone else. Dad, for the purpose of convenience (his own), ranked himself with the intermediate category.

In the last analysis, the person responsible for making the system work was Mother. Mother never threatened, never shouted or became excited, never spanked a single one of her children—or anyone else's, either.

Mother was a psychologist. In her own way, she got even better results with the family than Dad. But she was not a disciplinarian. If it was always Dad, and never Mother, who suggested going for a ride, Mother had her reasons.

She'd go from room to room, settling fights, drying tears, buttoning jackets.

"Mother, he's got my shirt. *Make* him give it to me."

"Mother, can I sit up front with you? I *never* get to sit up front."

"It's mine; you gave it to me. You wore mine yesterday."

When we'd all gathered in front of the house, the girls in dusters, the boys in linen suits, Mother would call the roll. Anne, Ernestine, Martha, Frank, and so forth.

We used to claim that the roll call was a waste of time and motion. Nothing was considered more of a sin in our house than wasted time and motions. But Dad had two vivid memories about children who had been left behind by mistake.

One such occurrence happened in Hoboken, aboard the liner *Leviathan*. Dad had taken the boys aboard on a sightseeing trip just before she sailed. He hadn't remembered to count noses when he came down the gangplank, and didn't notice, until the gangplank was pulled in, that Dan was missing. The *Leviathan's* sailing was held up for twenty minutes until Dan was located, asleep in a chair on the promenade deck.

The other occurrence was slightly more lurid. We were on our way from Montclair to New Bedford, Massachusetts, and Frank, Jr., was left behind by mistake in a restaurant in New London. His absence wasn't discovered until near the end of the trip.

Dad wheeled the car around frantically and sped back to New London, breaking every traffic rule then on the books. We had stopped in the New London restaurant for lunch, and it had seemed a respectable enough place. It was night time when we returned, however, and the place was garish in colored lights. Dad left us in the car, and entered. After the drive in the dark, his eyes were squinted in the bright lights, and he couldn't see very well. But he hurried back to the booths and peered into each one.

All of us had been instructed that when we were lost we were supposed to stay in the same spot until someone returned for us, and

Frank, Jr., was found, eating ice cream with the proprietor's daughter, back in the kitchen.

Anyway, those two experiences explain why Dad always insisted that the roll be called.

As we'd line up in front of the house before getting into the car, Dad would look us all over carefully.

"Are you all reasonably clean?" he would ask.

Dad would get out and help Mother and the two babies into the front seat. He'd pick out someone whose behavior had been especially good, and allow him to sit up front too, as the left-hand lookout. The rest of us would pile in the back, exchanging kicks and pinches under the protection of the lap robe as we squirmed around trying to make more room.

Finally, off we'd start. Mother, holding the two babies, seemed to glow with vitality. Her red hair, arranged in a flat pompadour, would begin to blow out in wisps from her hat. As long as we were still in town, and Dad wasn't driving fast, she seemed to enjoy the ride. She'd sit there listening to him and carrying on a rapid conversation. But just the same her ears were straining toward the sounds in the back seats, to make sure that everything was going all right.

She had plenty to worry about, too, because the more cramped we became the more noise we'd make. Finally, even Dad couldn't stand the confusion.

"What's the matter back there?" he'd bellow to Anne. "I thought I told you to keep everybody quiet."

"I'm trying to make them behave, Daddy. But no one will listen to me," Anne would reply.

"I don't want any excuses; I want order. You're the oldest. From now on, I don't want to hear a single sound from back there. Do you all want to walk home?"

By this time, most of us did, but no one dared say so.

Things would quiet down for a while. Even Anne would relax and forget her responsibilities as the oldest. But finally there'd be trouble again, and we'd feel pinches and kicks down underneath the robe.

"Cut it out, Ernestine," Anne would hiss.

"You take up all the room," Ernestine would reply. "Why don't you move over. I wish you'd stayed home."

"You don't wish it half as much as I," Anne would say, with all her heart. It was on such occasions that Anne wished she were an only child.

We made quite a sight rolling along in the car, with the top down.

As we passed through cities and villages, we caused a stir equaled only by a circus parade.

This was the part Dad liked best of all. He'd slow down to five miles an hour and he'd blow the horns at imaginary obstacles and cars two blocks away.

"I seen eleven of them, not counting the man and the woman," someone would shout from the sidewalk.

"You missed the second baby up front here, Mister," Dad would call over his shoulder.

Mother would make believe she hadn't heard anything, and look straight ahead.

Pedestrians would come scrambling from side streets and children would ask their parents to lift them onto their shoulders.

"How do you grow them carrot-tops, brother?"

"These?" Dad would bellow. "These aren't so much, friend. You ought to see the ones I left at home."

Whenever the crowds gathered at some intersection where we were stopped by traffic, the inevitable question came sooner or later.

"How do you feed all those kids, Mister?"

Dad would ponder for a minute. Then, rearing back so those on the outskirts could hear, he'd say as if he had just thought it up, "Well, they come cheaper by the dozen, you know."

This was designed to bring down the house, and usually it did.

When we would stop to eat our picnic lunches, Dad would keep looking around for something that might be interesting. He was a natural teacher, and believed in utilizing every minute. Eating, he said, was "unavoidable delay." So were dressing, face-washing, and hair-combing. "Unavoidable delay" was not to be wasted.

If Dad found an ant hill, he'd tell us about certain colonies of ants that kept slaves and herds of cows. Then we'd take turns lying on our stomachs, watching the ants go back and forth, picking up crumbs from sandwiches.

"See, they all work and they don't waste anything," Dad would say, and you could tell that the ant was one of his favorite creatures. "Look at the teamwork, as four of them try to move that piece of meat. That's motion study for you."

Or he'd point out a stone wall and say it was a perfect example of engineering. He'd explain about how the glaciers passed over the earth many years ago, and left the stone when they melted.

If he saw a factory, he'd explain how you used a plumb line to get the chimney straight and why the windows had been placed a certain

"Look there," he'd say. "What do you see? Yes, I know, it's a tree. But look at it. Study it. What do you *see*?"

But it was Mother who spun the stories that made the things we studied really unforgettable. If Dad saw motion study and team-work in an ant hill, Mother saw a highly complex civilization governed, perhaps, by a fat old queen bee who had a thousand slaves bring her breakfast in bed mornings. If Dad stopped to explain the construction of a bridge, she would

way to let in the maximum light. If the factory whistle blew, he'd take out his stopwatch and time the difference between when the steam appeared and when we heard the sound.

"Now take out your notebooks and pencils and I'll show you how to figure the speed of sound," he'd say.

He insisted that we make a habit of using our eyes and ears every single minute.

find the workman in his blue jeans, eating his lunch high on the top of the span. It was she who made us feel the breathless height of the structure and the relative puniness of the humans who had built it. Or if Dad pointed out a tree that had been bent and gnarled, it was Mother who made us sense how the wind, beating against the tree in the endless passing of time, had made its own relentless mark.

We'd sit there memorizing every word, and Dad would look at Mother as if he was sure he had married the most wonderful person in the world.

Before we left our picnic site, Dad would insist that all of the sandwich wrappings and other trash be carefully gathered, stowed in the lunch box, and brought home for disposal.

"If there's anything I can't stand, it's a sloppy camper," he'd say. "We don't want to leave a single scrap of paper on this man's property. We're going to leave things just like we found them, only even more so. We don't want to overlook so much as an apple peel or a single crust of bread."

Sometimes, in order to make sure that we left no rubbish behind, he'd have us form a line, like a company front in the army, and march across the picnic ground. Each of us was expected to pick up any trash in the territory that he covered. The result was that we often came home with the leavings of countless previous picnickers.

On the way home, when it was dark, Bill used to crawl up into a swivel seat right behind Dad. Every time Dad was intent on steering while rounding a curve, Bill would reach forward and clutch his arm. Bill was a perfect mimic, and he'd whisper in Mother's voice, "Not so fast, Frank. Not so fast." Dad would think it was Mother grabbing his arm and whispering to him, and he'd make believe he didn't hear her.

Sometimes Bill would go into the act when the car was creeping along at a dignified thirty, and Dad finally would turn to Mother disgustedly and say, "For the love of Mike, Lillie! I was only doing twenty."

He automatically subtracted ten miles an hour from the speed whenever he discussed the matter with Mother.

"I didn't say anything, Frank," Mother would tell him.

Dad would turn around, then, and see all of us giggling into our handkerchiefs. He'd give Bill a playful cuff and rumple his hair. Secretly, Dad was proud of Bill's imitations. He used to say that when Bill imitated a bird he (Dad) didn't dare to look up.

"You'll be the death of me yet, boy," Dad would often say to Bill after one of his imitations.

As we'd roll along, we'd sing three-and-four-part harmony, with Mother and Dad joining in as soprano and bass. "Bobolink Swinging on the Bow," "Love's Old Sweet Song," "Our Highland Goat," "I've Been Working on the Railroad."

"What do only children *do* with themselves?" we'd think.

Dad would lean back against the seat and cock his hat on the side of his head. Mother would snuggle up against him as if she were cold. The babies were asleep now. Sometimes Mother turned around between songs and said to us, "Right now is the happiest time in the world." And perhaps it was.

What Is Your Opinion?

This selection was taken from the book, *Cheaper by the Dozen*. It is the true story of the Gilbreth family. Keeping this in mind, answer the following questions. Be prepared to give reasons for your answers.

1. What do you think makes the story humorous?
2. What episode did you especially enjoy? Why?
3. From what you learned of him in the story, what kind of person do you think Mr. Gilbreth was?
4. Do you think the children feared him?
5. In what way was Mrs. Gilbreth a typical mother?
6. How does the story show a true family spirit?
7. What episode do you think is most typical of family life?

Interpreting Phrases

Locate the following phrases in the story and express their meaning on paper in your own words.

1. whistle assembly
2. fraught with peril
3. perpetual optimist
4. inanimate steel
5. entered the fray
6. process charts
7. duly initialed
8. intermediate category

34

To the Little House

DEAR LITTLE HOUSE, dear shabby street,
Dear books and beds and food to eat!
How feeble words are to express
The facets of your tenderness.

How white the sun comes through the pane!
In tinkling music drips the rain!
How burning bright the furnace glows!
What paths to shovel when it snows!

O dearly loved Long Island trains!
O well remembered joys and pains.
How near the housetops Beauty leans
Along that little street in Queens!

Let these poor rhymes abide for proof
Joy dwells beneath a humble roof;
Heaven is not built of country seats
But little queer suburban streets!

JOHN VAN DRUTEN

The Graduation Present[1]

CAST
(In the order of their appearance)

KATRIN, *a schoolgirl* (*In the Prologue she is a young lady*)
CHRISTINE, *a younger sister*
MADELINE ⎱ *school friends*
DOROTHY ⎰
PAPA (Lars)
MAMA (Marta)
DAGMAR, *the youngest sister*
AUNT JENNY ⎱ *Mama's sisters*
AUNT TRINA ⎰
NELS, *Katrin's older brother*

This play is based on the musings of Katrin, one of the members of an immigrant Norwegian family.

The time of the play is about 1910. The place is San Francisco.

The stage is so arranged that different parts are lighted for playing the different scenes.

[1]A scene from *I Remember Mama*, copyright, 1944, 1945, by John van Druten. Copyright, 1952, by John van Druten (revised). Reprinted by permission of Harcourt, Brace and Company, Inc.

The amateur acting rights are controlled exclusively by the Dramatists Play Service, Inc., 14 East 38th Street, New York, N. Y., without whose permission in writing no amateur performance of it may be made.

PROLOGUE

Katrin, in a spotlight, is seated at a desk at the right in front of the curtain, facing the audience. She is writing. Katrin is somewhere in her early twenties. Her blonde hair, when we see her first, is in a modern "up" style, capable of being easily loosened to fall to shoulder length for the childhood scenes. She wears a very short dress, the skirt of which is concealed for the Prologue by the desk behind which she is seated.

Katrin writes in silence for a few moments, then puts down her pen, takes up her manuscript, and begins to read aloud what she has written.

KATRIN. (*Reading*) "For as long as I could remember, the house on Steiner Street had been home. Papa and Mama had both been born in Norway, but they came to San Francisco because Mama's sisters, Aunt Jenny and Aunt Trina, were here. All of us children were born here. Nels, the oldest and the only boy—my sister Christine—and the littlest sister, Dagmar."

(*She puts down her manuscript and looks out front*)

SCENE I

Lights up and down front R. Katrin and Christine enter from right, in front of the curtain in school clothes, wearing hats. They are on their way home from school. Christine carries schoolbooks in a strap. Katrin is reciting.

KATRIN.

"The quality of mercy is not strained,
It droppeth as the gentle rain from heaven
Upon the place beneath: it is twice blest;
It blesseth him that gives and him that takes . . .

(*She dries up*)

. . . him that takes. It blesseth him that gives and him that takes . . ."

(*She turns to Christine*) What comes after that?

CHRISTINE. I don't know. And I don't care.

KATRIN. Why, Chris!

CHRISTINE. I don't It's all I've heard for weeks. The school play, and your graduation, and going on to High. And never a thought of what's happening at home.

KATRIN. What do you mean?

CHRISTINE. You see—you don't even know!

KATRIN. Oh, you mean the strike?

CHRISTINE. Yes, I mean the strike. Papa hasn't worked for four whole weeks, and a lot you care.

Why, I don't believe you even know what they're striking *for*. Do you? All you and your friends can talk about is the presents you're going to get. You make me ashamed of being a girl.

(*Two girls, Madeline and Dorothy, come from right, talking*)

MADELINE. (*To Dorothy*) Thyra Walsh's family's going to add seven pearls to the necklace they started for her when she was a baby. Oh, hello, Katrin! Did you hear about Thyra's graduation present?

KATRIN. (*Not very happily*) Yes, I heard.

MADELINE. I'm getting an onyx ring, with a diamond in it.

KATRIN. A real diamond?

MADELINE. Yes, of course. A *small* diamond.

DOROTHY. What are *you* getting?

KATRIN. Well—they haven't actually told me, but I think— I think I'm going to get that pink celluloid dresser set in your father's drugstore.

DOROTHY. You mean that one in the window?

KATRIN. (*To Madeline*) It's got a brush and comb and mirror—and a hair-receiver. It's genuine celluloid!

DOROTHY. I wanted Father to give it to me, out of stock, but he said it was too expensive. Father's an awful tightwad. They're giving me a bangle.

MADELINE. Oh, there's the streetcar. We've got to fly. 'By, Katrin. 'By Christine. See you tomorrow. Come on, Dorothy.

(*The two girls rush off L.*)

CHRISTINE. Who said you were going to get the dresser set?

KATRIN. Nobody's said so—for certain. But I've sort of hinted, and—

CHRISTINE. Well, you're not going to get it.

KATRIN. How do you know?

CHRISTINE. Because I know what you *are* getting. I heard Mama tell Aunt Jenny. Aunt Jenny said you were too young to appreciate it.

KATRIN. What is it?

CHRISTINE. Mama's giving you her brooch. Her *solje*.

KATRIN. You mean that old silver thing she wears that belonged to Grandmother? What would I want an old thing like that for?

CHRISTINE. It's an heirloom. Mama thinks a lot of it.

KATRIN. Well, then, she ought to keep it. You don't really mean that's *all* they're going to give me?

CHRISTINE. What more do you want?

KATRIN. I want the dresser set. My goodness, if Mama doesn't realize what's a suitable present— why, it's practically the most important time in a girl's life, when she graduates.

CHRISTINE. And you say you're not selfish.

KATRIN. It's not selfishness.

CHRISTINE. Well, I don't know what else you'd call it. With Papa not working, we need every penny we can lay our hands on. Even the Little Bank's empty. But you'll worry Mama into giving you the dresser set somehow. So why talk about it? I'm going home.

(*She goes off left. Katrin stands alone with a set and stubborn mouth, and then walks slowly to the right and resumes her place at the desk. Lights down except for spotlight on Katrin*)

KATRIN. (*Musing*) Christine was right. I got the dresser set. They gave it to me just before supper on graduation night. Papa could not attend the exercises because there was a strike meeting to decide about going back to work. I was so excited that night, I could hardly eat; the present took the remnants of my appetite clean away.

SCENE II

The curtains part on the kitchen, a large comfortable room which is really the center of their lives. It has a dresser holding china; a big table with chairs on both sides and an armchair at either end; a large stove; and a low Norwegian chest under the window. Papa, Mama, and Dagmar at table, with coffee. *Christine is clearing dishes.*

CHRISTINE. I'll just stack the dishes now, Mama. We'll wash them when we come home. (*She carries them into the pantry*)

PAPA. (*Holding up a cube of sugar*) Who wants coffee-sugar? (*He dips it in his coffee*) Dagmar? (*He hands it to her*) Katrin? (*From the right Katrin comes slowly into the scene for the sugar*)

MAMA. You get your coat, Katrin; you need it.

(*Katrin goes out back L.*)

DAGMAR. Aunt Jenny says if we drank black coffee like you do at our age, it would turn our complexions dark. I'd like to be a black Norwegian. Like Uncle Chris. Can I, Papa?

PAPA. I like you better blonde. Like Mama.

DAGMAR. When do you get old enough for your complexion *not* to turn dark? When can we drink coffee?

PAPA. One day, when you are grown up.

(*There is a knock at the street door L.*)

MAMA. There are Jenny and Trina. (*She goes to the door*) Is good. We can start now.

(*She opens the door. Jenny and Trina come in*)

JENNY. Well, are you all ready? Is Katrin very excited?

PAPA. She ate no supper.

(*Mama has started to put on her hat, and to put on Dagmar's hat and coat for her. Christine comes back from the pantry. Papa gives her a dipped cube of sugar*)

JENNY. Is that *black* coffee you dipped that sugar in? Lars, you shouldn't. It's not good for them. It'll—

PAPA. (*Finishing for her*) Turn their complexions black. I know.

JENNY. Lars, really!

(*Katrin returns with her coat*)

KATRIN. Aunt Jenny, did you see my graduation present? (*She gets it from a chair. Christine gives her a disgusted look, and goes out back L. Katrin displays the dresser set*) Look! It's got a hair-receiver.

JENNY. But I thought—Marta, I thought you were going to give her—

MAMA. No, you were right, Jenny. She is too young to appreciate that. She like something more gay—more modern.

JENNY. H'm. Well, it's very pretty, I suppose, but— (*She looks up as Mama puts on her coat*) You're not wearing your *solje*!

MAMA. (*Quickly*) No, I do not

wear it tonight. Come, Trina, we shall be late.

TRINA. Oh, but Peter isn't here yet.

MAMA. Katrin has her costume to put on. He can follow. Or do you like to wait for Peter?

TRINA. I think—if you don't mind—

MAMA. You can stay with Lars. He does not have to go yet.

JENNY. I hope Katrin knows her part.

PAPA. Sure she knows it. *I* know it, too.

TRINA. It's too bad he can't see Katrin's debut as an actress.

MAMA. You will be back before us, Lars?

PAPA. (*Nodding*) I think the meeting will not last long.

MAMA. Is good. We go now.

(*Mama, Jenny, and Dagmar leave. Nels and Christine enter back L and follow. Katrin puts on her hat and coat and gets the dresser set*)

PAPA. (*To Trina*) You like we play a game of checkers while we wait?

TRINA. Oh, I haven't played checkers in years.

PAPA. Then I beat you.

(*He rises to get the checker set. Katrin kisses him*)

KATRIN. Good-by, Papa.

PAPA. Good-by, daughter. I think of you.

KATRIN. I'll see you there, Aunt Trina.

TRINA. Good luck!

PAPA. I get the checkers.

(*Katrin goes out L. Papa gets the checker set from a cupboard under the dresser, brings it to the table and sets it up as the curtain falls*)

The following part of the scene is played outside in the street in front of the curtain where Christine and Nels have waited for Katrin.

CHRISTINE. (*Contemptuously*) Oh, bringing your cheap trash with you to show off?

KATRIN. It's not trash. It's beautiful. You're just jealous.

CHRISTINE. I told you you'd devil Mama into giving it to you.

KATRIN. I didn't. I didn't devil her at all. I just showed it to her in Mr. Schiller's window—

CHRISTINE. And made her go and sell her brooch that her very own mother gave her.

KATRIN. What?

NELS. Chris, you weren't supposed to tell that!

CHRISTINE. I don't care. I think she ought to know.

KATRIN. Is that true? Did Mama —Nels—?

NELS. Well, yes, as a matter of fact, she did. Now, come on.

KATRIN. No, no, I don't believe it. I'm going to ask Papa.

NELS. You haven't time.

41

KATRIN. I don't care.

(*She rushes back to the house and dashes into the kitchen as the curtains open. Christine goes off down L. Nels follows her*)

KATRIN. Papa—Papa—Christine says—Papa, did Mama sell her brooch to give me this?

PAPA. Christine should not have told you that.

KATRIN. It's true, then?

PAPA. She did not sell it. She traded it to Mr. Schiller for your present.

KATRIN. (*Near tears*) Oh, but she shouldn't—I never meant—

PAPA. Look, Katrin. You wanted the present. Mama wanted your happiness; she wanted it more than she wanted the brooch.

KATRIN. But I never meant her to do *that*. (*Crying*) She *loved* it so. It was all she had of Grandmother's.

PAPA. She always meant it for you, Katrin. And you must not cry. You have your play to act.

KATRIN. (*Sobbing*) I don't want to act in it now.

PAPA. But you must. Your audience is waiting.

KATRIN. (*As before*) I don't care.

PAPA. But you must care. Tonight you are not Katrin any longer. You are an actress. And an actress must act, whatever she is feeling. There is a saying—what is it—

TRINA. (*Brightly*) The mails must go through!

PAPA. No, no. The show must go on. So you stop crying, and go act your play. We talk of this later. Afterwards.

KATRIN. (*Pulling herself together*) All right. I'll go.

(*Sniffing, she picks up the dresser set and goes off L. Papa and Trina exchange glances, and then settle down to their checkers*)

PAPA. Now we play.

(*The lights fade and the curtains close*)

SCENE III

Spot up on stage L. Dorothy and Madeline are dressing in costumes

for "The Merchant of Venice" before a plank dressing table.

DOROTHY. I'm getting worried about Katrin. If anything's happened to *her*—

MADELINE. (*Pulling up her tights*) I'll forget my lines. I know I will. I'll look out and see Miss Forrester sitting there, and forget every single line. (*Katrin rushes in from the L. She carries the dresser set, places it on the dressing table*) We thought you'd had an accident, or something.

KATRIN. Dorothy, is your father here tonight?

DOROTHY. He's going to be. Why?

KATRIN. I want to speak to him.

(*As she pulls off her hat and coat*) Will you tell him—please—not to go away without speaking to me? After—after the exercises.

DOROTHY. What on earth do you want to speak to Father for?

KATRIN. I've got something to say to him. Something to ask him. It's important. *Very* important.

MADELINE. Is that the dresser set? (*Picking it up*) Can I look at it a minute?

KATRIN. (*Snatching it from her, violently*) No!

MADELINE. Why, what's the matter? I only wanted to look at it.

KATRIN. (*Angrily*) You can't. You're not to touch it. Dorothy, you take it and put it where I can't

see it. (*She thrusts it at her*) Go on—take it! Take it! Take it! (*Blackout*)

SCENE IV

Curtains part on the kitchen. Mama and Papa in conclave at the table with cups of coffee.

MAMA. I am worried about her, Lars. When it was over, I see her talking with Mr. Schiller—and then she goes to take off her costume, and Nels tells me that he will bring her home. But it is a long time, and is late for her to be out. And in the play, Lars, she was not good. I have heard her practice it here, and she was good, but tonight, no. It was as if—as if she was thinking of something else all the time.

PAPA. I think maybe she was.

MAMA. But what? What can be worrying her?

PAPA. Marta—tonight, after you leave, Katrin found out about your brooch.

MAMA. My brooch? But how? Who told her?

PAPA. Christine.

MAMA. (*Angry*) Why?

PAPA. I do not know.

MAMA. (*Rising with a sternness we have not seen before, and calling*) Christine! Christine!

CHRISTINE. (*Emerging from the pantry, wiping a dish*) Were you calling me, Mama?

MAMA. Yes. Christine, did you tell Katrin about my brooch?

CHRISTINE. (*Frightened, but firm*) Yes.

MAMA. Why did you

CHRISTINE. Because I hated the smug way she was acting over that dresser set.

MAMA. Is no excuse. You make her unhappy. You make her not good in the play.

CHRISTINE. Well, she made *you* unhappy, giving up your brooch for her selfishness.

MAMA. Is not your business. I choose to give my brooch. Is not for you to judge. And you know I do not want you to tell. I am angry with you, Christine.

CHRISTINE. I'm sorry. But I'm not sorry I told.

(*She goes back to the pantry with a set, obstinate face*)

PAPA. Christine is the stubborn one.

(*Nels and Katrin have approached the house in front of curtain, left. They stop and look at each other in the lamplight. Katrin looks scared. Then Nels pats her, and she goes in, Nels following. Mama looks up inquiringly and searchingly into Katrin's face. Katrin turns away, taking off her hat and coat, and taking something from her pocket*)

NELS. What happened at the meeting, Papa?

PAPA. We go back to work to-morrow.

NELS. Gee, that's bully. Isn't it, Mama?

MAMA. (*Absently*) Yes, is good.

KATRIN. (*Coming to Mama*) Mama—here's your brooch. (*She gives it to her*) I'm sorry I was so bad in the play. I'll go and help Christine with the dishes.

(*She turns and goes into the pantry*)

MAMA. (*Unwrapping the brooch from tissue paper*) Mr. Schiller give it back to her?

NELS. We went to his house to get it. He didn't want to. He was planning to give it to his wife for her birthday. But Katrin begged and begged him. She even offered to go and work in his store during her vacation if he'd give it back.

PAPA. (*Impressed*) So? So!

MAMA. And what did Mr. Schiller say?

NELS. He said that wasn't necessary. But he gave her a job all the same. She's going to work for him, afternoons, for three dollars a week.

MAMA. And the dresser set—she gave that back?

NELS. Yes. She was awful upset, Mama. It was kinda hard for her to do. She's a good kid. Well, I'll say good night. I've got to be up early.

PAPA. Good night, Nels.

NELS. Good night, Papa.

(*He goes out back L.*)

MAMA. Good night, Nels.

PAPA. Nels is the kind one. (*He starts to refill Mama's coffee cup. She stops him, putting her hand over her cup*) No?

MAMA. (*Rising, crossing R. and calling*) Katrin! Katrin!

KATRIN. (*Coming to the pantry door*) Yes, Mama?

MAMA. Come here. (*Katrin comes to her. Mama holds out the brooch*) You put this on.

KATRIN. No—it's yours.

MAMA. It is your graduation present. I put it on for you.

(*She pins the brooch on Katrin's dress*)

45

KATRIN. (*Near tears*) I'll wear it always. I'll keep it forever.

MAMA. Christine should not have told you.

KATRIN. I'm glad she did. Now.

PAPA. And I am glad, too. (*He dips a lump of sugar and holds it out to her*) Katrin?

KATRIN. (*Tearful again, shakes her head*) I'm sorry, Papa. I—I don't feel like it.

(*She moves away and sits on the chest under the window, with her back to the room*)

PAPA. So? So?

(*He goes to the dresser*)

MAMA. What you want, Lars?

(*He does not answer, but takes a cup and saucer, comes to the table and pours a cup of coffee, indicating Katrin with his head. Mama nods, pleased, then checks his pouring and fills up the cup from the cream pitcher which she empties in so doing. Papa puts in sugar, and moves to Katrin*)

PAPA. Katrin. (*She turns. He holds out the cup*)

KATRIN. (*Incredulous*) For me?

PAPA. For our grown-up daughter. (*Mama nods. Katrin takes the cup, lifts it*)

Listening as You Read

As you read the play, did you feel that you were listening to the characters? Could you hear the way they spoke? Identify the characters who spoke the lines below and write the words which, in your opinion, would be emphasized by the speaker.

1. Did you hear about Thyra's graduation present?
2. You mean that old silver thing she wears that belonged to Grandmother?
3. But you must care. Tonight you are not Katrin any longer.
4. I'll look out and see Miss Forrester sitting there, and forget every single line.
5. And you say you're not selfish.
6. Well, I'll say good night. I've got to be up early.
7. It is your graduation present. I put it on for you.

JACK HARRISON POLLACK

The Cobbler and the Archbishop

THIS IS THE STORY of a kindly Jewish cobbler and an alert young Irish boy who grew into a great priest of the Catholic Church—and of their warm and touching friendship that bridged two generations and two religious faiths.

Here in New Britain, where the two once lived on opposite sides of Lawlor Street, they still tell the story, speaking familiarly of "old Sam" and his young friend. Old Sam Greenberg is dead now, but his friend still lives, archbishop of one of the greatest sees in America, and he still holds their friendship dear.

In keeping with his wishes, the modest archbishop will not be named; in this story, he will be called "Jack," although his real name is more distinctly Irish than that. But in the town of New Britain nearly everybody knows who he is, and so do many of his million-member flock.

The story of old Sam and young Jack needs no names. The important thing is the spirit of brotherhood that pervades it.

[1]Reprinted from *Parade*, February 16, 1958, by permission of *Parade* and the author.

The story really begins in Kiev, Russia, more than a half-century ago, where lived a young cobbler named Samuel Greenberg. When the Czarist government began slaughtering Jews, he set out for America.

Alone, he came to Hartford, Connecticut. Carrying a battered satchel, he walked miles to New Britain and opened a shoe store in a poor neighborhood. Occasionally he sold a pair of shoes, but mostly he repaired old ones. If his neighbors couldn't afford to pay, Sam would mend their shoes free. Whenever he heard that a child couldn't attend school because he had no shoes, Sam promptly gave the youngster a pair.

"But we'll end up in the poor house," protested his young bride Sonya.

"I found heaven in America," smiled Sam. "It's more important, wife, to live a good life here than just to become rich."

Sam, who was then childless, took a fatherly interest in all the youngsters in the neighborhood. Some of the children were unkind. They teased Sam because of his poor English, because he kept the

Sabbath on Saturday and went to the synagogue.

Among the neighborhood boys was twelve-year-old Jack, who lived with his widowed mother and brother across the street from Sam. Jack didn't see Sam, or anyone else, as an object of ridicule. A thoughtful lad, he deeply respected the simple cobbler, and he was impressed by Sam's belief that there was more to this life than living by bread alone. Jack's father had died when he was young, and Jack soon became very fond of the good, simple shoemaker.

Sam advised Jack's mother, "Open a grocery store downstairs and, with God's help, you'll make a few pennies to send Jack to school." The plucky woman did so, and her store soon prospered.

Sam grew to love Jack as a son. "The boy has something special," Sam confided to his wife. "He isn't like other boys." For one thing, Jack was versatile. He was an excellent student, a nimble baseball player (he could run one hundred yards in ten seconds), and quick with his fists, if need be. One day he used them on a bully who slandered Sam.

The man and the boy had long talks while Sam worked. They discussed their respective religions and Sam's youthful dream of studying to become a rabbi. "Education is the greatest thing in the world," Sam used to tell Jack. "You can lose money, but you can never lose your education." Many evenings when he returned to his cobbler's bench, Sam would be pleased to see Jack studying by lamplight in his house across the street.

As Jack grew older, he became deeply religious. When he was an altar boy at St. Mary's Church, he told Sam that he wanted to enter the priesthood. "You'll make a wonderful priest, Jack," Sam encouraged him. "The world needs people like you to do God's work."

After graduating from St. Thomas Seminary in Hartford at seventeen, Jack sailed to France to study theology. At the start of World War I, he was recalled to this country to complete his training at St. Bernard's Seminary in Rochester, New York. In 1916 he was ordained at Hartford.

"Jack, you're now a priest!" Sam joyously greeted him. "My dream is starting to come true. You are doing God's work."

The young priest's first assignment was as an assistant pastor in a nearby town and, in 1919, he was called to an important office in the Hartford Diocese. He served there for fifteen years. During that time, he regularly visited his mother in New Britain. And, each time, he dropped in to see his old friend

Sam. Together the educated Catholic priest and the unschooled Jewish cobbler would discuss every topic in the universe.

Sam followed his friend's career with fatherly pride. In the 1930's, Jack was consecrated bishop of another New England diocese. He was the youngest bishop in the United States. Sam frequently visited him in his new city.

During a time of financial depression, idealistic Sam lost his shoe store. He paid all his bills and decided that he, too, would now spend all his time doing God's work. He organized a Hebrew Free Loan Society which lent money without interest to needy persons of all faiths. Almost single-handed, Sam launched dozens of local projects, ranging from a Golden Age Club for elderly folks to a Christmas toy collection for children. Despite his patched clothes, he was made a welfare commissioner, a park-board member, an adviser to mayors. He was dubbed "Mayor of Hartford Avenue." Hundreds came to him with their troubles, and he listened and helped.

One day Sam picked up the newspaper and read with excitement that his friend the bishop was being considered as archbishop in one of America's most historic cities. Sam, the Jewish student of Catholic history, was delighted. "I've always told Jack that that was the place for him," he exclaimed to Sonya.

Soon afterward, following World War II, Sam's dream came true; his friend the bishop had been elevated to archbishop. "I'm so happy!" Sam cried, tears salting his eyes. "We never had a son, my dear Sonya, but I couldn't feel any closer to one than I do to Jack."

Sam was sick in bed when arrangements were being made to install—during Brotherhood Week—his Jack as archbishop. One morning invitations arrived for him and Sonya to attend the installation ceremony. Arrangements also were made for railroad tickets. Sam got out of bed. He said, "I can't miss seeing Jack made archbishop."

Sam did not realize that only a few of the archbishop's many friends and relatives could be invited. The basilica seated only eight hundred persons, and there were hundreds of prominent Catholic churchmen and laymen who had to be accommodated. But room had been found for Sam and Sonya, who were not relatives and also were of a different faith.

At the railroad station a priest met them and escorted them to the Cathedral. They were promptly ushered into a pew reserved especially for them. Then they saw that the Cathedral brimmed with dignitaries of church and state, including archbishops, bishops, governors, senators, and mayors.

Most of all, Sam was awestruck by the breath-taking scene of medieval splendor. He had read many of Jack's books on church history, but he had never dreamed that the consecration of an archbishop was such an impressive ritual. Overhead was a baldachin, a canopy of jeweled metal with a white dove suspended in the center. Behind the throne hung the red Cardinal's hat of one of the archbishop's predecessors. The altar sparkled like a jewel.

The ceremony began—a ceremony hallowed in antiquity when America was still a wilderness. After the colorful procession of churchmen, a century-old bell tolled overhead as the organ rang out and the choir sang "Ecce Sacerdos Magnus"—Behold the Great Priest! The new archbishop was led to his marble throne after a young priest read, first in Latin and then in English, the Papal Decree of Appointment. From the Apostolic Delegate to the United States the new archbishop received the symbol of his office, a golden crozier—a long staff hooked at one end like a shepherd's crook.

After his elevation, the archbishop walked slowly down the aisle, blessing clergy and laymen. A quarter of the way down, he caught the eye of a familiar face. Handing his crozier to a nearby priest, he left the procession of church dignitaries. Approaching the pew of a little old man, he leaned forward, placed his hand on the man's arm, and, amid the stilled silence, said simply, "Hello, Sam. How are you?" Sam was too dumfounded to answer.

The new archbishop then rejoined the procession, greeting no one else by name.

Sam Greenberg's stunned face was flushed. His lips trembled, his heartbeat quickened. In those glowing minutes, he felt more than rewarded for any good he had ever tried to do.

"Hot tears from God fell from my eyes," he said later. "It was the greatest moment of my life."

That evening Sam and Sonya were escorted to a dinner-reception for the archbishop. There, amid the Catholic festivities, they learned that a kosher meal had been specially prepared for them. The archbishop invited them to remain as his guests for a week, but they could stay only two days.

Each year the archbishop celebrates the anniversary of that day. The humble cobbler who helped to shape his character is no longer there to see it, for recently Sam Greenberg died. Those who knew him say that one of the happiest memories he took to his grave was his true bond of brotherhood with another humble yet noble man.

Contrasting and Comparing

1. This true story is full of contrasts. Make a chart showing four or five contrasts between the two characters. An example is given below.

	Sam	Jack
Place of Birth:	Russia	America

2. Write a paragraph to summarize your data. Mention three ways in which Sam and Jack were alike and three ways in which they differed.

Drawing Conclusions

Select the answer which best completes this statement. The story "The Cobbler and the Archbishop" illustrates the fact that

a. many Jewish people found refuge in America when they were persecuted in Europe;
b. a man who is truly religious shows it in his dealings with his neighbor;
c. gratitude is a mark of a truly noble man;
d. the Church's ceremonies make a deep impression on even those who are not of the faith.

Knowing Homonyms

The following words are found in the story. Copy them on a paper and write a homonym beside each word.

great	needs	pair	altar	read
dear	way	here	told	aisle
real	heard	son	scene	days

Phyllis McGinley

The Legend of Befana

Befana, the housewife, scrubbing her pane,
Saw three old sages ride down the lane,
Saw three gray travelers pass her door—
Gaspar, Balthazar, and Melchior.
"Where journey you, sirs?" she asked them.
And Gaspar answered, "To Bethlehem,
For we have news of a marvelous thing:
Born in a stable is Christ the King."
"Give Him my welcome!" Balthazar smiled,
"Come with us, mistress, to greet the Child."
"Oh, happily, happily would I fare
Were my dusting through and I'd polished the stair."
Old Melchior leaned on his saddle horn,
"Then send but a gift to the small Newborn."
"Oh, gladly, gladly I'd send Him one
Were my cupboards clean and my weaving done.
I'd give Him a robe to warm His sleep,
But first I must mend the fire, and sweep.
As soon as ever I've baked my bread,
I'll fetch Him a pillow for His head,
And a coverlet, too," Befana said.
"When the rooms are aired and the linen dry,
I'll look to the Babe." But the Three rode by.
She worked for a day and a night and a day,
Then, gifts in her hands, took up her way.
But she never could find where the Christ Child lay.
And still she wanders at Christmastide,
Houseless, whose house was all her pride,
Whose heart was tardy, whose gifts were late;
Wanders, and knocks at every gate,
Crying, "Good people, the bells begin!
Put off your toiling and let love in."

Sister Louis Bertrand, O.P.

My Dad and the Rosary

I used to think it was my mother who had "all the religion" in our family. It was she who saw to it that we said our morning and evening prayers. It was she who asked us if we had been to Mass; and if she were at all in doubt about the boys, she demanded a rather full account of the sermon. Woe betide the one who couldn't give it! And I recall vaguely that on one occasion one of the boys had done something wrong—what, I do not remember.

"Kneel down and say the Act of Contrition," said my mother.

"O my God, I am heartily sorry," he began.

"You're *not* sorry," she interrupted.

I often wondered how she knew. But I suppose it was mother love which caused her to be concerned with the salvation of her children.

I was a very small child in those days; I couldn't stop to consider that my dad was earning the living for a family of thirteen and didn't have time to go to daily Mass. After a few years I came to know him better, and one of my first recollections is his gathering the family for the evening Rosary.

"Come on, time for prayers," he'd say shortly after supper.

"O Dad!" came the universal shout. "They are all waiting for us to go skating. They're out there already."

"That's all right. I'll call them in too. Won't hurt them a bit." And he did—the Clearys, the Morrows, the Clancys, and others. Somehow or other they never refused.

On one occasion my cousin happened to be present. Our family Rosary started with the Creed, took in a meditation on the mysteries, and ended with the Hail Holy Queen and the concluding prayer. Apparently my cousin wasn't used to so much, because at every good stopping place—or so she considered it—she started to rise from her knees, five times in all. Since it was wartime and some of our boys were in camp, the Rosary was followed by five Our Fathers and five Hail Marys for the soldiers. At the conclusion my cousin suffered intensely from a combination of rheumatism, lumbago, and housemaid's knees! The next morning she went to school and exclaimed, "Sister, did you know that Marion's

54

dad should have been a priest? I never saw anyone who could say so many prayers at one time."

When I finished high school, I entered a convent. My sister shortly followed me. One of my brothers was already a priest.

The morning after Dad retired from business, he went to Mass. For the next ten years, rain or shine, warm or cold, he was present at the Holy Sacrifice, his rosary beads slowly moving through his gnarled fingers. At the times when we were home for our summer vacation, we often saw him sitting in an old rocking chair out under the trees. If by accident we came upon

him and began to talk, he would hold the beads up in his hand to let us know that he didn't want to be disturbed. That picture of him is now one of my sweetest treasures.

Then he became ill. He was eighty-three and still active until a stroke made him bedridden. For days we did not expect him to live, but gradually he came back to his old self except that he couldn't get out of bed. During those last weeks I came to know more surely the beautiful side of his character.

One night, as I was leaving to say my prayers, he said, "Say some with me." I knelt and gave out a decade of the Rosary. He held my beads and tried to answer, but couldn't keep the Hail Marys and the Holy Marys straight. When I went back later, he was going through the motion of fingering the beads, although he had no rosary in his hands.

He died in October, Mary's month, the month of the Rosary. I think he would have chosen to go just then.

"Mother," I said one day shortly afterward, "was Dad always as good as he was the last ten years or so? I used to think when I was little that he didn't pray much."

"My dear," she replied, as the tears slowly gathered in her eyes, "your father taught me all the religion I know except what I had learned from my mother. I was just sixteen when we married. He had among his possessions the first Bible history I ever saw, Butler's *Lives of the Saints*, and a history of the Catholic Church. I often used to stand at the door of our little home and watch him out in the field. Many a time he stopped his plow, knelt in the field, and said his Rosary. After he came to town and started in business in the butcher shop, he delivered meat to the country homes. On the long, slow rides, between his calls, he spent his time saying the Rosary."

I recalled then how I used to wonder why Dad was so silent on those selling trips along the country roads, which had been one of my greatest childhood joys. He had been praying always. No wonder we loved him as we did!

Expressing Opinions

This character sketch is a tribute to the author's father. Answer the questions below and then write a ten-sentence summary of it.

1. What is the mood of the selection?
2. What part do you think family prayer and good example played in the three religious vocations in the family?
3. What is taught by the fact that the author's father did not go to daily Mass when the family was young and he was employed?
4. How does the selection teach that it is possible to pray always?

CHARLES L. O'DONNELL, C.S.C.

Our Lady Passes

WHEN down the street Our Lady went,
   No stir possessed the little town,
And yet the sun for this event
   Put on a golden gown.

Shopkeepers did not pause as sweet
   Their windows saw her pass,
But cobblestones thrilled to her feet
   Like daisies in the grass.

A blind man at the corner asked
   Why were the airs, that day, like spring,
A deaf man in a doorway basked
   And heard a robin sing.

2. Under the Wide and Starry Sky

THESE are the distant places:
where God's great might and purpose roll
the gleaming earth from pole to pole;
where softly, far from surging crowds,
drift the great shining silver clouds;
where first frail rain spreads like a shadow
across the slumbering brown of meadow,
leaving sharp colors and new smells
on frosted glass and icebound dells;
where, when the singing rain is over,
wild creatures leap from under cover,
and stars, as once at Bethlehem,
shine down upon the hopes of men.

These are the mountains:
where winter comes and wild winds blow
across the spaces of the snow;
where white-tipped peaks in broken lines
stand sentinel above dark pines;
there eagles nest and coyotes cry
and rivers rush and clouds ride high;
there hoot owls shriek from canyon stone
and gray wolves cry, "Alone! alone!"
while stars, as once at Bethlehem,
shine down upon the hopes of men.

This is the sea:
where rivers end and long waves thunder
and wild storms tear gray hulls asunder;
where ships from out of Aberdeen
from Amsterdam and New Orleans,
from Liverpool and Tampico,
from Staten Island and Bordeaux
pass in the sea lanes, sound a bell
that, in the silence, cries, "All's well!"
Their quest is but an odyssey
as old as the unchanging sea,
and stars, as once at Bethlehem,
shine down upon the hopes of men.

These are the quiet places:
where summer twilights softly fall
and God's great peace is over all;
where man has scorn for meaner plans
and, trusting God, his spirit spans
to where ships sail and white birds fly
and eagles nest and coyotes cry;
where first frail rain spreads like a shadow
across the slumbering brown of meadow;
there man, apart from crowds and things,
sings glory to the King of Kings,
and stars, as once at Bethlehem,
shine down upon the hopes of men.

Salt Water[1]

AT EARLIEST MEMORY, at the farthest back that I can take myself, the waters and the shore of Narragansett Bay were familiar.

The shore is always a place on which a group of boys, or one boy alone, can become utterly absorbed and self-forgetful. Exploration of the little basins, the animals, the rocks, is never completed or exhausted. As soon as we could swim, we put out in rowboats for ourselves. ("We" are the three La Farge brothers and a cousin who is indistinguishable from a brother.) We rigged sails for anything that would float, slowly learning how to make the most unlikely tubs move to windward, acquiring unconsciously the feel of wind, boat, and water.

Growing a little older, we progressed to canoes, and then to sailing dories, the most seaworthy of small craft when properly handled, and the most easily capsized. Although we thought little of it, we must have become pretty skillful, for now I can see that in all innocence we performed some surprising feats. We had no intention of being foolhardy, but, for instance, felt as boys will that we really should get home somewhere around the time at which we were expected, rather than lying over in a safe place, waiting for a bad blow to pass. It never would have occurred to any of us to tie canoe or dory up and telephone for someone to fetch us by land.

My mother was most anxious to avoid building up fears in us; she wanted her children daring, and so she swallowed her own fears without a murmur. When, for instance, we had brought a canoe across two miles of open water in a strong northwester, she would confine herself to pointing out, rather mildly, that it would have been all right if we'd stayed on the other side of the bay, provided we had telephoned her. Beyond that she did not blame us nor did she praise, since she hated a stuck-up boy as much as she did a coward.

In time we graduated to the *Windigo*, a sloop, and were allowed to take her out alone. Now a new element of delight came in, the sense of mastery. On land I might be clumsy and slow on my feet,

[1]From *Raw Material*, by Oliver La Farge. Reprinted by permission of Houghton Mifflin Company.

slow in my reactions; at school I might be the sad specimen whose development into a high jumper, an oarsman, were incongruous exceptions, but afloat I was something else. At the helm of the *Windigo*, now at last I was altogether Oliver La Farge as he longed to be, competent, sufficient, sure of himself. Imagination could still run free, but it did so less and less as the task and the endless changing beauty of sight, sound, smell, and motion absorbed me. In moments of fast maneuver, in narrow waters and tricky shoals, there was the use of body, mind, and training all together; in foul weather there was the great satisfaction of violence and effort to the extreme of one's capacity.

There was no doubt in the minds of any of us that the *Windigo* was a most superior boat, that to sail her competently was an achievement. She was a smart nineteen-foot sloop, built to special order. She was not built for racing, but she was unusually fast, very handy, and able to stand up to a terrific pounding. Her chief fault was that

she was headstrong; she always made the steersman work to keep her from heading up into the wind, and sometimes in a heavy blow, running before the wind, she could not be held on her course. This fault saved us once from real disaster, and so I can't kick about it too much.

My younger brother and I were caught out in Vineyard Sound heading for Vineyard Haven, in a blow of real power. It was a northeasterly storm in which, not far from us, a four-masted schooner sank at her anchors; and it did enough damage along the coast to get into the newspapers. We had underestimated the wind, thinking the *Windigo* could handle it easily with the mainsail double-reefed and her ordinary large jib. Also, when we were well away from land, the wind increased on us.

62

We were serious enough about it. I assumed my technical authority as older brother for the only time in all our cruising, to the extent that I insisted on staying at the helm. We were in a region of shoals and reefs which we had never sailed before. I knew that sails could blow out and masts carry away, and if any such thing happened, we should be driven onto the coast of Martha's Vineyard, harborless and rock-strewn. To reach shelter, we had to get around the clifflike point of West Chop; until then, disaster lay to leeward of us. It was no place for an accident, and the prospects of losing the boat were excellent. I was no more competent than my brother, but if she went, I was responsible; so I should steer her.

This meant that when we saw she could no longer carry the big jib, my brother had to go forward to take it in. The only help I could give him was to hold her nose as straight as possible into the wind and waves, and with that, of course, she swooped madly down the slopes and shipped water by the bucketful around his feet and legs. There is no pleasure whatever in remembering my brother up there on the deck, water swashing round him, balancing to the dives and rises as he worked. He was quick about it, as a matter of fact, but to me it seemed an age before he was safe in the cockpit again.

On our course, we carried the wind a little forward of abeam, so that the seas were striking about against the highest part of her windward side. These seas ran steep and high enough so that again and again we shipped green water into the cockpit, no more than the pump could readily handle, but constant reminders of what could happen. There is always something rather sickening about seeing green water pouring inboard. We were, of course, under a constant, generous bombardment of spray. My brother was moved to song, and I was particularly irritated because his favorite tune was "Oh, do it again," the words usually coinciding with a new dousing. It was a long, slow fight, the water being much too rough for us to make good time under the little canvas we were carrying. It was exhausting at the tiller. Yet both of us enjoyed ourselves enormously.

We rounded West Chop finally, and bore round into Vineyard Haven. The Haven is a great V, directly open to a northerly wind. But the chart showed a semicircular breakwater across the narrow part of the V, with a passage at each end of it. I chose the western passage as being the nearer. To make it, we had to run dead before the wind.

Now we really moved. With storm and sea behind her she tore like a runaway horse. She made you want to shout. But I have said she was headstrong; with the pressure of that much wind on the mainsail and no jib to counterbalance it, it was impossible to hold her on her course. I had to let her swing around to the eastward spilling a little wind out of the sail, and run for the eastern entrance to the harbor. We made it in grand style, came round, and anchored with deep relief.

Later, according to our custom, we rowed around the harbor and explored it. We went, of course, to the western entrance we had failed to make, to see what the passage was like. There wasn't any western entrance. The breakwater there was so low the tide covered it. The chart showed a passage; it looked like a passage. Had we been able to hold our course we should have piled up at full speed on solid rocks in a foot of water, and there would have been nothing left of the *Windigo*, perhaps not much of us.

Skimming to Prove Points

Read the sentences below and then skim the story to find proof for each statement. Write the page number, the number of the paragraph, and the first and last words of the sentence which is proof of each statement.

1. A boy will find that there is enough of interest on the seashore to hold his attention for a long time.
2. The La Farge boys were very close to their cousin.
3. The boys took a great many risks without realizing that they were doing so.
4. The boys' mother concealed any apprehension she had concerning their daring adventures.
5. Oliver La Farge felt a sense of self-fulfillment when at sea which he seemed to lack on land.
6. The *Windigo* was a very good boat in many respects, but she was difficult to steer.
7. On one particular occasion the fact that the *Windigo* was headstrong saved the two La Farges from disaster.

Understanding Sea Language

The following words and phrases are the language of the sea. Copy the list on your paper and beside each word write its meaning. Use the Glossary to help you.

dory	abeam	cockpit
sloop	jib	tiller
schooner	helm	dead
mainsail double-reefed	leeward	windward

ARTHUR HUGH CLOUGH

Where Lies the Land

WHERE lies the land to which the ship would go?
Far, far ahead, is all her seamen know.
And where the land she travels from? Away,
Far, far behind, is all that they can say.

On sunny noons upon the deck's smooth face,
Linked arm in arm, how pleasant here to pace;
Or, o'er the stern reclining, watch below
The foaming wake far widening as we go.

On stormy nights when wild northwesters rave,
How proud a thing to fight with wind and wave!
The dripping sailor on the reeling mast
Exults to bear, and scorns to wish it past.

Where lies the land to which the ship would go?
Far, far ahead, is all her seamen know.
And where the land she travels from? Away,
Far, far behind, is all that they can say.

Miracle at San Carlos

I. Rancho Nevería

From the time she was a little girl, barely able to crawl to the top of the hill, Teresa Nevería loved the place where she had been born. She loved the high mountains, red in the sunshine under the far blue sky, which she always called the Cloak of Our Lady. She loved the flowers of the near valleys, flowers that blossomed so briefly and so gorgeously after the infrequent rains had rushed down the mountain slopes. Most of all, although she came to know the poverty and bareness of the land, she loved the few acres on which her father worked.

With the pride of her people, the Spaniards who had settled these stark mountains of New Mexico, the girl clung to their love of the land. Sometimes, looking out over the nearer hills, she dreamed herself one of those Neverías who had, long ago, ridden over thousands of acres to some happy *fiesta*. But oftener, seeing the few poor acres of her father's rancho and the little adobe house where she lived, Teresa prayed for a miracle which would make the land what it had

been in those earlier, happier days. *"O Madre de Dios,"* she lifted her plea above the purple of the mountain summits, the blue of the sky, "do you not see our land? And will you not help our land?"

For the land was poor.

There had been a time—although the Neverías could not remember it—when the New Mexican hillsides had been rich pastures. That had been when one Don Antonio Nevería, ancestor of all the Valerios and Cardenos and Neverías who now lived around San Carlos, had owned thousands and thousands of acres. On these acres he had lived like a king. But when he died, his kingdom had been divided among his many children. Then, generation after generation, the land had been divided among their children until now the ranchos were small —and poor.

Year after year, the gully-washing rains of the Southwest had rolled the soil of the hillsides down the slopes and the little farms grew barer. Year after year, the descendants of Don Antonio labored to make a livelihood from their soil-stripped acres while the labor grew harder, the results poorer.

67

Papa Juan, toiling with the others, knew the hopelessness of his efforts. Always, however, he had tried to make himself believe that tomorrow would be a better day, the next year would bring what this year had denied. But there came at last a day when he said, "We must rent our rancho to our neighbor Rafael. I can find work with the sheepherders."

"*Ai, ai!*" Mama Zita mourned. Then, staring hard at Papa Juan, she demanded, "How can Rafael make this rancho pay if you cannot do it?"

"Rafael has his own rancho," said Papa Juan. "And he has rented Miguel's rancho, and José's and Pedro's. These all lie beside one another, just as they lie beside ours. That gives him one big farm. On it he will make a little money."

"Will Rafael also rent our home?" Mama Zita cried. She looked around the low adobe house as if it were a palace. "Will he rent the bed my father gave me for a wedding gift? Will he rent the chair my grandfather made for me? Will he rent the red curtains I made with my own hands?"

"The house goes with the land," said Papa sadly.

"But where shall we go?" young Luis asked. "With the sheepherders?"

"No," said Mama Zita. "I will cook for the railroad men. We will live in Jones Junction. You can go to high school there, Luis and Teresa. Papa will come there when he can get away from the sheepherders' camp."

"I don't want to be an *anglo*," Luis said. "*Anglos* are English-Americans, they are not Spanish-Americans. The boys who go to the high school at Jones Junction all want to be *anglos*. I am American, an American of Spanish ancestry. Our people have been here in New Mexico for a long, long time. They have always tilled the soil. I want to do what they did."

"It is no longer possible, Luis," Papa said. "There is no use trying to do anything with this little rancho. It is too small, too poor."

"We'll see," said Mama Zita. "And, Juan, you will not sign any paper for Rafael until we find out if there is not another way."

"There is no other way," said Papa.

"Have you prayed?" Teresa asked.

"Of course I have prayed," said Papa. "Every time I go into town, I go to the Mission of San Carlos. There I pray, pray hard, that God will help us."

"But you must pray all the time, Papa," said Teresa, "not just when you go into San Carlos. You must pray as Mama does. She prays when she washes, and when she scrubs, and when she cooks."

"He prays," Mama Zita came to Papa's defense, "but he does not pray aloud as I do."

"You do everything aloud, Mama," Luis said.

"Hear him!" Mama shouted. "Hear my own son speaking so of his mother!"

"I don't mean anything wrong," Luis said. "It is only that you like to do everything with other people, and Papa likes to do everything alone."

"Each to his own way," said Mama. "But if Pedro and José and Miguel and your papa had joined together, as I told them to join, they would not all now be renting to Rafael. If Rafael can make money on their ranchos, they also can make money."

"There is not enough good soil on any one rancho to make money," Papa said patiently. "No, I will go with the sheepherders."

"Better the Bellamy rancho," said Mama. "But you will do nothing, Papa, until I have talked with other people."

"Talk!" said Papa. "What good is talk?"

"How else can I find out what I want to know?" asked Mama.

If Mama did not find out at once what she wished to know, she at least started a considerable amount of conversation in the neighborhood of San Carlos. She talked to the wives of Pedro and José and Miguel. She talked to the wives of the storekeepers in San Carlos. She talked to the old Padre of the Mission. Something, she declared loudly, must be done about a situation which forced men and women to break up their homes. Everyone agreed with her that something must be done. But no one suggested what that something might be until Teresa, usually as quiet as her father, came home one afternoon from the Mission school, quivering with excitement.

"Mama Zita, Mama Zita!" she cried. "There is a way to make land better. I learned about it today!"

"Oh, sí, sí," said Mama. "I know all about that. You buy fertilizer and put it on the soil. But where have we the money for fertilizer? And why put anything on soil that will wash down with the first rain?"

"No, no, Mama," Teresa said. "You don't understand. This is a way to keep the soil from washing down with the first rain."

"How can anyone do that? The rain comes, and the soil goes."

"But, Mama, there is a way. The government has found a way."

"The government in Washington? There, in a city? What do men in a city know about the land?"

"Some of the men have lived on farms and ranchos, where they have tried ways to help farmers and ranchers. They have made laws to give that help."

"Laws?" said Mama Zita. "How can laws keep soil on hills when storms start to sweep it down into the valleys?"

"But they do something, Mama. Truly, they do." Teresa paused, baffled by her mother's doubts, then turned to her father as he came into the little adobe house. "Please," she pleaded, "will you listen to this?" Then, at his nod, she went on. "Nita Vicente's uncle has come from Santa Fe to visit them. He was telling us, just this afternoon, that there is a way to prevent this loss of soil from the hills here. He doesn't know much about how it's done, because he's not a farmer himself, but he says he knows the plan is good. The government at Washington has found that way, but the people themselves have to use it."

"We have no money, Teresa," her father said.

"Nita's uncle said this plan doesn't require money as much as it requires co-operation. People who own the land, who work on the land, must get together to carry it out."

"But how?" Papa asked.

"What have I always said?" Mama Zita put in. "I have always said that you get nowhere by working alone."

"But how can I work with other people when I have so small a piece of land?"

"I don't know yet," Teresa said.

"I'll find out," said Mama Zita. "Watch the pot on the stove," she bade Teresa, "while I go around San Carlos."

II. MAMA ZITA GOES INTO ACTION

For all Mama Zita's inquiries, it was Luis who really brought home the information about the Soil Conservation Act. He had gone with a truck-driver into Jones Junction and there had met Manuel Reyes, once of San Carlos. Manuel, who had political ambi-tions, was working for Judge Draper. There was nothing, said the young man, which he, Manuel, did not know about the operation of Federal laws in New Mexico.

"Then what is this law to keep soil on the hillsides?" asked Luis.

"That is the Soil Conservation Act," said Manuel. He stood for an hour upon the broad street of Jones Junction, explaining it to Luis. Later Luis, at home in the adobe house, explained the Act to his family.

There had been, said Luis, a great loss of land every year through what the *anglos* called erosion. Erosion meant the washing away of soil by rain, the blowing away of topsoil by wind. Every year the United States lost the use of millions of acres through this erosion. In some years dust storms had swept over most of the country, carrying away the fertile topsoil. Then the farmers could not raise crops. Rains, too, like the rains here in New Mexico, washed good soil down the hillsides. Then the ranchers could raise nothing on the slopes. And in the valleys the washed-down soil covered the fields and wrecked the planting.

After a while the government at Washington set out to help the farmers and ranchers. It put experts to work, men who could find out ways of stopping this erosion.

71

"Why have they not come here?" Mama Zita asked.

"Because the farmers, the ranchers, have to send for them," Luis reported Manuel's words. "By writing to Washington? Oh, no! This Act says that the work of helping the farmers must be done through state laws. Forty-five states have already passed laws to do it."

"Has New Mexico passed this law?" Papa Juan asked.

"Oh, yes," said Luis. "New Mexico has a good system. This is the way it works. There's a state soil-conservation committee in Santa Fe. If some of the ranchers who live in San Carlos would sign a petition and send it to the committee, saying that they wanted it to organize a soil-conservation district, the state committee would hold a public hearing on the question."

"In Santa Fe?" asked Papa. "That's so far away."

"No, here in San Carlos, or, maybe, at the county seat. At the meeting all the ranchers of the territory would have an opportunity to talk. They could tell the members of the committee what they want, what they need. Then, if the committee thought that a soil-conservation district should be established here, its chairman would call for a vote."

"A vote!" Mama Zita was impressed.

"That's right," Luis continued. "All the ranchers in the territory of the proposed district would have the right to vote. If the majority voted against having the district, then that would end the matter. No district. No help. But if the majority voted for the district, then the state committee would take prompt action. The state would issue a certificate, and the district would become a real organization.

"Next," Luis went on, "two men from the district would be appointed by the state as supervisors for the district, and they would hold an election to select three more supervisors. Then all five representatives of the people would go to work together. They would study all the land of the district and work out a plan to prevent erosion. To help them, they would call in experts from the Federal and state services."

"These experts go all through the district," Manuel had continued. "They look over the land. They talk to the ranchers. They show how things need to be changed. Plowing must be done a different way."

72

"But that all takes money," said Papa Juan, "and money we have none."

There would be a way to overcome this difficulty too, Manuel had pointed out. There was an agency in the Federal government which lent money to farmers when they showed that the money would be used to improve their farms.

"You see," Luis ended, with a flourish which even Manuel Reyes would have envied, "it's already worked out. All you need do, Papa, is to sign the petition to have this land around San Carlos made into a district."

"I have no such petition," said Papa Juan.

"I'll find one," said Mama Zita.

There was, however, no one in San Carlos who knew, as Luis did, about the creation of a soil-conservation district. Miguel and Pedro and José, coming in from the sheepherders' camps, had never heard of petitions for any such purpose. Neither had their neighbor Rafael, who did not like the idea of any change and who told Mama Zita that she might as well get ready to move to Jones Junction. The Sisters at the Mission school advised Mama Zita to write to the state committee at Santa Fe. But Mama Zita never believed in writing where talking was possible, and so one morning she set out with Luis upon a truck that he had borrowed from a friend. Being a

woman of direct action, she went not to Manuel, as Luis suggested, but to Judge Draper. Dramatically, with flashing eyes and waving hands, she told him the story of the Nevería rancho. "A poor, small rancho," she ended her discourse, "but all we own now of the great lands once owned by that splendid soldier Don Antonio Nevería."

"I see," said Judge Draper, who knew and loved these descendants of the pioneers who had sailed unknown seas and crossed unknown lands to set the flag of Spain and the Cross of Christ in this wide Southwest. One of the *anglos* who had come much later into the territory, he had never—as some of his fellows had—felt that the civilization his people had brought was better than the one they had found. The friend of everyone in the county, he had made it his business to know ways of helping the people. Instead of looking now in a dusty lawbook, he drew out a paper from a pigeonhole of his desk. "Here you are, señora," he told Mama Zita. "Have your husband sign on the first line. Then have him get twenty-four other ranchers to sign their names on the other lines. Bring it back to me, and I'll see that it gets to the right place."

"*Gracias, gracias*, señor," Mama Zita said. "I'll pray for you every night," she promised him.

"Why not mornings?" he laughed.

"There is so much to do in the mornings," she said seriously, "that I can only pray for my own family then."

"Tell your husband to get that petition signed as fast as he can," he bade her.

"I'll tell him what you say," said Mama Zita, "but I'll take the paper myself to the men who will sign it."

"In that case," the judge said gallantly, "I am sure that no man will refuse to sign."

It was not as easy as that, however, in spite of Mama Zita's whirlwind drive for signatures. Pedro was not sure that he had the right to sign the petition, since he had leased his land to Rafael. Rafael declared that he had no right at all to sign for the lands that he, Rafael, rented. José was willing to sign, but his wife feared that any signature on any paper was sure to bring disaster. She had, she said, a cousin who had once signed a paper and had lost his rancho when he was unable to pay money to the banker who held the paper.

In time, however, Mama Zita wore down all the resistance of their near neighbors except that of Rafael, who was certain that the whole plan was an unfair scheme to get him off the lands that he wanted to gain.

74

"I would trust you, Juan," he told Papa sadly, "but I'm afraid of your wife."

There were times when Teresa wondered if her father also did not fear her mother. They never quarreled, perhaps because Papa Juan never grew angry at Mama Zita's scoldings. His wife's sharp words never drove him into swift action, but even Teresa saw that they had an effect on his conduct. Perhaps, she thought, the family would be far worse off than they were if it were not for her mother's ambition to keep what was left to them of the Nevería land. In that, her heart was with her mother; but in her love of quiet she was very like her father. Like him, too, she saw tomorrow as a better time for action than today.

At no time did the girl come closer to her father than in the evenings when his work was done. Then, while Mama Zita and Luis studied the applications and charts and booklets which the state committee had sent them, Papa Juan and Teresa went out into the short twilight of the mountains and climbed to the crest of the hill above the little adobe house. Sometimes they barely spoke to each other; but, even without words, Teresa knew that her father and she were sharing a deep and beautiful experience in their love of the land.

"Do you think Mama and Luis love this—as we do?" she once asked.

"Yes," said Papa. "Why else would they work so hard on those papers? They must love their rancho very much to go through so many troubles to keep it. You see," he explained slowly, as if he were groping through an idea new to him, "people are not all alike, although we all are children of the good God. Your Mama and Luis must act when they think deeply. That is their way. You and I wish to stand here on the hilltop, looking out over our home. That is our way."

"Do you believe," Teresa asked him, "that someday we shall stand here and see below us a beautiful green rancho, a rancho that will give us food to sell and food for ourselves?"

"I do not know," Papa said. He sighed deeply. "I wish I believed that, Teresita. Do you?"

"Oh, yes, yes," she said eagerly. "I believe that God will work a miracle for us someday. Then the earth will be as green below us as the sky is blue above us, not green for one day only, as it sometimes is now, but green long enough to let us grow what we need."

"My mother once told me," Papa Juan said, "that if you believe something long enough and deeply enough, it will come true."

"I know it will," Teresa said.

For a time, however, it looked as if even Mama Zita's efforts would be in vain. Through talk which must have wearied even her busy tongue she won thirteen signatures for the petition. These, with Papa Juan's, made fourteen. For more than a week, she could not obtain another. For reasons she could not discover, man after man refused to sign. Then she crossed the line into the Mexican settlement on the other side of the town.

Within an hour after she had gone into the Mexican settlement she was the friend of all the men and women she met.

Carefully she explained to them what the signed paper would do. It would bring men who would help the ranchers to help themselves. The Mexican ranchers, called in from their tiny fields by their wives and mothers, smiled pleasantly at her. But no one signed. "Why not?" she demanded. "Why not?"

The answers came slowly. "Sign here," she bade them, remembering the instructions which Luis had brought her from Manuel. Then, after a great deal of talk, she discovered that only seven of them owned the land they tilled. She took down seven signatures; and she left the settlement, having made new friends but not too cheerful.

Four more signatures to get! Where could she get them?

She trudged the dusty road grimly, turning possibilities over in her mind. Already she had asked everyone she knew and many she did not know. What could she do now?

The bus had just stopped at the little plaza as she came into San Carlos. Four men, *anglo* ranchers from the valley beyond the Nevería rancho, were moving toward a little car.

"Señores, señores!" Mama Zita called, and ran across the plaza toward them.

They paused, staring at her in puzzled surprise. Rapidly, in a combination of English and Spanish which only a New Mexican resident could understand, she outlined to them the purpose of the petition. Then, with a blaze of dark eyes and a flash of white teeth, she waved the paper before them. "Please, señores, sign," she pleaded. "For the good of all our land!"

"I believe she's right," one of the men said. He read the petition carefully. "Maybe this is the answer," he told the other three. "God knows we've suffered enough from erosion. We're in the flatlands and can use irrigation, but first of all we must stop the wash-down from the slope ranchos, which wrecks our land. Well, here goes." He signed his name below the names of the Mexicans, then handed his fountain pen to the men beside him. "Come on in," he bade the three. One after another, they signed. The first man handed the paper back to Mama Zita.

"Twenty-five," Mama Zita slowly counted. "Twenty-five!" she repeated in triumph. She flung out her arms as if she would embrace the world. "*Gracias a Dios!*" she sobbed, and ran across the plaza to the Mission to pray in gratitude for His blessings.

Luis mailed the paper to Judge Draper. Manuel, returning to San Carlos for a brief visit, reported to Luis that the judge had sent the petition to the state committee. In time, said Manuel importantly, the people of San Carlos would hear from the committee. Until then the ranchers could do nothing. Even he, Manuel Reyes, could do nothing.

III. SPRINGTIME IN SAN CARLOS

For Papa Juan and Teresa time. passed just about as usual, days of sunshine and clouds, nights of moonlight and starlight, work, meals, the happiness of everyday things, hope, and trust in the to-morrows. For Mama Zita and Luis time dragged. Mama Zita's query "When shall we hear?" became "Shall we ever hear?"

Then, just as she was about to send Luis to Judge Draper, a stranger came to the rancho, inquiring for Papa Juan. "I'm the county agricultural agent," he explained to the Neverías. "You seem to have bypassed me when you sent your petition directly to the state soil-conservation committee, but that's all right. We'll work together. A representative of the state committee will meet me here, and he will call all you people together in the Mission school to have a hearing on whether to hold an election for the proposed district."

"More waiting?" groaned Mama Zita; but she rejoiced in the activities which went with this waiting. There were letters and more letters coming to Papa Juan, who had ·become, in spite of himself, a local leader. He and Mama Zita read them all and directed Luis to answer them.

"Soon will come the vote," said Papa. "Perhaps the vote will go against us."

"It cannot," said Mama Zita.

In fear, however, that it might, she began a campaign which would have done credit to any politician. Every day, while Teresa helped with the housework before and after school, Mama Zita traveled through the district. Usually she walked; but drivers on the roads came to know her short, squat figure, and paused to invite her to ride with them. Before election day she had gone to every rancho in the district, homes of the Mexican-Americans, homes of the Anglo-Americans, homes of those Spanish-Americans who were the oldest inhabitants of them all. Over and over she repeated her message: "Join us in saving the land."

She found unexpected friends and unexpected enemies. The Bellamys, who owned the big rancho on the flatlands at the edge of the district, took up the cause enthusiastically. Some of her nearest neighbors, led by Rafael, did everything possible to win away votes. She was hopeful, but not too hopeful, when election day arrived. Then, as the day progressed, the little hope she had fell to zero.

To her disappointment, the vote was light. And what was worse, if she could judge by the number of men who greeted Rafael in friendly fashion, was that it seemed to be against the establishment of the district. At noon she realized that the success of the project depended upon the votes of the ranchers beyond the Mexican settlement. If they did not come to vote for the district, there would be none. "*Ai, ai!*" Mama Zita grieved within her heart; but she kept on smiling while she stood as near as she could go to the polling place.

There were no telephones to the ranchos beyond the Mexican settlement. The roads were bad. How could she get word to the ranchers out there that they must come, at once, to San Carlos? She herself could not go, for she must stay near the polls to encourage those who might waver at the last moment. Luis had already gone, on the borrowed truck, to the northern end of the district. Papa Juan was no messenger to send on an urgent errand. There was no one to send but Teresa, who was only a little better than Papa. And how could Teresa get to those ranchos to the southward?

As if in answer to Mama Zita's prayers, a station wagon swung into the plaza. The señor Bellamy had come to vote. The señora Bellamy was driving him to the polls. Almost before the señor was out of the wagon, Mama Zita was standing beside his wife. Would the señor be so kind as to inform the missing ranchers that they must come to vote?

The señor and señora would be quite willing, but the señor must, as soon as he had voted, take the bus to Jones Junction. The señora would be glad to go to the ranchos, but she could not speak Spanish. Was there anyone she could take as interpreter to carry Mama Zita's message?

79

There was Teresa, said Mama Zita. With delight for the ride with Mrs. Bellamy, but with panic at the thought of her task, Teresa climbed into the station wagon.

"Bring them back, every one," Mama Zita shouted after her.

Mrs. Bellamy talked swiftly and easily as she sped the station wagon over the road to the southward. What was Teresa studying in school? Geometry? Not really? And she knew how to figure out problems of curves and angles? And chemistry? And English? What did she like best? Music? Of course. Mrs. Bellamy had studied music. Would Teresa come to the rancho sometime and sing with her? They were old friends before they reached the first rancho; and

Teresa was sorry to have to put away thought of music for her immediate errand of picking up a rancher for the voting at San Carlos.

It was not hard, however, to persuade the men to come with them. Most of them had failed to go to the voting merely because they had something else to do. Of course they wanted a district established. Of course they would vote for it. Only at Marcelino Mora's did Teresa have difficulty. Marcelino, crabbed as an old walnut, declared that he would never vote for anyone but the Senator Cutting.

"But the Senator Cutting is dead," Teresa told the old man in Spanish. "He has been dead a long time. This is not a vote for a man. It is a vote for saving the soil, the soil on your rancho."

"Once I made a promise," old Marcelino told her, "that I would never vote for any man but Senator Cutting. He was our friend. He did what was good to help our people. He understood us. He liked us."

Mrs. Bellamy caught enough of the conversation to understand its meaning. "Tell him," she bade Teresa, "that Senator Cutting would want him to vote for this. And talk like your mother if you want to convince him."

"I cannot talk like Mama Zita," Teresa said, but she plunged into a declaration that in this election there was no opposition to the long-dead Senator Cutting.

Gradually old Marcelino began to understand. "Oh, sí, sí," he said at last. "The senator, in heaven, finds this way for his friends on earth." Stiffly he climbed up into the wagon and, cheered by Mrs. Bellamy's smile, which was more for his words than for himself, took his place between her and Teresa. "We go," he told them.

They went as fast as the señora could drive over the bad roads. A wagonful of them, they pulled up before the polling place just twenty minutes before the closing of the polls.

"Fast, fast!" Mama Zita called to them from her post down the street. "Vote right! Vote right!"

They must have voted right, for the count showed that the majority of the voters of the district had chosen the soil-conservation program. Before long, word came that the state had issued the certificate which would make the San Carlos soil-conservation district a real organization. Now there would be local supervisors to plan the work, two appointed by the state committee and three elected by the people of the district.

Again Mama Zita went into action. She wanted the señor Bellamy to be one supervisor. She wanted one of the Mexicans to be another. She was willing, though not anxious, to have Pedro for the third. It was Luis who suggested that Papa Juan should be a supervisor.

"Oh, no, no," said Mama. "Papa cannot boss anyone."

"But if Papa is a supervisor, you can do the bossing," Luis said.

"You have truth there," said Mama Zita.

For once, however, she did not know how to go about getting what she wanted. It was not proper that a man's wife should say that he should be elected to any office. She was standing before a blank wall of inaction when the señor Bellamy himself declared that he wanted Juan on his ticket.

"If I can talk him into it, señor, he will accept," Mama Zita told him.

"I hope you will be able to do that, señora," Bellamy said solemnly.

Papa Juan protested, of course, although he and Teresa knew that his protests would avail him nothing. His name went on the ticket with Bellamy's and the Mexican's, and they were easily elected. For a day Papa went around with an air of vast importance, then settled back into his usual, not too hopeful, round of hard work.

From that time the district buzzed with activity. For weeks the government experts studied the hillsides and valleys. There were men in corduroy suits and high boots and sombreros, marching back and forth over the hills. There were men with surveyors' instruments measuring the ground. Then, at last, they told the supervisors what they thought should be done to prevent erosion.

There was a great deal to be done, they said, if the hillside ranchos were to produce crops for the ranchers. Forests must be planted on some of the land. By maps and charts they showed how other hillsides should be terraced. The ground should then be plowed to follow the shape of the hills.

Several different crops certain to grow should be planted, not merely the single crops that the ranchers had been planting just because their fathers and grandfathers and great-grandfathers had planted them. There were long months of work ahead; but in the end, promised the experts, the district would no longer be poor.

Slowly at first, then with deeper belief, the ranchers undertook the labor. There were many days when even Mama Zita was discouraged. But in faith that all the plans must mean something, the men kept on. Miguel and José and Pedro, who had come back from the sheepherders' camps to do their ranching, grew hopeful, although Rafael, reduced now to his own acres, declared that he had no faith in the new way.

"But his land also will be helped," Mama Zita said.

Every day the springtime advanced. To Teresa's eyes the hillside of the Nevería rancho looked little different from the way it had looked in other springtimes except that the rows ran around the slope instead of up and down the hill. The seeds had not yet sprouted above the soil. Until they did, even Mama Zita could not claim success for the experiment which had cost so much in time and work.

"I keep on praying," Teresa told her father.

"That is the best any of us can do," said Papa Juan.

There was no school during Holy Week, the week after the planting; and while Papa worked on the rancho, Mama Zita and Luis and Teresa walked every morning to the Mission at San Carlos. There, in the old church which had seen the Baptisms and the First Communions, the Confirmations and marriages and requiems of so many Neverías, Teresa, the youngest of them, prayed with a fervor that no other of them could have excelled. For, while Mama and Luis prayed mostly for favors received from the good God and for favors to come from Him, Teresa prayed for souls, for her own soul, for the souls of those dear to her, and for the souls of people she had never known and would never know. Something of the old spirit of the old Spain, which had fought for God and country against heretics and invaders, burned within the girl's spirit. She was so sure of the goodness of God that a miracle would have been no surprise to her; sometimes she came out into the plaza with the expectation of seeing the hillsides blossoming like the valleys of the Psalmist.

On Good Friday Papa Juan put aside his work and went with Mama and Luis and herself to the Mission. There, all day, they prayed with the hundreds of other men and women and children from the neighborhood, joining the sorrowing procession which followed the old Padre from Station to Station of the Cross. Then, sadly, for the death of Christ upon the Cross was vividly real to them, the Neverías walked homeward past hills which showed no sign of green to prove the worth of the labors of men against the forces of nature.

On Holy Saturday, only Luis and Teresa went to church. Mama Zita had much to do that day—the cleaning of the little adobe house, the baking of Easter delicacies, the sewing of a dress for Teresa to wear on the morrow. The day was cloudy as Teresa and Luis walked homeward, and Luis frowned at the sky.

"Rain," he sighed. "What will happen to our crop?"

"It will hold now," Teresa said, and her voice was as certain as ever Mama's had been. "God will not fail us."

The house seemed clean and quiet when they went in.

"Disturb nothing," Mama Zita told them. "On Easter morn all must be in order for the Resurrection. And go to bed early if you wish to be awake to see the sun dancing as it comes over the mountains."

"It doesn't really dance," said Luis.

"Of course it dances," Mama Zita said.

Perhaps because the thought lingered in her mind through the night, Teresa woke before dawn. She heard no sound in the little house as she quietly dressed; but as she stepped out from the low doorway, she saw Papa Juan standing in the dim grayness. He was staring toward the eastward, waiting, she thought, for the sun to come up beyond the mountains. She moved to his side, and put her hand within his work-worn one. "Christ is risen," she said.

This was, the girl told herself, a great moment in a great day—the dawn of Easter. Long ago, on such a dawn, the Marys had gone to the tomb where Christ had been laid after Calvary, and had found Him risen. Always, in the centuries between, the world had awakened to memory of His Resurrection. Today, watchers again, the two of them seemed to be waiting as the faithful had waited at the tomb.

"Christ is risen," her father repeated.

Then, above the line of the hills, came the rosy clouds of dawn. Below them the sun was rising. Slowly, over all the east, the sky grew bright. Then, at last, in golden glory, the sun rose above the summits, flooding the hillsides and valleys with brightness.

"See, see!" Teresa cried, and clutched her father's arm. "The sun is dancing, the sun is dancing on the hilltops!"

Papa Juan smiled at her. "Perhaps," he said. Then his own eyed widened in glad amazement. "Look!" He almost choked on the word. "Look, Teresita!" Tremblingly he pointed to the terraces where he had planted the seeds of the new crop. There, gleaming in bright, young green, stood the first promise of the plants which would make the crop. "The good God has brought them," said Papa.

Swiftly he went down upon his knees while tears streamed down his brown cheeks. For a moment he was silent; then he spoke as he stood up. "Call Mama," he bade Teresa. "She will want to see this miracle of Easter, although"—his

smile shared a secret with his daughter—"Mama will probably think that she was the one who really made it."

"God made it through Mama's plans and your work," Teresa said.

"*Sí, sí*," said Papa Juan. "Many and many a miracle has been made that way."

Organizing Material

1. In Part II, "Mama Zita Goes into Action," the five principal steps necessary to form a soil-conservation district are described. List on a paper the five necessary steps. The first step is done for you as an example.

Steps

Step 1. A signed petition is sent to
the state soil-conservation committee.

2. Write a paragraph telling how each of the five steps was carried out in San Carlos. Refer to the selection if necessary. You will find that some of the steps cover a number of pages, and others are described in a few paragraphs.

Using Local Color Words

As you recall, local color words are those which name things belonging to a particular area. An author uses them to make a story more vivid and realistic, to add a distinctive flavor to his work. Make a list of local color words which the author of this selection used to give a picture of America's Southwest, which the Spanish had settled centuries ago. Look them up in the Glossary and dictionary if you are not sure of their meanings.

The West Wind

It's a warm wind, the west wind, full of birds' cries;
I never hear the west wind but tears are in my eyes.
For it comes from the west lands, the old brown hills,
And April's in the west wind, and daffodils.

It's a fine land, the west land, for hearts as tired as mine,
Apple orchards blossom there, and the air's like wine.
There is cool green grass there, where men may lie at rest,
And the thrushes are in song there, fluting from the nest.

"Will ye not come home, brother? Ye have been long away,
It's April, and blossom time, and white is the may;
And bright is the sun, brother, and warm is the rain,—
Will ye not come home, brother, home to us again?

"The young corn is green, brother, where the rabbits run,
It's blue sky, and white clouds, and warm rain and sun.
It's song to a man's soul, brother, fire to a man's brain,
To hear the wild bees and see the merry spring again.

"Larks are singing in the west, brother, above the green wheat,
So will ye not come home, brother, and rest your tired feet?
I've a balm for bruised hearts, brother, sleep for aching eyes,"
Says the warm wind, the west wind, full of birds' cries.

It's the white road westwards is the road I must tread
To the green grass, the cool grass, and rest for heart and head,
To the violets and the warm hearts and the thrushes' song,
In the fine land, the west land, the land where I belong.

IRMA H. TAYLOR

Balto's Race against Death[1]

THE PALE FACE of Dr. Curtis Welch grew very serious as he looked about the hospital room. He knew that he faced a hard fight— and all alone! He was the only doctor in the little town of Nome, Alaska, that bitter, cold winter in 1925.

Already three people were dead.

On the hospital beds lay twenty-five sick people. They had diphtheria, a terrible throat disease. If it should get out of control, it would sweep like wildfire over hundreds of square miles. Eleven thousand Eskimos and white people were in danger!

"We've got to have help," Dr. Welch said in a worried voice. "I mean help from the outside!"

"Yes, it's getting away from us," agreed a nurse. "Maybe some town can send us more doctors. If we were only on the railroad, or if the sea weren't frozen! This load is too much for you alone."

"It is not doctors or nurses we need," said Dr. Welch. "It is medicine. I have hardly five shots of antitoxin left, and that is six years old. Maybe it is no good." He clasped his thin fingers. If he could shoot fresh antitoxin into the arms of the people who were well, they probably would not get sick.

The nurse spoke eagerly, "Can't you radio to Washington for antitoxin?"

"Yes, but it will take six weeks to get here. By that time we may have one of the worst disasters in history."

"But, Doctor, couldn't they reach us sooner with airplanes?" broke in the nurse.

"Not through this weather. No pilot could make it, and it is fifty degrees below zero." The doctor looked very grave. "Our only hope is to get antitoxin from some place closer. Take care of that Eskimo woman's throat while I call the radio station."

A few minutes later the cry for help was flashing across the snows. As people heard the bad news, they were much alarmed. Nome was more than six hundred miles from the nearest railroad and frozen in by the sea. Yet help must be sent at once.

A doctor in southern Alaska heard the message. He happened

[1] From *Perilous Journeys*, by Irma H. Taylor, copyright 1940, by Harcourt, Brace and Company, Inc.

to have a good supply of antitoxin, and immediately wired Dr. Welch: "I am sending antitoxin to Nenana on today's train." Nenana was the town closest to Nome on the railroad.

So the precious twenty-pound package was started on its journey. After the three hundred miles by train, it must be carried six hundred and fifty miles over the cruel snowbound trail stretching between Nenana and Nome.

Only dogs could make it!

Again the radio sent out a call— this time for drivers of dog teams. These drivers are known as mushers and their dogs as huskies, a good name for what are sometimes called Eskimo dogs. At once brave mushers picked out their strongest dogs, hitched them to their sleds, and hurried to the trail. The six-hundred-and-fifty-mile trail had never been covered in less than nine days. But this was a race against death, with eleven thousand lives at stake!

At eleven o'clock on Tuesday evening, January 27, the package on which so many lives depended was taken off the train at Nenana. The first musher, waiting with his dog team, took it eagerly and set out on the trail.

The great relay race had begun. Each musher struggled on until he reached the next man, twenty-five to one hundred miles away.

We do not know much about the first heroes who carried the medicine. We know their names and the route they took. But the greatest honor has been paid to the two mushers who bore the most dangerous part of the journey. Of course, their skill and daring would not have been enough. The others had to do their part also, but to these two fell the greatest tests of heroism. Their courage and that of the huskies who led their teams would have been hard to equal.

Shannon was the first musher. Every inch of the trail was familiar to him as he hurried down a frozen stream bed toward the Yukon River. Even in the dark he recognized which Indian dwelling he was passing. He knew he was making good time—more than five miles an hour.

Wednesday noon Shannon, tired but happy, turned the package over to the second musher. It was time for Shannon to stop, because his dogs were worn out. Losing no time, the second stout team plunged down the trail. By seven o'clock in the evening they had reached the Yukon River.

One hundred and fifty miles in twenty hours!

The next teams kept up the pace! Just twenty-four hours later the antitoxin was three hundred and fifty miles on its way.

Friday afternoon it was placed in the hands of Leonard Seppala, known far and wide as "the king of dog-team drivers." This daring musher had come out from Nome to meet the medicine. He had covered two hundred miles of difficult trail in four days. Now, with no chance to rest, his picked team of Siberian dogs turned back on the trail.

Seppala hoped to carry the antitoxin all the way back to Nome so that it would get there Saturday afternoon. This would mean covering those two hundred miles in one day! Even in the fresh fallen snow! And with the temperature down below zero!

His team soon came to the edge of the ice-covered Norton Bay. Anxiously he looked out over the frozen surface, for the direct route to Nome lay across this bay. It would be safer to take the land route around it, but that would add almost another hundred miles. If he followed the land, maybe the antitoxin would arrive too late. Seppala decided quickly. It would be the short, dangerous way.

"Gee, Togo!" he cried, and the beautiful forty-eight-pound husky dog headed over the ice.

The musher watched the sixteen-year-old dog with a thrill of pride. Togo was a natural leader. He was a wonder at picking up the trail, and the other dogs knew they must obey him.

It was now dark. The condition of ice worried Seppala. Any minute it might break up and drift out to sea. Sometimes, before they realized that the ice was free, travelers have been carried for miles on a loose ice cake. Some have been blown out into Bering Sea and drowned.

Horrible thoughts crowded into Seppala's mind. "Suppose the bay ice should suddenly crack up. We would be carried to open water and drift helplessly all night. Nobody could rescue us. My dogs would freeze to death—and so would I—if we did not drown first. And the antitoxin would be lost, somewhere on the bottom of the sea. They trusted it to me, and I must get through."

Speed—there lay his safety. Togo picked his way carefully as the team raced along. Each husky seemed to know that Seppala was depending upon him. They loved this master who never struck with a whip.

Midnight came. Seppala wondered whether they were halfway across. How cold it was! Didn't he hear a creaking noise? His heart stood still! Togo raced on as if he knew the danger.

At last the sky turned gray. The musher looked eagerly for signs of land. Ahead lay only an icy stretch.

No, wasn't that a shadowy coast line a bit to the right? A few minutes later he was sure. Another mile slipped by. They would make it safely—the ice would hold!

"My good dogs!" he cried proudly. "Gee, Togo!"

Togo led the team up on the snowy bank, and the treacherous bay ice was left behind. Seppala hummed a little song. Now if this team he loved could only go the rest of the way.

Suddenly, as he rounded a turn, he saw a dog team and master waiting on the trail. Much as he would have liked to go on himself, he knew it would be wiser to let this fresh team of dogs take over.

"Hello, Olson," he called, stopping his sled beside the new team. "Here is the antitoxin."

Olson's fingers soon were busy tying the package to his sled. "You made wonderful time, Seppala." Then Olson and his seven dogs were off. Before their twenty-five-mile run was over, these dogs were almost frozen.

With great relief Olson handed the antitoxin to the last musher. Gunnar Kasson, who lived in Nome, had been waiting in an empty cabin for two days and nights. He had not even slept, because he was afraid he might miss Olson. Thirteen stouthearted dogs made up his team.

He said to Olson, "I am going to take the antitoxin into the cabin for a few minutes. The terrible wind may have frozen it."

Although the men waited inside the cabin for two hours, the weather kept getting colder. It was thirty degrees below. Snow began to fall. Every time they looked outside, the flakes were pelting down all the faster. A snowstorm meant dangerous going, Kasson knew. But he said, "There is no use waiting any longer."

Stepping outside, he called his lead dog, "Hey, Balto!"

Thirteen balls of fur scrambled out of their warm nests in the snow.

"Here, Balto. Here, boy!"

A handsome husky with a glossy coat ran to his place at the head of the traces. As Kasson fastened the dog into the harness, he said, "Tonight we'll have a hard pull. We have to make it through, boy!"

The dog pricked up his ears and raised intelligent eyes as if he understood.

Thirty-four miles away lay the next town, a little place called Safety. They must reach it before snowbanks could pile up and block the trail.

"Mush!" cried Kasson.

The dogs headed out bravely on the trail following the coast. It was terribly hard pulling. Although animals and sled sank into the heavy snow, the team struggled on.

"Whew, I never felt a colder wind!" thought Kasson, trying to pull his long reindeer coat closer

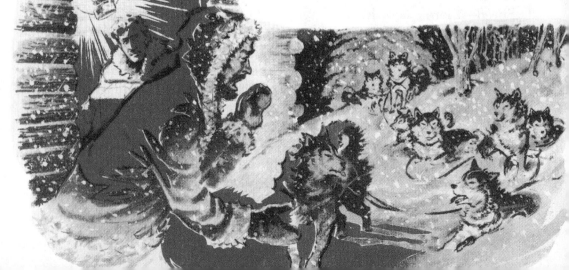

around him. Sealskin boots reached to his hips, and over these he wore sealskin trousers. His head was protected by a reindeer hood. But the fierce eighty-mile gale whipped right through the skins.

Their way led straight into the wind. How could he or the dogs face it? He feared they would all freeze to death. Even though they kept going, how long could they stay on the trail?

Something else made Kasson very uneasy. The ice under his feet was in constant motion from ocean ground swells. He turned the dogs in closer to the shore line. Now he was crossing the mouth of a frozen river.

Suddenly he realized that Balto was in trouble.

The lead dog had stepped into a pool of water, an overflow that had run up on the ice. Unless Balto's feet could be dried off immediately, the skin would stick to the ice and be torn off. Then he would have to drop out—and he was the only lead dog in the team. It was a bad moment. Just then Kasson saw the one thing which could save Balto's feet—a snow-drift a few yards away.

"Gee, Balto!" he shouted, and the dog turned sharply to the right.

When Balto felt the soft snow, he knew what to do. He worked his paws in the snow until they were dry. Now the skin was safe. Kasson breathed a sigh of relief.

Starting off again, he headed the team up a six-hundred-foot hill. Here there was nothing to stop the fury of the wind howling in off the sea. Kasson's lips set tightly. This hill was the spot he feared more than any other. Near the top he discovered that his right cheek had no feeling. It was frozen. He grabbed some snow and rubbed the cheek until it felt alive again.

He was glad to leave the hill behind. Next came a flat stretch six miles long. He wondered whether they would ever get across it, for the wind was picking up masses of snow and hurling them. Kasson was choked and blinded. He strained to catch sight of the dogs. The dog nearest the sled was not even a blur. He held up his hand —no use, he could not see it!

His heart sank. Lost—he was hopelessly lost. The antitoxin would never reach Nome. Yet the sled was moving steadily on. There was one hope left—that the dogs could keep the trail themselves. Kasson thought, "Balto will not fail me!"

The heroic lead dog never hesitated. Hurrying straight ahead, he scented the trail on the glaring, wind-swept ice. For two hours the musher held to the sled and trusted everything blindly to Balto.

95

They entered the tiny village of Solomon. Kasson did not even see the cabins. In this village a message was waiting for him: "Stop in Solomon until the storm clears. Then go on to Safety. Ed Rohn is there with a fresh team. Let him finish the race."

Kasson sped on through the storm, not knowing that he had passed Solomon—not dreaming he had missed an important message.

If anything, the wind grew more bitter in the next twelve miles. Kasson was filled with joy when finally he caught sight of an old log store. He was in the village of Safety. His wonderful Balto had followed the trail!

Kasson saw that all the houses were dark. Not knowing that another musher was waiting here, he thought, "Shall I stop for help? It would mean a long delay. There may not be any dogs in town strong enough to mush through the storm. Balto knows the trail; there is no other dog like him."

Speeding past the dark hotel, the team soon left Safety behind. Just twenty-one miles to go. The trail followed the shore of Bering Sea.

An angry wind whipped in from the sea. "I will tear you off the sled!" it seemed to cry. Kasson clung the tighter.

He was growing very tired. The dogs too were slowing up, almost worn out by the long, cruel grind. Deep drifts made the pulling terribly hard. Yet they struggled bravely on. They would reach the goal—or die in the traces!

Kasson was thinking of many things—the rosy flames of a warm fire, how wonderful it would feel when he got to Nome. Would all his dogs make it through? Too bad to lose even one—it must not be Balto! What wouldn't he give for a drink of steaming hot coffee? How far away was Nome? Fifteen miles? Twelve miles? How many more sick people had died? He must hurry—hurry—

Just then Kasson felt the sled pitch roughly. The next instant he was flung into the snow. As the sled overturned in a great drift, Balto slowed down and stopped the team. The dogs began to bark and fight, tangling up their harness.

Kasson jumped up and put the sled back on both runners. Then, lashing his whip, he quieted the dogs. It took him some time to straighten their harness in the dark. When they were ready to start again, he reached down to see whether the antitoxin was securely fastened.

What a horrible moment—the antitoxin was gone!

Crawling on his hands and knees, he hunted frantically in the snow. The sled had turned over on the right. Surely he would find the metal can there—if he had not lost it miles back on the trail. Could that have happened?

No, thank heaven, here it was!

His heart began to beat again. This time he tied the package very securely.

As they set out, the snowfall seemed lighter. At times he could see a bit of trail ahead. Then in the half-light he saw that two dogs were suffering—the two that had been frozen a few weeks before. The poor creatures were limping stiffly. Stopping the team, he fastened rabbitskin covers over these two dogs; but it didn't help much, for the cold went right through. If they should die, he would leave them and press on. If all the dogs should die, he would still go on, carrying the antitoxin in his arms. Nome—he must get to Nome!

He wished for morning as the hours dragged by. Now he was running behind the sled, for the team was staggering. "Keep going, Balto!" he cried. "We're almost there!" It seemed that the team could not last another mile.

He was straining his eyes looking for the lumber mill at the edge of Nome.

At last it appeared out of the falling snow. Thank God, they had made it—they had made it to Nome! It was 5:36 in the morning of Monday, February 2—just five and a half days after the start at Nenana.

The dogs seemed to know that the end of the great race was here. They hurried past the mill, past a row of wooden houses. Kasson heard people shouting, knew they were running after him. He turned to the left—there was the hospital. The next thing he knew, Dr. Welch was wringing his hand.

"You got here in time!" cried the doctor. The crowd shouted.

Half frozen and almost blinded, Kasson dropped down into the snow. With tears in his eyes he started to pull ice splinters out of Balto's paws.

"Balto!" he cried. "Wonderful dog! You brought us through!"

Evaluating Statements

Copy the statements below and beside each write *F* if it expresses a fact and *O* if it expresses an opinion.

_____ 1. A diphtheria epidemic raged through Nome, Alaska, during the winter of 1925.
_____ 2. Antitoxin generally counteracts the dread disease.
_____ 3. The hospital at Nome was poorly staffed and badly equipped.
_____ 4. Dog-team drivers are called mushers, and their dogs are referred to as huskies.
_____ 5. Alaskans are a brave, energetic people.
_____ 6. Eskimos enjoy the sub-zero weather, and they pay little attion to wind and snow.
_____ 7. Nome is in the Arctic Circle, hundreds of miles removed from a rail center.
_____ 8. Leonard Seppala had a reputation for being outstanding among dog-team drivers.
_____ 9. Credit for bringing the antitoxin to the hospital on time to save the diphtheria victims belongs to Balto.
_____ 10. The trip from Nenana to Nome took the mushers five and a half days.

Knowing Synonyms

Write a synonym for each of the following words:

disaster	eagerly	realized	handsome	constant
alarmed	route	treacherous	gale	hesitated

JAMES DAUGHERTY

The Trail Breakers

WE REMEMBER, we do not forget, oh Trail Breakers searching
The river courses to their secret sources,
Platte, Yellowstone, Sweetwater, Columbia,
Seeking out the passes over the shining mountains across
The Big Horns, Bitterroot, Medicine Bow,
The Tetons, the Cascades, the Sierras.
The wind in the Great South Pass remembers the lost trappers.

Under the red bluffs the wagon trains pass, the prairie schooners,
The white tops in dusty processions along the Oregon Trail, the Santa Fe,
Bringing the Prairie Breakers, the plowmen, the bull-tongued plows
To cut the tough sod in Nebraska, in the Dakotas.
Armies of green corn for Iowa, for Minnesota the golden sea of wheat . . .
Pioneer mothers listening to wilderness cries in the twilight
In the sod huts of the Kansas prairie. . . .

Mule train, stage coach, pony express, pushing through the mountain
    passes;
The Iron Horse rolls spouting black clouds and cinders;
The Continental Express roars on, faster, faster, faster.
On the six-lane highways the sleek speeders are streaking west.
The Airliner drones across the sky, nine hours to California.
The Jet Plane, the Supersonic Rocket, the mushroom blast of the Atomic
    Age!

Astoria, the log fort forgotten between the forest and the sea
Lost in the white sea fog and the drip of the perpetual forest.
For the time is not ripe for the dream, a bound rushing ahead
Of slow destinies, for Astor's encompassing dream.
The vision is true but the hour has not come, only the voice
Calling in the wilderness, "The vision is yet for an appointed time
But in the end it shall speak, and not lie;
Though it tarry, wait for it, because it will surely come,
It will not tarry."

On Cartridge Pass[1]

"IT's a tough break, Cress." Dr. Jim Estabrook finished bandaging her blistered feet, and Cressida Pomeroy, disappointment written all over her face, bent to lace up her boots. "Those broken blisters are so deep," he continued gently, "that you can't possibly walk out of here tomorrow morning. You'll have to ride one of the horses to Marion Lake. It's going to be a hard trek—one of the hardest of our whole trail trip. First we have to get to the bottom of the canyon here below us." A long arm gestured toward the opposite side of the lake nestling high in the Sierra Mountains. "Then we crawl straight up over Cartridge Pass and down the other side. After that we follow down Cartridge Creek, I don't know how many miles."

Dennis Pomeroy, who had spent his college vacations as a member of the Sequoia Hiking Club staff, smiled gently down from his lanky height. "Don't take it so hard, Sis. Just a little tenderfoot luck."

[1]An adaptation based on *Hoofbeats on the Trail*, by Vivian Breck. Copyright 1950 by Vivian Gurney Breckenfeld. By permission of Doubleday & Co., Inc.

At seven the following morning Cress stood waiting beside the roped-off corral. One of the older women, her bandaged ankle out in front of her, sat with the other riders under a tree. Cress climbed on top of a rock where she could watch the hikers starting down the trail with their knapsacks. With all her heart she wished she were among them.

A few walked directly toward the rim of the canyon. These were the select ones—rock climbers, long-legged youths, and practiced mountaineers. She thought of them bounding lightly down the steep slide of rock debris, pausing just long enough to enjoy the gardens of purple columbine flourishing where the outlet from Bench Lake trickled down the canyon wall. But the main flow of the hiking traffic wound away through the forest to follow the little piles of rock—the ducks—which Scott, their leader, had set up yesterday.

By now most of the animals had been brought in—mules which were to be packed with equipment and horses which were to be ridden by the packers. But some were

100

still missing and there was no horse yet for Cress.

"Horses go up high," muttered old Joe, their Indian guide. "Early morning, horse get cold. Go up high on mountain for get sun."

By ten o'clock most of the packers had found their animals. Cress watched them saddle up and ride away, leading the mules toward the now deserted camp, where piles of equipment lay waiting.

The saddle-horse boy gathered his small group of riders together and looked questioningly at Cress.

"Don't wait for me," Cress said. "Please don't. I'll overtake you easily."

"Okay, miss. You're sure that's all right? You know how to ride?"

"Oh, yes. I've ridden before."

The boy touched his buckskin cow pony with one spur, wheeled, waved, and led off across the clearing. The other riders waved good-by and followed.

For what seemed at least an hour Cress sat alone. She counted the animals tied to the trees. Mules all of them, except Socks, a heavy old "truck horse." Suddenly, galloping hoofs brought Cress to her feet, and Mitch, one of the packers, came into view. He swung out of the saddle and came toward Cress, spurs clanking.

"Listen, Cress. You better get aboard Socks and get going. The other horses must have gone farther than we thought. If you're going to get to Marion Lake before

dark, you'll have to beat it now."
He grinned. "That Cartridge Pass
is dangerous. I'll wait because I
can take my mules down the short
trail and save hours. But you'll
have to go by the regular animal
trail." He gestured to indicate the
direction. "You ride three miles
back along this bench, the same
way you come in to Bench Lake.
There's a junction there and you'll
see some signs. Take the trail
leadin' left, down to the river.
That's the headwaters of the South
Fork. After you cross it, turn sharp
left again and come the same three
miles back again along the river
bed. Got a map?"

"Yes."

Mitch handed her the reins. He
helped her into the saddle, looped
her knapsack over the pommel, and
waved good-by.

The trail through the woods was
studded with hoofmarks all the
way to the junction, and, as Mitch
had said, the junction was plainly
marked with signposts. Socks,
however, had no intention of turning down toward the river. In fact
he had positive ideas about going
back the way he had come.

Annoyed, Cress yanked on the
reins and kicked at the massive
ribs. The big horse merely lum-
bered round and round in maddening and deliberate circles. Finally
Cress rode him to a place where

she could twist a branch from a
tree. Beating his haunches till the
branch broke in her hands, she got
him headed at last in the right direction.

The trail still seemed to be running the wrong way, but at least
it was winding downhill toward
the bottom of the canyon. It was
weird riding alone. She had not
realized before what a comforting
sense of companionship she had received from the other members of
the club, even those whom she
scarcely knew by name. They were
all far ahead of her now. Mitch
would cross the South Fork long
before she did. Only Coke, the

102

head packer, and old Joe, the Indian guide, were still behind. If they also went down the ducked trail, there would be no one behind. No one at all. These and a thousand thoughts like them whooshed through her head as Socks picked his way slowly along the descending trail.

Several hours later, when they came to the river, it was impossible to believe this small bubbling stream was the torrent she had seen, earlier on the trip, foaming past Zumwalk Meadow. Even Socks made no fuss about crossing. Cress was hungry and very thirsty. Sliding off the saddle, she tied Socks to a tree and drank eagerly from the clear, cold water. She ate the crackers and liver sausage which constituted today's rations, washing them down with another cup of water. The dried fruit she stuck in the pocket of her jacket to munch as she rode.

Before remounting she took a good look at the map. It was easy to find the exact spot where she was sitting now; the dotted trail line crossed the blue line of the river at this ford. At last she was going to turn west. Studying the closely drawn contour lines which indicated the ridge to the north, Cress realized that the climb over Cartridge Pass would be all that Mitch had said.

Getting back in the saddle turned out to be a problem. Socks was too high to mount from the ground, and when she led him to a log or a rock on which she could stand, he had a maddening way of moving off just as she was about to put one foot in the stirrup. Turning this big hulk around took moral persuasion, physical strength, and infinite patience. By the time Cress landed in the saddle again, her arms ached from pulling and hauling.

"I bet I could ride an elephant after this," she giggled to herself, as the four white feet took up their plodding progress downstream.

On the north side of the river the trail was less clear than before. Cress had to keep alert every second. There were fresh animal tracks visible now and then, indicating that pack trains had gone this way. Then again there seemed to be no hoofprints at all. Deer trails added to the confusion. Twice Cress got off on one and wound up in a dead-end thicket of brush. Then laboriously she made the unwilling Socks rightabout-face and go back to the meeting of the two pathways. She began looking for blazes cut into the tree trunks, or for ducks, but there were none.

If the main body of walkers had been following a trail as obscure as this, Cress knew that Scott, their leader, would have led the way, marking any questionable turns with paper arrows. But today this was the packers' route only, and the experienced packers knew where they were going.

A startled buck crashing off into the underbrush set Cress's heart pounding with fright. Her knees, unaccustomed to the saddle, were beginning to cramp. She would have liked to walk awhile. But considering her struggle to remount at lunchtime, she decided against it. Mitch's remark about being caught on the pass by darkness rang in her ears as she kicked and kicked at the horse's heavy flanks.

The trail came out of the timber and turned sharply toward the water. Right to the river's edge it ran —and stopped. The place didn't look like a ford. The water was swift, full of large rocks, and there was no trail continuing on the other side—nothing but a dense thicket of scrub willow. She must have got off on another deer trail. Cress turned her horse around and stuck him so sharply with her heel that he broke into a gallop. She rode back about a quarter of a mile, picked up mule tracks, turned around, and landed back at the river again. There *was* no other trail.

Once more she took out the map. The trail plainly crossed the river from north to south and back again

before starting on the long grind over the pass. The reason for this was equally plain. On the northern bank the way was barred by a rocky slope. Jumbled blocks of granite as large as stoves had broken off the mountain and rolled right to the river's edge. No horse could possibly travel here. The trail must cross the river. But it didn't.

Grateful for a chance to stretch her legs, Cress slid off the saddle, tied Socks to a bush, and set out to explore. Scrambling and slipping, using both hands as well as her feet, she started over the rocks. Panic was churning in her now. Yet she knew it was silly to be panicky. The trail must be there somewhere. But where?

"A trail just isn't any use if you can't find it," she sobbed aloud.

She got back on the horse again and tried to ride him across the stream. Socks put two forefeet into the swirling water, sniffed it, and refused to budge.

"Do I have to carry you over?" Cress yelled. "You clumsy old elephant!" Slowly Socks withdrew his feet from the water and stood like a rock.

Actually Cress didn't blame the beast. The channel looked treacherous and deep. It was hard to gauge depth because of the white water eddying around the boulders

in midstream. Certainly the South Fork was much more of a river here than at the spot where they had crossed at lunchtime. A sickening thought attacked her mind. Was that the place she had made her mistake? Were the tracks she had been seeing those of some other pack train and not those of the Sequoia Club at all?

Once more Cress got off. In a mounting frenzy she waded straight into the river and began hauling on the reins. "All right, if you won't walk I'll drag you across!" Above the noise of rushing water she shrieked, "Come on, Socks."

With a sudden lunge he followed her into the stream. The water rose quickly over the tops of her boots,

but Cress was past caring. She struggled one step forward, bracing herself against the pull of the current; turned back, yanked with all her strength, plunged forward again in a rush to get out of the way of the great black legs. Dear heaven, she thought, suppose I get this dopey creature halfway over and then he decides to go stubborn again—to stay right here for the night. "Socks! Come on!"

Plunge by plunge they approached the opposite bank. How she was going to ride through the thickets of brush on the other side she didn't know. Then suddenly, as the bank came within striking distance, Socks gave a mighty jump and landed on dry ground. Cress

threw herself flat in the water to avoid the great legs flailing the air, but she was not quick enough. As the horse sprang past, one hoof grazed her ankle. She collapsed into the river in a white-hot spasm of pain.

Trailing his reins, Socks went crashing off into the head-high brush. Using all her will power to pull herself out of the water, Cress crawled up the bank and unlaced her boot. At least the ankle wasn't broken, she decided, as she wiggled it gingerly back and forth. The blow had taken off a couple of layers of skin, but the intense pain, already diminishing, was because of being struck directly on the ankle-bone. She squeezed the water out of her socks and dragged them back

on, then stood up, dripping, to see what had become of Socks. He was standing, stock-still as usual, nibbling willow tips about fifty feet away.

Cress scrambled through the tangle of bushes till she reached her steed. Then, bending a dense thicket of brush to serve as a mounting block, she managed to get into the saddle.

"Socks! Look!" The words came with a squeal of joy as Cress urged him toward a rock cairn a short distance upstream.

The whole story was plain enough now. And when they had finally penetrated the willow jungle to reach the cairn, the trail itself was equally plain. The ford was a long diagonal crossing, going in what was apparently the wrong direction in order to avoid some large rocks.

Since the stones had been piled up to mark the crossing, the willow had grown so tall that the cairn was invisible from the other side of the river.

When they reached the next crossing of the South Fork, Socks, unpredictable as ever, stumped over the sandy bottom as if he had been ambling across his own corral.

More than once Cress had wondered why so careful a head packer as Coke had brought Socks into the mountains as a saddle horse for inexperienced riders. But as he carried her up the heartbreaking grade toward the top of Cartridge Pass, she began to understand.

Socks's strong body, his sturdy heart and lungs, were carrying her willingly up and up through steep heavy sand. It was an old trail—a perpendicular model—which ran straight to its destination at the top of the ridge without bothering to zigzag. At times Cress leaned forward and grabbed the horse's mane to counteract the sensation that she was about to slide off backward. No wonder Coke had hesitated to take loaded mules up this grade. No wonder she had heard old Joe say, "We gotta rope them mules good today. Else we gotta stop and rope over again goin' up."

Timberline lay below. Relentlessly an unshaded sun beat down on Cress's head. Her knees ached, and she knew for certain that she had been sitting a long time on hard leather. But not for anything would she have checked this steady upward progress by getting off to rest. Higher and higher the trail wound, until she could look straight down into the faces of the tiny ice-blue lakes below the pass. Rock-rimmed, treeless, and bleak, these lakes, yet strangely exciting. She forgot physical discomfort to enjoy the piercing color of them, the violent thrust of the cliffs.

Socks's heavy withers gave a last scramble up over the rocks and stopped dead. Cress gasped. Here it was. The top of Cartridge Pass. But the trail dropping off into space below looked like no trail at all. The north side of the ridge was not only rougher, bleaker, stonier than the south; it was also steeper. She couldn't ride down over those boulders with the horse slipping and sliding under her. Even if Socks could be persuaded to carry her down, she dared not try. She would have to lead him to the bottom of this first steep pitch.

Mitch must be far ahead now. Only Coke and old Joe were behind her. Or perhaps none of them were behind. It was lonely standing on the top of the world by herself, lonelier than anything Cress had ever imagined.

She was startled by the noise of

a rolling rock. She looked up to see old Joe on his pinto just rising over the top of the pass.

"Oh, Joe!" cried Cress. "Is Coke behind you?"

The old Indian nodded, lifted a hand in salute, and was gone. She stood watching the brown-and-white pony with the big head stepping down the mountainside as if it had been a stretch of prairie. As long as Joe was in sight she stood looking, trying to see where the trail led through the rocks. Then, picking up her own reins, she started down the steep slope, hauling Socks behind her.

It was not easy. His big, clumsy hoofs did not move nimbly, as the pinto's had. Sometimes his back feet slid so that he seemed to be sitting on his tail. Again he lunged forward so suddenly that Cress had to jump aside to keep out of the way. His lumbering hulk followed so close behind that his muzzle brushed her neck.

At last, as abruptly as it had plunged down from the pass, the trail leveled out into a wide, stony basin. With a fervent sigh of relief Cress turned to look back at the wall she had just descended. There, like ants against the skyline, she saw Coke on his chestnut horse followed by a string of mules coming over the crest. The light made the tiny figures look black.

At times the animals on the mountain seemed to stand still, feeling their way. Then they slid downward a few more feet, halted again. It was a grueling descent. The ground tilted so steeply that, from where Cress stood, it looked as if all six were hung dangling on a string. Watching held a kind of gloomy fascination. If one of the mules slipped, certainly the rest would be pulled head over heels to destruction with him. In the distance the rocks looked like pebbles, but Cress knew how big they were, how slippery with melting snow. Her own boots, which had begun to dry out after wading the river, were sopping again from the water sluicing down Cartridge Pass.

Now Coke and the mules were moving diagonally across the slope. Cress remembered the place. The trail was completely obliterated by a snowbank. She had left Socks standing while she hunted a possible route around the gray glacier-like mass. Seeing the animals now in profile, she recognized the packs. The lead mule was balancing one of the sheet-iron stoves precariously on its spine.

With a sharp gasp Cress clapped both hands over her mouth, withdrew them tensely. "Oh no!" The words were a whisper of horror.

The lead mule, the one which

seemed to be dangling directly above Coke's head, was rolling. It all happened so fast that afterward Cress could scarcely sort out the sequence of events. Coke went flying through the air. The rolling mule came to a stop and did not rise again. A whirl of arms and legs jolted from rock to rock. Then Coke, too, lay still.

Cress waited for him to get up. The seconds were hours. He did not move. The rest of the pack train ground to a halt. Socks pawed at the ground and gave an unearthly whinny that echoed from peak to peak around the vast granite basin. Still Cress stood, waiting and wondering, listening to the terrified beat of her own heart.

She forgot that she had blistered feet, forgot that she was not supposed to walk. Even if she had to crawl on hands and knees, she knew she had to get to Coke. Nothing mattered now except helping Coke. But how? What am I going to do when I get to him? Suppose he's dead. Appalling thoughts boiled in her head. Oh, dear God, help me! Help me to know what to do.

She untied the coil of rope from her saddle and anchored one end as best she could under a large stone. If Socks took off he'd have to go, that was all. Coke was hurt and alone. The mountains had seemed big before. Now every crag was magnified. The thin air seemed otherworldly. The whole place had a hollow feel, void. Socks felt the loneliness, too. He kept tossing his head and pawing the rock to express his longing to get close to the other animals.

Cress began climbing back toward the pass as fast as her legs would propel her. It was difficult going. Her muscles were tense, her breath came in gasps, and the raw flesh on her heels gave her merciless jabs of pain.

When she reached him, Coke was lying on his side, limp, motionless, his eyes closed. Not twenty feet above him the mule lay wedged against a boulder with all four feet in the air, the stove still under its back.

"Coke! Coke! Are you all right? Can you hear me?" There was no answer. She lifted one limp arm, fumbling for a pulse. Not a quiver ran through his veins. Perhaps she wasn't feeling in the right place. She opened the blue denim jacket, laid her ear directly against his shirt, and cried out with joy. Distinctly she had caught the throb of a heartbeat.

"Coke! Speak to me. It's Cress. Cress Pomeroy." Still no response came from the motionless form on the ground. But she could feel the rhythm of his breath, incredibly slow, far off, but perceptible. The nearby rocks were wet with melting snow. Cress sopped her bandanna in the trickle and laid the cold cloth over Coke's forehead, moistening his lips with a finger. Still Coke made no sound.

Perhaps the best thing would be to ride on to Marion Lake for help. One idea was fixed firmly in Cress's mind. If Coke was suffering from concussion, or if his bones were broken—or his back—he mustn't be moved without a stretcher. Still trying to make up her mind what to do, she moved up the hill toward the fallen mule.

The frayed end of the rope

which had fastened the pack animals together lay on the ground. Cress looked down at it with a sudden realization of the terrific pull it had taken to jerk those tough fibers apart. In that moment the rope itself seemed to crystallize into a symbol of man pitted against the fierce, dynamic force of these mountains—man pitted and broken. She, Cress Pomeroy, was not the center of the world. She was only a solitary speck on a spinning globe. A hundred and fifty people traveling together, she thought with awe, but you're still alone. In a tight place it's still every person for himself.

She stared at the rigid legs of the mule sticking into the air and turned away. There was nothing she could do about that. But Coke was alive. Unconscious, but breathing. She had to get help to him before dark.

Heavy-hearted and with shaking knees, she hurried down the rock pile. With less trouble than usual she climbed aboard Socks and began urging him frantically to speed up his maddening pace. Ducks of rocks were piled up here and there as guides. Over and over, just as Cress thought she had lost the way, another duck came into sight ahead. The trail wandered all over the landscape, and the way to find it was to look for the easiest place to go. Several times she had to ride around in circles to locate the next marker. Then panic grasped her, and she rode with desperate urgency. The sun had already dropped out of sight in the west, and a chill in the air gave warning of the quick, cold mountain night. When Coke regained consciousness, Doctor Jim must be there with something to deaden the pain.

When she came to a small meadow where the sod was worn into an unmistakable rut, meaning many hoofs had trodden here, the certainty was sweet as honey. She took out the contour map again to look closely at the trail before dark. Marion Lake was off to the left—somewhere. And by now somewhere shouldn't be very far. A low ridge separated the lake from Cartridge Creek, down which she was traveling. The main trail went straight downstream all the way to Simpson Meadow. Somewhere— and surely soon—Cress had to turn left onto a minor trail winding around the ridge which walled in the lake. If the turning was obscure, she felt certain Scott would have tacked an arrow on a tree. However, if the light grew too dim, she might easily overlook such a mark. In that case she might go riding on and on, down through the rugged canyon of Cartridge Creek. There would be nothing to stop her from riding all the way to Simpson Meadow four thousand feet below.

It seemed queer that she could not look down onto the lake. Not once since coming over the pass had she even glimpsed it. Was it possible that already she had ridden too far? Marion Lake, which Cress had heard described as a small blue sapphire at the bottom of a bowl, lay at an elevation of ten thousand feet. The thickening of the forest as well as the steepness of the trail made her feel that she might be below this level.

Breaking off a branch to replace the one long since worn out, she began lashing Socks. Her right arm flailed and her heels kicked until finally the big horse broke into a trot that almost jolted her out of the saddle.

He thundered along like an old fire horse until the pitch of the trail made anything except a walk impossible. With every additional step downward Cress felt her heart sinking. She was positive now that she had overshot the junction.

It was not for herself now that she was afraid. In a pinch she could sit out the night alone with a fire. But Coke! He might come to and find himself in a torture of pain. Dr. Jim Estabrook's quiet reassurance, codein, hands to lift and help him—these were the things

he needed. Or perhaps he would never regain consciousness.

The trail swerved sharply to avoid an old giant of a tree, and there, taped to a fallen stump, bright and warming as the blazing hearth of home, hung the orange paper arrow pointing off to the left. Socks whinnied and crashed over broken twigs onto the little-traveled trail. Within five minutes the ruddy glow of campfires was visible in the twilight sky.

On a small grassy flat at the outlet of the lake the entire camp seemed to be assembled. Three or four small fires were burning, and droves of people were milling about, getting in one another's way. Not only both stoves, Cress realized, but the big nest of cooking pots had been packed on Coke's mules. Dinner was, of course, delayed.

Scott was sitting by himself on a rock at the edge of the water, staring across the lake at a wall of granite which rose sheerly to a fluting of snow. Smoke circled his head, but he seemed unconscious of it. Half running, Cress stumbled toward him.

He flung around. "Cress! Am I ever glad to see you! What happened? Have you seen Coke?"

Cress's heart thudded like a stone. Breathlessly she blurted out the story: her own late start, Coke's fall, the dead mule lying on top of a stove. Scott listened, tightening his lips. Cress noticed the tension in him. When he took off his glasses to wipe them on a bandanna, she noticed his eyes—red-rimmed, whether from sun glare or sitting in the smoke she did not know. Responsibility for other people was a heavy thing. In time of stress the whole weight of it lay on the leader. His decisions could mean life or death.

"Dennis, get over to the packers' camp on the double. We'd better have six horses. Tell old Joe to pick them. Doctor Jim and you and I will go, and three packers."

Long hours later commotion started on the fringes of the crowd. Shouts rose. "He's here! Hi! He's in. It's Coke!"

Cress pushed her way through the surging people and stood gaping at the familiar figure in the black ten-gallon hat, the tilt and twist of it as much his own as his face. And suddenly tears of relief were spilling down her cheeks as he rode slowly down the trail.

Sensing Emotions

Number your paper from 1 to 16. Then read the following statements which recall events of the story. Beside each number write, from what you learned in the story, the feeling conveyed by each of the statements.

1. The doctor ordered Cress not to walk on her blistered feet.
2. Socks, an old horse, was slow and stubborn, and Cress beat him with a switch which she had made from a branch of a tree.
3. Cress had never before realized how much companionship means.
4. After consulting her map, Cress knew that the trip over Cartridge Pass was going to be dangerous.
5. Cress laughed to herself at the slow, old horse she was riding.
6. Cress's heart pounded as a startled buck crashed into the underbrush.
7. She began to wonder if she had followed the tracks of some other pack train and not those of the Sequoia Club.
8. Socks gave a mighty jump and Cress threw herself into the water to avoid the great legs flailing the air, but one heavy hoof grazed her ankle.
9. On the other side of the stream, Cress found the trail whose markers she could not see from the other side because of the tall willows.
10. There Cress stood completely alone, looking down from the height of Cartridge Pass at the world below.
11. At last the trail leveled out into a wide, stony basin.
12. Looking up, she saw Coke and the string of mules coming over the crest.
13. Cress saw the mule tumble, then Coke went flying through the air.
14. It seemed that she should have reached Marion Lake by this time. Had she missed the mark? Had she ridden too far?
15. Scott, the leader, tightened his lips as he heard Cress's report of the accident.
16. Tears streamed down Cress's cheeks as she saw Coke riding down the trail.

Robert Frost

The Runaway

Once, when the snow of the year was beginning to fall,
We stopped by a mountain pasture to say, "Whose colt?"
A little Morgan had one forefoot on the wall,
The other curled at his breast. He dipped his head
And snorted to us. And then he had to bolt.
We heard the miniature thunder where he fled,
And we saw him or thought we saw him dim and gray,
Like a shadow against the curtain of falling flakes.
"I think the little fellow's afraid of the snow.
He isn't winter-broken. It isn't play
With the little fellow at all. He's running away.
I doubt if even his mother could tell him, 'Sakes,
It's only weather.' He'd think she didn't know!
Where is his mother? He can't be out alone."
And now he comes again with clatter of stone
And mounts the wall again with whited eyes
And all his tail that isn't hair up straight.
He shudders his coat as if to throw off flies.
"Whoever it is that leaves him out so late,
When other creatures have gone to stall and bin,
Ought to be told to come and take him in."

The Earth, the Sky, and the Psalms

His Holiness, Pope Pius XII, in his encyclical *Mediator Dei*, said: *"To all who are born to life on earth the Church gives a second, supernatural kind of birth,"* and, in the same document, he reaffirmed the principle: *"The most pressing need of Christians is to live the liturgical life, and increase and cherish its supernatural spirit."*

How does the liturgy of the Church apply to this unit, "Under the Wide and Starry Sky"? It applies in the knowledge that God created all things out of nothing; that He made all things in heaven and in and on the earth.

The liturgy of the Church sings of the goodness of God, His wisdom and power, His beauty and majesty.

The liturgy proclaims that creatures of God prove His existence by their own existence, and by their lives, their movements, their order and design.

The liturgy explains that the earth and all other bodies of the universe move in regular order according to the law of God, that God made man greater than all other creatures on the earth by giving him an immortal soul made in His image.

Feasts and seasons of the Church, time of sowing and time of harvest, fill the pages of Holy Scripture, for they are the stories of God's love for mankind. Holy Scripture and the liturgical year are closely related, and nowhere is the handiwork of God upon earth more vividly phrased than in the Psalms.

A magnificent hymn, praising the majesty and power of God, was written by David, King of Israel. In it, the psalmist sings of the marvels wrought by God—sea and sky, streams and field, sun and moon, day and night. It is called "Hymn of All Creation to the Almighty Creator," also known as Psalm 148.

Praise the Lord from the heavens,
  praise him from the heights;
Praise him, all you his angels,
  praise him, all you his hosts.
Praise him, sun and moon;
  praise him, all you shining stars.
Praise him, you highest heavens,
  and you waters above the
    heavens.
Let them praise the name of the
  Lord,
  for he commanded and they
    were created;
He established them forever and
    ever;
  He gave them a duty which
    shall not pass away.

Everything in the universe reflects the wisdom, the power, and the providence of God. All of nature follows the law of God and gives glory to Him. Man alone, above all creatures, can *will* to follow God's law and give Him praise by free choice, and so merit the reward of eternal happiness in heaven.

The liturgical movement is one name for all those interconnected and interdependent works being carried on in the Church today to restore the faithful to their rightful inheritance of a fully sacramental Catholic life.

Using Reference Material

As you grow older, you will find that your reading will expand the knowledge which you already have acquired in your studies. On the other hand, our background knowledge should make our reading more meaningful. See how well you can apply your knowledge by answering the following questions which are raised in the selection. If you need help, use your religion book or some other reference book.

1. What is an encyclical?
2. When does the "supernatural kind of birth," of which the selection speaks, take place?
3. What is the liturgy?
4. When does the liturgical year begin?
5. What is the liturgical movement?

Interpreting a Psalm

1. What was the psalmist referring to when he wrote "Praise him, you highest heavens, and you waters above the heavens"?
2. What did he mean by "for he commanded and they were created"?
3. What is meant by the line, "He gave them a duty which shall not pass away"?
4. Why is the praise which man can give to God superior to that of all other creatures?

Using the Dictionary

Use your dictionary to locate the meanings of the following words:

reaffirmed	cherish	universe	vividly	reflects
principle	proclaim	immortal	phrased	providence

ARTHUR GUITERMAN

Heritage

THIS is the land that we love; where our fathers found refuge,
    Here are the grooves of their plows and the mounds of their graves;
These are the hills that they knew and the forest and waters,
    Glorious rivers and seas of rejuvenant waves.

This is our heritage, this that our fathers bequeathed us,
    Ours in our time, but in trust for the ages to be;
Wasting or husbanding, building, destroying or shielding,
    Faithful or faithless—possessors and stewards are we.

What of our stewardship? What do we leave to our children?
    Crystalline, health-giving fountains, or gutters of shame?
Fields that are fertile, or barrens exhausted of vigor?
    Burgeoning woodlands, or solitudes blasted by flame?

Madly we squander the bounty and beauty around us,
    Wrecking, not using, the treasure and splendor of earth;
Only in grief unavailing for glory departed—
    Only in want do we count what the glory is worth.

Now let us heal and restore where we trample and plunder,
    Cleansing and saving our shallowing rivers and rills,
Lending new life to the fields we have ravaged and beggared,
    Calling new forests to gladden the desolate hills.

Then though we pass from the land that our fathers bequeathed us,
    Mountain and river and wood shall our message renew:
"This is the land that we loved; oh, be faithful, our children!
    Fair was it left to us; fairer we leave it to you!"

3. American People

THESE are our people:
farmers who break the soil and plow the fields,
who dig the furrows, and who plant the seeds;
the men who sow and grow the mighty crops
that fill the cupboards of our nation's needs;
men of the hills and of the ocean's shore,
of the lake country and the mountain's crest,
of midland prairies and of sprawling plains,
of purple mesas and of golden west;
laboring in the dawn and in the dusk,
backs often bent beneath their heavy loads,
but pausing, for a little, from their tasks
as neighbors pass upon the country roads.

These are our people:
miners who burrow in the earth for coal,
miners who scoop vast shovels of iron ore,
miners who dredge salt from the ocean depths,
miners with nuggets on the river shore;
men blasting granite from the mountainsides
for churches to arise with gleaming domes,
men making bricks from sticky fields of clay,
or hewing trees to make a nation's homes;
men building dams to harness surging power
and serve the valleys that the waters spanned;
men lifting derricks that black gold may flow
in steady streams across a needing land.

These are our people:
drivers who steer great trucks on highways wide,
roaring through little villages at night,
feet on the pedals, driving steadily
to reach their markets by the dawning light;
crews of the railroads who take mighty trains
up steep-sloped mountains and through narrow dales,
moving through heat or cold or snow or sand,
as massive engines pound the shining rails;
sailors at work on decks or in the holds
as the long ships set out for lands afar;
and airplane pilots winging through the blue
within a ship that glistens like a star.

These are our people:
the men and women of the little towns,
the sprawling cities, and the lonely heights;
the young, the old, the workers in the dark,
the toilers of the day and of the night;
the girls of offices and factories,
the buyers and the sellers in the marts;
the builders of majestic enterprise,
and those who only do their tiny parts;
united in one thought, our nation's good—
merger of many lands and many climes,
the rich, the poor, the many-millioned mass—
our brothers, under God, in these, our times.

First Part of the Declaration of Independence

July 4, 1776

As citizens of the United States we may be inclined to take our freedom as a matter of course. But we know better. The great documents that contain "the words that set men free" are like markers showing the stages of our difficult progress. Underlying this first marker, the famous Declaration of Independence, is one all-important idea which is basic to freedom. What is that idea?

WHEN in the Course of human events, it becomes necessary for one people to dissolve the political bands which have connected them with another, and to assume among the Powers of the earth, the separate and equal station to which the Laws of Nature and of Nature's God entitle them, a decent respect to the opinions of mankind requires that they should declare the causes which impel them to the separation.

We hold these truths to be self-evident, that all men are created equal, that they are endowed by their Creator with certain unalienable Rights, that among these are Life, Liberty and the pursuit of Happiness.—That to secure these rights, Governments are instituted among Men, deriving their just powers from the consent of the governed.—That whenever any Form of Government becomes destructive of these ends, it is the Right of the People to alter or to abolish it, and to institute new Government, laying its foundation on such principles and organizing its powers in such form, as to them shall seem most likely to effect their Safety and Happiness. Prudence, indeed, will dictate that Governments long established should not be changed for light and transient causes; and accordingly all experience hath shown, that mankind are more disposed to suffer, while evils are sufferable, than to right themselves by abolishing the forms to which they are accustomed. But when a long

123

train of abuses and usurpations, pursuing invariably the same Object evinces a design to reduce them under absolute Despotism, it is their right, it is their duty, to throw off such Government, and to provide new Guards for their future security.—Such has been the patient sufferance of these Colonies; and such is now the necessity which constrains them to alter their former Systems of Government. The history of the present King of Great Britain is a history of repeated injuries and usurpations, all having in direct object the establishment of an absolute Tyranny over these States. To prove this, let Facts be submitted to a candid world.

Summarizing

Write a paragraph summarizing, in your own words, the rights to which the citizens of the United States felt themselves entitled.

The Ratification of the Constitution[1]

Eleven troubled years after the Declaration of Independence, our Constitution was submitted for ratification to the thirteen original States, which were loosely united under the Articles of Confederation. In Virginia and some other States there was a bitter struggle over ratification. As you listen to this pretended "on-the-spot" broadcast of the Virginia convention, in 1788, what arguments seem to you to have a curiously modern sound?

As you know, important events being broadcast today are covered by many reporters. Microphones from various spots are synchronized into one continuous program. Several different broadcasters are therefore used in this script to help create the "on-the-spot" feeling:

BROADCASTERS

JOHN DALY—*Convention Hall*
NED CALMER—*Headquarters Booth*
DON HOLLENBECK—*Governor's Mansion*
KEN ROBERTS—*Street outside Convention Hall*
STATION ANNOUNCER

CAST

EDMUND RANDOLPH, *governor of Virginia*
PATRICK HENRY, *leader of the anti-Constitution party*
JAMES MADISON, *delegate*

THOMAS HALLOWAY, *woodsman*
RALPH BARKER, *tobacco merchant*
EDMUND PENDLETON, *president of the convention*
OTHER DELEGATES AND CITIZENS

CAST. *Main Studio. Thirty delegates talking excitedly in background.*

DALY. This is John Daly at Convention Hall, Richmond, Virginia. On this 25th day of June, 1788, in a move which has taken this Virginia ratifying convention completely by surprise, Mr. Randolph, present governor of Virginia, has come out publicly *in favor* of the proposed Federal Constitution for the United States of America. Governor Randolph, a delegate to this decisive convention, and hitherto a leader in

[1]Written by Michael Sklar and presented by the Columbia Broadcasting System, Inc., on their program "You Are There," broadcast September 19, 1948. Copyright by Columbia Broadcasting System, Inc.

the campaign *against* ratification, has just told reporters that he will speak and vote *for* ratification when the convention reconvenes . . . a few minutes from now.

CAST. (*Fades*)

DALY. (*Fading*) Thus the Constitution, which would unite the thirteen American States under a strong central government, has found a powerful new friend. Governor Randolph's action is bound to affect the delegates here, and may very likely influence many votes. Governor Randolph has much prestige in Virginia.

MAN. (*Echo*) June 25th, 1788 . . . Convention Hall, Richmond, Virginia . . . YOU ARE THERE!

ANNOUNCER. (*Normal*) Virginia, key State in the plan to form the thirteen original States into a united America, stands undecided, and the Constitution hangs in the balance. Columbia Broadcasting System takes you back a hundred and sixty years to the day that determined whether Americans could go forward from revolution and establish a strong, stable central government. All things are as they were then, except for one thing. When CBS is there . . .

MAN. (*Echo*) YOU ARE THERE!

DALY. (*Fading in*) Governor Randolph made his surprise announcement before a group of reporters a few minutes ago. Asked why he is turning from the party of Patrick Henry to the party of James Madison, Governor Randolph said that he will give his reasons on the floor of the convention. We hurried to this microphone, to bring you this news. Ned Calmer has been analyzing Governor Randolph's action, and is ready now with his report. So over to our CBS headquarters in Convention Hall and Ned Calmer.

CALMER. Governor Randolph's sudden change to the Federalists may have a decisive effect upon this convention. There are one hundred sixty-six Virginia delegates here who are more or less evenly divided. Roughly half of them represent the cities and towns, the tidewater planters . . . and the other half come from the back country. They are small farmers, frontiersmen from the Western District.

Most of the planters and the businessmen are in favor of a national Constitution. They are haunted by memories of Daniel Shays's rebellion in Massachusetts last year, and they want the Constitution as an instrument to end social chaos. On the other hand, the rural delegates, by and large, oppose the Constitution. Most of them are saddled with heavy mortgages. At present they are paying their debts with cheap state paper money, and they fear that national currency reforms would work to their disadvantage. Governor Randolph has much influence among these country delegates. His change may very well swing the necessary votes.

What happens here in Virginia today may decide the destiny of America. As you know, nine States must ratify the Constitution if it is to become the basic law of the Union. Eight States have already ratified, and four others most likely will not. Virginia is the key State. If Virginia fails to ratify, the Constitution is likely to be doomed. Just a moment . . . Governor Randolph has granted a brief interview. So over to Don Hollenbeck at the Governor's Mansion.

HOLLENBECK. Governor Randolph, sir—will you tell us why you have made this last-minute turn from the anti-Constitution party to the Federalists?

RANDOLPH. I have joined the Federalists because the anti-Constitution party has caused far too much delay on the pressing issue of a strong central government.

HOLLENBECK. And you feel that a strong central government is needed?

RANDOLPH. It is imperative. The Union of the States sags apart for want of it. But Mr. Henry fails to see the danger. He attacks various parts of the Constitution without realizing that the measure, as a whole, is desperately needed.

HOLLENBECK. Well, Governor, do you endorse the proposed Constitution without amendments?

RANDOLPH. No, I hope and trust certain amendments will be adopted . . . such as a Bill of Rights and a clause forbidding the importation of Negro slaves. But all that can come later. Time is running out, and we cannot go on under the Articles of Confederation.

HOLLENBECK. Thank you, Governor Randolph. This is Don Hollenbeck returning you to John Daly on the floor of Convention Hall.

DALY. About eighty of the delegates are now here in the hall, among them the fourteen delegates from the Kentucky district of Virginia. These backwoodsmen in their buckskins and fringed shirts, with hair tied in pigtails, Indian fashion, look out of place and uncomfortable in this huge, formal room.

VOICE. Mr. Henry! Mr. Henry!

DALY. (*No pause*) (*Up*) Mr. Patrick Henry, former governor of Virginia and leader of the anti-Constitution party, has just entered the hall. He is wearing the ill-fitting wig and shabby black coat for which he is famous, and his hawklike face is grim and forbidding. (*Up*) Mr. Henry, sir—would you care to comment on Governor Randolph's change from the anti-Constitution party?

HENRY. (*Fifty-two—eloquent—fiery—touch of backwoods—with angry scorn*) Governor Randolph, pah! My opponents are welcome to him. Like them he has turned his back on the revolution. He has divorced himself from the common people and embraced the monster, Property.

DALY. Do you mean to suggest, sir, that the Constitution favors the property-holding classes?

HENRY. Suggest? Nay, I *charge*

it! The worship of private property is implied in every article of that document. One year ago, sir, at Philadelphia the Constitution stank so badly that Governor Randolph refused to sign it. Does it smell any sweeter now? No, the Constitution remains unchanged. It is Randolph who has changed—with the wind from the tidewater!

DALY. Are you implying that Governor Randolph has yielded to pressure from the tidewater plantation-owners?

HENRY. No, no, the explanation of Randolph's action is simpler than that. Randolph was born with a golden spoon in his mouth. He is rich; he has many slaves. He is also a politician, and as such he flirted briefly with the ideas of liberty and equality. But now he has seen the light; property is the thing that counts.

DALY. Wouldn't you say that the protection of private property is important?

HENRY. Important, yes—but human rights are equally important. And where, I ask—where do you find one single mention of human rights in this Constitution? Those scoundrels at Philadelphia provided for everything that would gladden the hearts of the rich. But did they write a Bill of Rights for the common man into the Constitution? No, they did not!

DALY. But Governor Randolph says that a Bill of Rights will probably be added after . . .

HENRY. Why this talk of "after"? Do intelligent men enter into a compact without first settling the terms? No. And honest men would not offer such a crooked bargain.

DALY. How do you explain that eight States have already ratified?

HENRY. The citizens of those eight States would bargain away their heritage of freedom for a mess of pottage. For my part—give me liberty, greatest of all earthly blessings—and you may take everything else!

DALY. Thank you, Mr. Henry.

CAST. Mr. Madison! If you please, Mr. Madison!

DALY. (*Up*) And here comes Mr. Madison now. He is greeting friends and supporters as he walks down the aisle. Mr. Madison is a small, frail man, but although small of stature and quiet of voice, he yields to no man in intellectual capacity. Indeed, Mr. Madison is as famous for the logic of his arguments as Mr. Henry is for the brilliance of his oratory.—(*Up*) Mr. Madison—sir —Mr. Henry has just charged that the Constitution places property rights above human rights.

MADISON. (*Thirty-seven—intellectual—scholarly—keen—smiling*) Has he now, eh? Well, that's an interesting phrase. Patrick Henry is

a master of interesting phrases. If I remember correctly, one of them helped to start our revolution. The trouble is, Mr. Henry is in a constant state of revolution. He should remember that the war is over and that his opponents in this hall are not redcoats.

DALY. (*Encouraging further discussion*) Yes, Mr. Madison—but what about his argument?

MADISON. Ah, yes—property rights above human rights. Well, now, suppose we examine that, without the benefit of oratory, shall we? Mr. Henry would give you the impression that this is a struggle between the rich and the poor, the strong and the weak.

The fact is, sir, that there are wealthy men who loathe the Constitution, and poor men who love it. The point is that all Americans, rich and poor, are in trouble today because we have no strong central government. Mr. Henry poses as the shining knight of liberty—but where, sir, is liberty without order? Order is what we need, not at the expense of human rights, but precisely to keep them secure.

DALY. It's been reported, Mr. Madison, that Mr. Thomas Jefferson, our Ambassador to France, is against the Constitution.

MADISON. That, sir, is not accurate. Mr. Jefferson is a friend of mine. I am in constant correspondence with him. It is true that he disagrees with some parts of the Constitution, but, on the whole, he favors it. It would be well for Mr. Henry to remember that there are other patriots of the War for Independence who stand behind the Constitution; not only Thomas Jefferson, but General Washington, Benjamin Franklin, Alexander Hamilton, and a host of others.

DALY. Thank you, Mr. Madison.

MADISON. A pleasure, sir.

DALY. Mr. Madison said that the Constitution would be of great benefit to all Americans. Well, outside this hall people are waiting for the result of the vote. Ken Roberts is out there, so let's switch to him and find out how these people feel about the Constitution. . . . Go ahead, Ken Roberts.

SWITCH. *Out Daly and delegates —in men and women in street; a large crowd talking in b. g.; wagons going by ad lib on cobblestones; Roberts on halter mike.*

ROBERTS. In this crowd, judging by their dress, are people from every section and class of Virginia. I see men who are obviously planters, others who must be tradesmen, and a large number of farming folk. Some of them must have come a long way to be in Richmond at this fateful hour. Here, for instance, is a tall man wearing a fringed shirt and a coonskin cap. Where are you from, sir?

WOODSMAN. (*Fifty*) I be from Pineville, in the Western District.

ROBERTS. You're a delegate, sir?

WOODSMAN. Nay. I came here to watch o'er the delegates. I want to be sure they vote the way they're supposed to.

ROBERTS. And how are the delegates of the Western District supposed to vote, Mr. —uh—?

WOODSMAN. Halloway—Thomas Halloway. And they're still supposed to vote against the Constitution, and Governor Randolph will be paying for being a turncoat—come next election.

ROBERTS. Would you mind telling us why you're against the Constitution, Mr. Halloway?

WOODSMAN. You see this bullet wound in my left arm? I received it ten years ago come September. I received it fighting to free Virginia from the rule of King George.

ROBERTS. Don't you mean you were fighting to free the United States?

WOODSMAN. Nay—to free Virginia.

ROBERTS. But aren't you a citizen of the United States?

WOODSMAN. Nay—I'm a citizen of Virginia. We fought to be rid of the Third George and we want no fourth to take his place.

ROBERTS. You think that the Constitution will result in a King?

WOODSMAN. Aye, if there be a Constitution—there'll be a President—and if there be a President—he'll waste no time making himself into a monarch.

ROBERTS. But, Mr. Halloway, it's generally agreed that if the Constitution is ratified, the first President will be General Washington.

WOODSMAN. Aye. He'll waste no

time making himself into a monarch. And he could do it. According to the Constitution, the President would have *his own standing army!*

ROBERTS. Yes, but wouldn't the army be subject to Congress?

WOODSMAN. With a gun at its throat—what could the Congress do? He'll be making himself monarch—Congress or no.

BARKER. (*Interrupts. Off, angrily*) That, sir, is a ridiculous statement! It's evil! Treasonable!

ROBERTS. (*Quickly*) Mr. Halloway has just been interrupted by a well-dressed man in the crowd. . . . Thank you, Mr. Halloway. Now, sir . . .

WOODSMAN. He'll tell you naught. He's an empty head!

BARKER. (*Interrupts*) Abuse! That's the way of you rascals. You impute the lowest motives to the patriots who framed the Constitution. You don't want the truth. Scum of the backwoods, that's all you are.

WOODSMAN. Now, be holding your tongue if you value your head.

BARKER. Scum, scum. I'll say it again.

ROBERTS. Please, gentlemen, let's get back to the Constitution.

BARKER. Indeed! The Constitution! I predict, sir, that unless the Constitution is ratified the mer-chants of this country will be ruined.

ROBERTS. Are you a merchant, sir?

BARKER. Certainly. I trade in tobacco, fine Virginia leaf.

ROBERTS. And you feel that the Constitution would help business?

BARKER. Absolutely. Business is bad today, very bad. My warehouse is bursting with unsold tobacco. The country is in a depression. It's because of the money situation.

ROBERTS. Will you explain that, Mr. Barker?

BARKER. My word, there are so many different kinds of money in circulation that it drives a man insane. Doubloons, pistoles, gold johanneses, English and French crowns, guineas and Spanish dollars! And to cap it all, the States are issuing money that isn't worth the paper it's printed on! Take the dollar—it's idiotic! A dollar is worth 8 shillings in Virginia, but in Pennsylvania it's worth 7 shillings, in Georgia 5 shillings, and in South Carolina 32 shillings and sixpence! Now how on earth can a merchant do business under such conditions?

ROBERTS. It must be difficult.

BARKER. Difficult! It's impossible! And that's not all . . .

DALY. (*Interrupting*) This is John Daly in Convention Hall. We have interrupted Ken Roberts. Governor Randolph has just come in by a side door to avoid the crowd. He is walking down the aisle . . . and the tension here is so thick one can literally feel it. Mr. Patrick Henry, whose eyes met those of Governor Randolph momentarily, now turns his head away with no sign of recognition. The snub was unmistakable. His face pale, the Governor sits down, shakes hands with Mr Madison . . . and now the gavel sounds. Mr. Pendleton, president of the convention, is calling the delegates to order. . . . The final debate will begin in a few moments . . .

SOUND. *Gavel*

PENDLETON. Order, please . . . The gentlemen will please come to order. This session of the Virginia convention is hereby declared to be officially convened. The final speech in opposition to ratification will be made by Mr. Patrick Henry. He will be followed by Mr. James Madison, who will speak in favor of ratification. I now recognize the first speaker, Mr. Henry.

CAST. *Low murmur, coughs*

DALY. Mr. Henry rises . . . he is mounting the platform. . . . His hawklike eyes, under that ragged wig, look piercingly around the room. Mr. Henry stares at Governor Randolph with contempt. Now Mr. Henry is about to speak. . .

HENRY. Mr. President—fellow delegates to this convention, it is my privilege to make the concluding address in behalf of the anti-Constitution party, which is the party of liberty. But I would first make a few remarks on the conduct of one of the delegates. I am referring to none other than Governor Edmund Randolph.

CAST. *Stir*

HENRY. Some months ago the Governor sent to the legislature a letter setting forth in strong terms the reasons why he had refused to sign the Constitution at the general convention last year in Philadelphia. It seems to me very strange that that which was then the subject of his disapproval should today become the object of his praise. Something extraordinary must have happened to work so great a change.

RANDOLPH. (*Off*) Mr. President! Mr. President!

SOUND. *Gavel*

DALY. Governor Randolph is calling for the floor. He's been ruled out of order.

HENRY. I yield, Mr. President, Let us hear what the "honorable" member has to say.

RANDOLPH. (*Angry*) The honorable speaker hints that I have changed my opinions for some hidden, and therefore discreditable, reason.

HENRY. I have no intention of offending. I merely do my duty.

RANDOLPH. The gentleman smiles when he says that. His conduct is not in harmony with the least shadow of friendship.

HENRY. (*Furious*) Does the member accuse me of malicious behavior?

RANDOLPH. I believe the meaning of my words is clear.

HENRY. Is the member prepared to back up his remarks with deeds?

RANDOLPH. If the gentleman seeks satisfaction, my seconds are ready.

HENRY. I thank the gentleman for his willingness to render satisfaction. Mr. President, I request a recess to arrange details of a matter of honor.

PENDLETON. (*Stumbling*) This—this—is most unusual. However—the member's request is granted. I declare a recess.

SOUND. *Gavel raps*

CAST. *Uproar*

DALY. Mr. Randolph and Mr. Henry are leaving the hall . . . no doubt to choose and confer with their seconds. This is a startling turn of events. The delegates are milling about on the floor, shouting, shaking their fists. . . . (*Up*) There's Mr. Pendleton! Mr. Pendleton . . . will the session resume in spite of this conflict between Mr. Henry and Mr. Randolph?

PENDLETON. Yes, I will reconvene in five minutes.

DALY. Thank you, Mr. Pendleton. The debate will continue and the vote will be taken despite this dramatic interruption. Mr. Henry is one of the principal speakers. He must be back. Now . . . Ned Calmer has been circulating among the delegates to learn how Mr. Henry's attack on the Governor will affect the vote. So over to Headquarters.

CALMER. On the basis of my brief conversations with the delegates, it is safe to say that Mr. Henry, by his open attack on Mr. Randolph, has restored the situation to what it was before the Governor came out in favor of the Constitution today. The delegates from the rural districts admire forceful speech and prompt action. No matter what outsiders think of Mr. Henry's conduct, his action sits well with them. Those rural delegates who might have been shaken by Governor Randolph's new allegiance to the Federalists are now back in the anti-Constitution fold. So now it looks as if the Constitution may fail of ratification. . . . Now, Mr. Pendleton has called the convention to order again . . . so . back to John Daly.

DALY. The delegates are again seated. . . . The convention has reconvened. . . . Mr. Henry is now speaking.

HENRY. (Off) The Republic itself, born in blood on the battlefield, is in extreme danger. Why? Because of this proposal of establishing nine States in a Confederacy to the exclusion of the four remaining States. Congress, under this Constitution, would have a tyrant's power. It could lay whatever taxes it chooses. With a standing army it could keep the people in submission. The President, if he should be merciless and able, could make himself an absolute ruler. I would rather have a king, lords, and a House of Commons!

Gentlemen, my opponents ask you to surrender not only the sword and the purse, but the very scales of justice. Ratify this Constitution and you place our State courts at the mercy of federal courts. I dread popular resistance to this proposed government, so vague, so indefinite in its assurances of liberty and human rights. Let me warn you of the dreadful effects if the people should resist. I beg the delegates to vote "nay, nay" on this resolution, lest they rouse the people to rebellion in defense of their God-given liberties!

CAST. *Excitement and applause*

DALY. Mr. Henry has left the platform, and Mr. Madison is coming up. He carries his hat in his hand. . . . Now he is . . . taking some notes out of his hat.

PENDLETON. The chair recognizes Mr. James Madison.

SOUND. *Gavel raps twice*

MADISON. Mr. President, fellow delegates, I yield to no man in my respect for the previous speaker. Yet I would point out that his objections arise out of misunderstanding. This is not strange, because the form of government we are proposing is new in the history of the world. Let the delegates therefore not measure it by old-fashioned standards.

The American States have stirred the admiration of the world by setting up free governments under the pressure of war. How much more will they win admiration if they should be able, peaceably, to establish one central government! Suppose only eight States ratify, and Virginia refuses to become the ninth, except on her own terms. Then, even if the others agree to our terms, which is doubtful, every State must call new conventions to consider the amendments. Agreement will be even more difficult to reach than it was in Philadelphia.

In short, if Virginia holds out today, the United States may never have a functioning central government. But if Virginia ratifies the Constitution, it may bring the most fortunate event in the history of mankind. I therefore respectfully submit that the honorable delegates vote "yea" on the resolution before us—the resolution containing the Constitution of the United States of America.

CAST. *Excitement and applause*

VOICES. Question! Question! Call the question!

DALY. Mr. Madison leaves the platform. Voices are calling the question. Mr. Pendleton raises his gavel. . . .

SOUND. *Gavel raps twice*

PENDLETON. The convention will now vote on the resolution embodying the proposed Constitution for the United States of America. The vote will be by a show of hands. A simple majority will decide. (*Pause*) Those delegates who are in favor, those who wish to vote "aye" will raise their right hands.

DALY. Hands are going up all over the hall. The tellers are moving about . . . counting. A total of 166 votes will be cast; 84 are necessary to carry or defeat the resolution. . . . It seems as if half the number of delegates here have their hands up, but it's impossible to tell exactly. It's going to be close . . . very close. . . . We'll know the result in a moment from the aye count. If it's 84 or over, the ayes will have it, and the Constitution will be ratified here in the Virginia convention . . . and will become the law of the land. . . . The tellers have completed their count. . . . They are reporting to the platform. . . . Mr. Pendleton is receiving their reports . . . checking the totals. . . . We'll know in a moment.

SOUND. *Gavel*

PENDLETON. (*Triumphant*) The tellers report in favor of the resolution—88 votes!

CAST. *Terrific excitement, applause . . . cheers*

DALY. The resolution is carried.

. . . Carried by 88 votes—4 votes more than necessary. . . . (*Fades*) The United States is now committed to a strong, central government. We're to have a President, a Congress, a Federal Judiciary . . . a national army under the Constitution. I have a copy here in my hand. Its preamble declares: "We the People of the United States, in order to form a more perfect union, establish justice, insure domestic tranquillity, provide for the common defense, promote the general welfare, and secure the blessings of liberty to ourselves and our posterity, do ordain and establish this Constitution for the United States of America."

MAN. (*Echo*) June 25th, 1788, Virginia ratifies the Constitution . . . and government of, by, and for the people begins![1]

[1] The Virginia convention debated and voted under the impression that they were the ninth necessary ratifying State. The ninth necessary State was actually New Hampshire. It had ratified five days earlier. Mr. Madison, Mr. Henry, and their associates did not know this because of poor communication.

Using Your Reasoning Power

Think of the events described in the play as you read the statements below. Copy the sentences on a paper and write C before each statement if it is correct and NC if what it says is incorrect. Decide what is wrong with the incorrect sentences and rewrite them so that they are accurate.

_____ 1. The Constitution could have become a basic law of the Union without the ratification of nine states.

_____ 2. The governor felt that no amendments to the Constitution were necessary.

_____ 3. Patrick Henry was formerly a governor of Pennsylvania.

_____ 4. Mr. Henry was fifteen years older than James Madison.

_____ 5. Madison's influence with the voters was largely due to his oratorical brilliance.

_____ 6. Madison favored the ratification because he felt that all Americans needed a strong central government.

_____ 7. Some of the people from the back country were afraid that a president would have too much control over the army.

_____ 8. The Constitution was ratified in Virginia by an overwhelming majority of votes.

MARY FABYAN WINDEATT

Project

Now it is well
That we should start
Planning a fortress
In the heart;

Building with things
Which will endure
Longer than Sorrow's
Signature.

(Take away stone,
Take away wood;
Faith is ten thousand
Times as good!

Take away steel,
Take away lead;
Charity, hope, will
Do instead!)

Thus when the years
Pile up the pain,
We can go seeking
Peace again,

Back of the walls
Heaven designed
Just for the hurts of
Humankind.

FREEMAN H. HUBBARD

A Statue of Mr. Lincoln[1]

VINNIE REAM, whose father had a government job in Washington during the unhappy years of the 1860's, had developed serious ambitions in art. Senator Trumbull, a friend of her father's, persuaded the successful sculptor, Clark Mills, to accept her as a pupil. But as the war dragged on, an uneasy conscience tempted Vinnie to give up sculpture and go back to full-time duty in the Washington Post Office. She felt she had no right to be shaping lifeless clay when the whole country was on the brink of disaster. Vinnie asked Mr. Mills if it was fair to let art shut her eyes to the misery in hospitals and prison camps.

"Yes," her teacher told her, without a shade of doubt in his voice. "One little girl would not make any great difference to the outcome of the war, but what you are learning to do may make a difference to the world. Steep your soul in beauty so that some day you will have something to give the world that will enrich it." But Vinnie was still plagued by doubts.

Abraham Lincoln had been chosen to run again for the presidency, but with the misgivings of his own Republican party. When the Democrats picked General McClellan to oppose him, the nation's faith in "Old Abe" sank to its lowest ebb.

Staunch as her loyalty was, Vinnie could not help being affected by this uncertainty. One day at the sculptor's studio, she told Mr. Mills that she was going to begin work on a bust of Abraham Lincoln right away. "I have wanted to do it ever since I began studying sculpture, but I waited because I didn't think I was ready for so great a subject."

"You weren't." Clark Mills was not the man to offer easy encouragement. "What makes you think you are ready now?"

"I don't. But I have a feeling I can't get rid of that if I don't start this bust very soon, I shall never do it. I want terribly to finish the job while he is still President."

Mills smiled down at the earnest small face. "Don't believe all you read in the papers, my dear! Lincoln isn't going to resign, and Lit-

[1]With permission of McGraw-Hill Book Co., Inc. from *Vinnie Ream and Mr. Lincoln*, by Freeman Hubbard, published by Whittlesey House. Copyright, 1949, by Freeman Hubbard.

tle Mac isn't going to run him out of the White House either. The people know a good man when they have one." Then he turned more serious and scowled. "Of course, if this war drags on much longer, they may do anything in sheer desperation. Maybe, after all, you had better start the bust."

"I have pictures of Mr. Lincoln in my scrapbook at home. I'll bring it in tomorrow. I keep everything I can find except those horrid political cartoons. They make me so mad that I throw them into the fire."

"And that's where you are wrong, my girl. Some of the cartoons are abusive enough, I'll grant you. But any caricature is worth study if you want to learn more about your subject's features and personality. No man admires Lincoln more than I do, but I have saved his enemies' most venomous lampoons."

The sculptor hauled out a portfolio bulging untidily with scraps, and together they pored over it.

"Pictures will help you a great deal in getting details," he said, "but if you want to achieve realism, you will have to cram your mind with fresh impressions of the man himself. Pictures show only the surface, and you have to give your subject three dimensions. To imagine depth is not easy, even with long experience. You need a very close look at Mr. Lincoln before you can even begin to mold his features with any vigor, or even with any life."

Vinnie was dismayed. "But how can I get close to him?"

"Well, every Thursday evening he holds an informal reception at the White House, and anyone can go in and shake his hand. That's your chance. Of course, you'd have to wait in line to get close to him."

"Oh, I'd wait forever."

"It won't be forever, but the longer the better, if you can keep him in sight. You're so tiny, you'll have to watch out that other people don't cut off your view."

At the supper table, Vinnie coaxed her mother to chaperon her visit to the White House. "Is Mr. Lincoln well guarded while so many people gather round him?" she asked her father.

Mr. Ream said he did not think so. However, a few precautions were taken for Mr. Lincoln's safety. Visitors had to leave their shawls and coats in the cloak room, and Sergeant Crook, the President's bodyguard, kept a close watch on the hands of everyone passing along the receiving line to see that they were not covered or hidden in any way.

"Well, it still seems risky to me," said Vinnie.

"And it is, undoubtedly, but Mr. Lincoln insists on being available to the people."

On Thursday evening Vinnie and her mother joined the slow-moving line in the White House, which inched along under the flaring gas chandelier. Mr. Mills had been quite right saying that the receptions were informal. Some of the visitors wore full evening dress; others were clad in homespun and backwoods bonnets. When she could not see the President, Vinnie studied the folks in the line. There was a tent preacher with the burning eyes of a fanatic, and a lady whose sky-blue silk was trimmed with point lace, while her hair shimmered with its powdering of gold dust, and diamonds gleamed upon her throat. No one acted as if the contrast were in any way remarkable, certainly not President or Mrs. Lincoln, nor the mischievous Tad who stood between his father and Sergeant Crook.

As long as Tad was in the receiving line with his parents, he shook hands solemnly with all comers. But before Vinnie and her mother got anywhere near the presidential party, he had discovered another boy of his own age and was playing tag with him, racing in and out among the visitors. Once he dived headfirst through the line right in front of Vinnie and tripped over her foot. She was quick to help him up and then close the gap so that his pursuer did not catch him. The little boy gave her a flashing grin and was gone.

Mr. Lincoln made no effort to restrain his son's high spirits, and the child was careful not to look at his mother, lest he should have to obey her warning frowns.

To the tiny Vinnie, who was two inches short of five feet in height, Mr. Lincoln towered astonishingly. He stooped slightly in his ill-fitting evening clothes and looked as if he were going through some mechanical routine. Each time the Marshal of the District of Columbia called out a name, Mr. Lincoln would smile and thrust out an arm that was as stiff as a pump handle.

A quick handshake, a single pleasant remark, and he turned to the next comer, and always with a faraway look as if his eyes were fixed on something beyond the moving line and beyond that room.

Desperately Vinnie tried to memorize every detail of the weary, cavernous face. The thick black hair was slightly disheveled as if a nervous hand had been run through it. The ears were large and the head abnormally high above them. But it was the architecture of the deep eye sockets that set Vinnie's forefinger to trying to trace them on her poplin skirt.

She was within two yards of the President when she caught Sergeant Crook's eye upon her, and remembered that the bodyguard kept a constant lookout for hidden hands. Swiftly she lifted both her own, with an instant's unreasoning terror that he was going to denounce her. The sergeant's lips twitched ever so slightly, and Vinnie's face burned with embarrassment at her own foolishness when he gave her a slow, solemn wink.

She was still flustered a moment later when an enormous white glove was thrust out at her. Shyly she put her own hand into the huge one and looked up into Mr. Lincoln's face. He glanced down at

her, and smiled kindly and impersonally with a murmured, "How do you do, my dear?"

In November, Abraham Lincoln was swept into a second term by the votes of a grateful nation. The day after the election, Senator Trumbull dropped in to see his artist friend. Vinnie was in the studio, just finishing her bust of the President and wondering glumly why it did not please her.

"That's a *very* good likeness," the Senator declared with enthusiasm. "I am no authority, of course, but I am sure the girl has done a fine job."

"You should have seen how hard she's worked on it," Mr. Mills replied. "She would have been here night and day if I had let her. But there is still something about this portrait that lacks reality. I wish Vinnie could have modeled the living man instead of having to use pictures."

"Maybe we could arrange it," Mr. Trumbull said, almost as if he were talking to himself. "I will see what can be done."

Instantly Vinnie was wild with excitement. "Do you mean you'll ask President Lincoln to pose for me?"

"I certainly do not mean anything of the sort. The President is much too busy to pose for anyone.

But I just might be able to persuade him to let you sit in a room with him while he is working or relaxing."

"Oh, please tell Mr. Lincoln that I'll be so still he won't know I'm there. Tell him I promise not to disturb him. Tell him how much it means to me. Tell him sculpture is my lifework. Tell him——"

The Senator laughed. "Yes, yes, yes! I'll tell him all that, but don't set your heart on it, for the chances are nothing will come of it."

A week later Mr. Trumbull visited the Reams one evening. With great deliberation he hung his cane and hat and overcoat, one by one, on the antlered hatrack in the hall. He went into the parlor and sat down by a blazing fire.

"It's a raw night and a bit of fire certainly feels good," he said.

Vinnie could not tell whether it was a twinkle or a reflection of the dancing flames that she saw in his eyes. At last she couldn't hold her tongue another minute. "Please, did you speak to Mr. Lincoln?"

"Of course I spoke to Mr. Lincoln. I often have occasion to do that."

"You're teasing me! You know what I mean."

"Vinnie!" protested Mrs. Ream. The Senator grinned. "I was teasing you. But I did ask him if you could come to the Executive

Mansion to work and record your impressions of him. I said you wouldn't talk to him, or annoy him, or do anything to disturb his routine——"

"And what did he say?"

"Well, at first he brushed aside the whole notion. He said he was constantly besieged by people wanting favors—and that is true. But when I said, 'She's young and poor and clerking at the Post Office to help support her family,' his expression changed. He said, 'Poor, is she? Well, that is nothing against her. Bring her to the White House tomorrow at noon' That was only half an hour ago, so you see I lost no time in letting you know."

Vinnie planted a quick kiss on the nose of the dignified Senator from Illinois. "Mr. Trumbull, you are a darling." Then she did not dare look at her mother, but if she had dared, she might have caught a smile that would have surprised her.

It was three minutes before noon the following day when she arrived at the White House with Senator Trumbull. Eagerly she trailed the doorkeeper across the hall and up to the family's private apartment on the second floor. They found the President very much at ease in an old-fashioned sitting room, quite unlike anything Vinnie had expected to see in the mansion. He was slouched in a sagging rocker, near a window that looked out over gardens and river and the red hills of Virginia. Slanting sails made a pretty picture on the sun-tipped water, and Mr. Lincoln was peering at them through a brass telescope.

As he laid aside the spyglass to greet his visitors, a little white dog uncurled himself on the sofa with a low growl. "That's part of our menagerie. He won't bite, but he takes himself seriously as a watchdog. My Tad is always adopting some new pet. Three weeks ago some friends in Delaware sent us a live turkey. Tad has been leading the bird around on a string ever since, and there isn't a chance that it will ever provide us with a good meal."

Mr. Trumbull chuckled, and Vinnie laughed shyly.

"But wait till you hear the rest of the story. On election day, Tad left his turkey in charge of a company of soldiers who were balloting out there on the lawn under the direction of a commission sent down from their own state. He rushed into my office and pulled me over to the window to look at the soldiers 'voting for Lincoln and Johnson!' I asked him if the turkey was voting, too, and he seemed perfectly serious when he told me that it wasn't of age yet."

Perhaps Mr. Lincoln had been

deliberate in putting Vinnie at ease, for he smiled down at her then from his great height.

"Now, Miss Ream, my old friend Trumbull tells me you want to make a clay model of me."

"Yes, sir."

"But I am so homely," he protested with his tired smile. "Why do you want to model me?"

Vinnie took a deep breath. "For the very same reason that millions of people voted for you, sir. I have already done one bust of you, but my teacher, Mr. Mills, says it lacks realism because I had to copy it from pictures."

"Yes, I can understand that it might." Mr. Lincoln pondered a moment. "All right then, young lady, you shall have your wish. I rest every noonday between twelve o'clock and half past, and you may come to my office at that time. Everyday except Sundays till you finish your model. But not more than half an hour."

Vinnie was seventeen years old when she began to model Mr. Lincoln in clay in the White House, but she still tipped the scales at a few ounces less than ninety pounds. The contrast between her elfin figure and the tall, rawboned President made many a visitor smile.

She was smiling, too, these days. This association with Abraham Lincoln was something that any girl in the land—that any American of either sex and in any position —might well envy her. Vinnie thought of it as the turning point of her life.

Later on, she promised herself, when the war need was over and her family had a little more money, she would resign her position at the Post Office. She intended to let nothing interfere with her career as a sculptress. She meant to devote her life to improving her art until its tools had become part of her own hand, controlled as accurately and surely as her fingers.

Vinnie hired an astonished drayman to cart her tub of moist clay to the White House, along with a carpetbag that held tools and smock. Then, precisely at noon on Saturday, she presented herself to the President, dressed in her best.

Mr. Lincoln was alone in his office. It was the room where he met his Cabinet, where he conferred with generals and statesmen. He was an untidy figure in a rusty black suit, green with age along the seams. But when he took off his eyeglasses to greet her, Vinnie thought she had never seen anything so beautiful or so kind as his smile.

"Here you are, my dear. We'll try to give you every chance to work out your ideas. Mrs. Lincoln

146

says you may have that closet over there to store your equipment. Now, is there anything else you need before you begin?"

"No, sir." Vinnie was choked with bashfulness now that she was alone with her hero.

"Then we won't disturb each other at all." He picked up a book from his desk. Vinnie slipped into her smock and tucked her ringlets up under her cap. She laid out her tools. Mr. Lincoln chuckled aloud over his book.

The first half hour passed like five minutes. Vinnie had scarcely begun to work when she noticed with dismay that the clock on the President's desk said twenty-eight minutes past twelve. She hurried to put everything away and was ready to leave as the hands pointed to twelve-thirty.

Mr. Lincoln laid down his book. "I see that you keep the rules, my dear. That is good. I reckon it's time for my dinner. Good afternoon!"

Day after day, Vinnie kept her appointment at the White House. Day after day, she put more clay onto her armature and cut more off. She molded and pressed and gouged. She roughened and smoothed, and because she was more experienced now, she roughened again. Gradually, the clay took on some resemblance to Abraham Lincoln.

"I do declare, you're getting him as he is," Mrs. Lincoln used to say sometimes when she came in with a mug of milk or an apple or a dose of cough mixture for her husband.

Tad was a frequent visitor, too, from the second morning, when Vinnie found the President of the United States galloping down the corridor with the boy piggyback on his shoulders. Both of them were hooting with laughter.

"I remember you," Tad told Vinnie when his father put him down and began to introduce them. "She came to one of your Thursday nights, Papa."

"Fancy you remembering that," Vinnie said.

"Well, of course I remember. If you hadn't picked me up when I stumbled, I would have been tagged."

"It would seem that more goes on at my receptions than I had any notion of," Mr. Lincoln said to Vinnie.

For the next week, Tad kept pestering Vinnie with questions, which had a quaint sound in the little boy's slight lisp.

"What is this for?"

"Why do you do that?"

"Why do you take mud off as soon as you put it on?"

"How did you learn about fooling around with mud like this?"

"Won't you do me now? Just as big as I really am?"

Vinnie answered all his queries patiently, explaining everything he

wanted to know, while his father looked on indulgently.

Inauguration Day was miserably cold and drizzly. As other bleak days followed one another, Vinnie felt that she was somehow drawing closer to the lonely gaunt man whose image she was creating. She saw Mr. Lincoln in many moods, but nearly always she detected an undercurrent of deep sorrow. The tragedy of the man etched itself into her brain and heart, and into her fingers as well.

At noon one day in April when Vinnie opened the door of the Cabinet room, she found Mr. Lincoln standing by the window, through which drifted the din from Pennsylvania Avenue. His gaze was fixed, but he didn't seem to be looking at the White House lawn, now touched by the magic of spring.

He stared beyond it, beyond the silvery Potomac and the green mantled heights of Arlington. After months of daily companionship with the sad-faced giant, Vinnie had grown used to his moods. She had seen him as firm as granite and as gentle as an April sunrise. Now he greeted her distantly, possibly because the weight upon his mind was too heavy for casual remarks.

Vinnie set to work. The clay model was all but finished. She rejoiced in its completion, but did not like to think that within a few days there would no longer be any reason for her to come here. She ran a critical eye over her work. There was so little more that she could do to it. The noble brow and rugged features stood out in the clay as true to life as she could make them.

Mr. Lincoln's voice brought her back to the moment. He towered over her, studying the figure. "Are you still happy now that your wish is almost fulfilled? I congratulate you on work so nearly finished."

Just before seven-thirty of a gray morning a few days later, the big wet flag that still hung outside the Ford theater was lowered halfway down its staff, to mark the end of the tragic scene enacted there the night before. Lincoln was dead.

149

The next day Vinnie went to the White House and arranged for the bringing home of her bust of the dead President and the rest of her gear. A newspaper reporter happened to be there at the time. He saw the tiny sculptress and wrote an account of her and her work that captured the imagination of the public. After that, a steady stream of visitors began making its way to the little house on North B Street. Some of them were old cronies of Mr. Lincoln's, but many more who had never seen him in life looked upon that bust as the portrait of their friend. All of them wanted to see the girl who had been so close to him during the last dark months.

"I am astonished at the life you've got into this," Mr. Trumbull told Vinnie. "This is Abraham Lincoln himself, as we know him. You are a genius, Vinnie."

"No, I'm not, Mr. Trumbull," Vinnie protested with utter sincerity and a clear-sighted appraisal of her own work. "You and Mr. Mills gave me my chance, and I did the best I could with it. But I still have to go on working hard. My best isn't good enough yet."

The Senator from Illinois came back time after time, and often he brought other men with him to show them the bust. Vinnie recognized the names of some politi-cal celebrities when he introduced them. Others she did not recognize.

One day when Senator Trumbull called, he told Vinnie, "I have just introduced a bill in the Senate authorizing the creation of a life-size statue of our late President, to be set up in the Capitol. A similar bill has been presented to the lower house. All Congress feels that Lincoln deserves a fine memorial."

"That's true," said Vinnie. "The contract will be given to Mr. Mills, won't it?"

"No, he doesn't want to compete for it. A lot of other artists have been trying to wangle something of the sort, sending in sketches and rough models and all that."

"I think it should be Mr. Mills. Are any of the others very good?" Vinnie asked wistfully.

"Not much, in my opinion. And here is what I came to tell you. Most of the members of Congress are so impressed with your bust of Mr. Lincoln and the circumstances under which it was done that they think you are the logical person to get that contract."

"Me?" Vinnie couldn't believe her ears. "There must be some mistake, Mr. Trumbull. There really must! I have had so little experience. And they would never let a girl do it."

"You will get the experience, my dear. There will be time. This is your chance to go to Europe. If you sign the contract, you will be given money enough to complete the statue in Rome if you want to. The marble would have to come from Italy anyway."

"But it is cruel to get up my hopes like this! The bill may not pass, and they would never choose me."

The Senator laughed then. "They have chosen you! And the bill has already been passed by both houses, and President Johnson has signed it. I thought I'd better break it to

you gradually in case you fainted on my hands or something. The nation has chosen you to honor Abraham Lincoln!"

Vinnie Ream had never fainted in her life, but she came close to it then. Her voice was very weak and far away when she promised to do her best, and tried to thank the Senator for all he had done.

"Tut, tut, no more than you deserve!" Mr. Trumbull patted her shoulder awkwardly. Then he pulled out his big handkerchief and blew his nose like a trumpet.

The contract awarded to Vinnie was signed on a hot August afternoon by James Harlan, the Secretary of the Interior. Vinnie's hand trembled when she wrote her name under his, and her penmanship would not have done much credit to a child of twelve.

She was to get five thousand dollars as soon as she finished a life-size plaster cast, full figure, of Abraham Lincoln, and an additional five thousand when she completed and delivered the marble statue. In each case the sculpture would have to meet the approval of the Secretary of the Interior.

Never before had the United States Government awarded a sculpture contract to any member of her sex. Never before had an American girl received such a distinction.

Today Vinnie Ream's statue of Lincoln stands in the rotunda of the Capitol.

Writing a Character Sketch

You are all familiar with the traditional stories about Abraham Lincoln—his poverty as a boy, his honesty and desire for education. In "A Statue of Mr. Lincoln," you get an insight into the great man who saved the Union. Write a ten-sentence character sketch of Mr. Lincoln from what you learned of him in this story. You will have to "read between the lines" in order to see the real Abe Lincoln.

Using Reference Books

From the encyclopedia and other reference books collect information about sculpturing and then write a brief answer to each of the questions below. State the name of the reference book, the number of the volume, and the page on which you found the information.

1. How old is the art of sculpture?
2. What materials did early sculptors use?
3. What is a figurine? What is its purpose?
4. What is meant by sculptures of heroic scale?
5. What materials did Egyptian sculptors use?
6. What is a kiln?

MILDRED PLEW MERRYMAN

Abraham Lincoln

REMEMBER he was poor and country-bred;
    His face was lined; he walked with awkward gait.
Smart people laughed at him sometimes and said,
    "How can so very plain a man be great?"

Remember he was humble, used to toil,
    Strong arms he had to build a shack, a fence,
Long legs to tramp the woods, to plow the soil,
    A head chuck-full of backwoods common sense.

Remember all he ever had he earned.
    He walked, in time, through stately White House doors;
But all he knew of men and life he learned
    In little backwoods cabins, country stores.

Remember that his eyes could light with fun;
    That wisdom, courage set his name apart;
But when the rest is duly said and done,
    Remember that men loved him for his heart.

The Jim Thorpe Story[1]

ARMY kicked off. The Indian caught the ball on his own ten-yard line. He picked up his interference. He was up to the twenty-, the thirty-, the forty-yard line. He passed the fifty-yard mark and shot out from behind his own men. He was in the clear. There was no stopping him. Straight down the field he ran, swift as a deer, till he passed the last chalk mark and looked out to the referee to raise his hands to signify another touchdown for Carlisle.

But the whistle had blown. Carlisle had been offside. Army breathed a sigh of relief and took the ball out of the Indian's hands.

They kicked off again. This time the Indian picked up the pigskin on his five-yard line. Again the interference. And again the yards were pealed off under his fast feet. Again he pushed out from his own interference and again he was in the clear. This time the referee's hands went up.

[1]Abridged by permission of Julian Messner, Inc. from *The Jim Thorpe Story*, by Gene Schoor; copyright date, October 22, 1951, by Gene Schoor. Abridgment copyright (c), 1956, by Harcourt, Brace and Company, Inc.

"I guess that was the longest run for a touchdown I ever made," the Indian would tell his listeners. "Ninety and ninety-five make one hundred eighty-five yards."

He was phenomenal. Deceptive, fast, leaving his would-be tacklers and his tacklers dazed on the field, he ran the highly touted Army team and its All-American candidates ragged.

When the final whistle blew to end the festivities the score was 27–6, and it was Carlisle that carted off the goal posts. The Indian? He played the full sixty minutes of the savage, clean, but hard-hitting game, without a substitute for a single play.

That Indian was the greatest athlete America has ever produced in its great history in the field of sports. His name is Wa-Tho-Huck. Translated from the language of the Sac and Fox Indians, the name means Bright Path. Indeed, in almost every possible athletic venture the great Indian blazed a bright path for himself and for the glory of his country. Everybody in the world who is in the least interested in athletics knows him better by that simple name, Jim Thorpe.

"I am not, as many believe," says Jim Thorpe, "a full-blooded Indian. I am five-eighths Indian; three-eighths Potawatami on my mother's side and two-eighths Sac and Fox on my father's side."

But when a ten-pound baby came to that one-room log cabin on the North Canadian River, just outside the Indian reservation, Charlotte View Thorpe felt that her newborn son had inherited all the valiant qualities of her heroic grandfather, the great Sac and Fox chief, Black Hawk.

Jim was fifteen years old when he reported to Carlisle Indian School in 1904. He was only a little over five feet tall and weighed a skimpy one hundred and fifteen pounds. There wasn't anything resembling a football uniform that wouldn't swim on him, but the game fascinated him. His eyes lit up as he watched the ball snapped back from center in varsity-scrub battles. His muscles tensed with the back carrying the pigskin. His shoulders ached to get into the melee, to throw a smashing block, to bull his way down the field.

This was a tough game, the competition keen. It called for stamina, for quick thinking, for sheer strength. Jim couldn't wait for the height and weight he needed to get into the middle of it. When the whistle blew for the end of the drill,

Jim was as exhausted as any of the players leaving the gridiron. He lived through every run, every kick, every smashing play he had seen and followed.

It would be three years before Jim Thorpe, standing five feet eleven and a half inches and tipping the scale at one hundred and eighty-one, would really begin to play the grueling game.

The first to really notice the great possibilities in the Indian was a man who has been pretty much forgotten. He was an assistant coach at the school. His name was Newman.

"Who's the boy who made that tackle?"

He was watching the Tailors' team playing the Carpenters' squad. The boys who couldn't make varsity organized a sectional league for the school. Jim was playing guard for the Tailors.

"Thorpe," said one of the boys on the bench. "Jim Thorpe."

Newman didn't hear him. He was watching the boy as he cut through the line, sure, certain, watched him nail the runner before he could get his feet in motion. He watched him block, run, kick. He watched him all afternoon.

"You're pretty good, young fellow," he said, as the boys came trotting off the field.

"Thanks," said Jim quietly. "I guess I like the game."

"I can see that," said Newman. "Report to the scrubs tomorrow."

Jim just looked at the coach. He could feel his heart beating fast.

"Aren't you going to say anything?" asked Newman.

Jim struggled to loosen his tongue. He never could release his feelings in a flow of words.

"Sure, Coach," he said. "I'll be there."

And he was there all right, but Glenn Scobey Warner, Pop Warner, one of the greatest track and football coaches of all time, took a little while in recognizing the great potentialities of the new boy Assistant Coach Newman had sent on to his scrub squad. It was on the track field and not on the gridiron that Jim Thorpe first excited the man whose fame was to grow almost step for step with the Indian's swift rise to athletic glory.

Jim had been playing a pickup game of ball, as he often did after the day's classes. On the way back to school he crossed the field where some members of the track team were practicing high jumping. He stopped to watch them. Anything that involved athletic competition interested Jim. He had never done any high jumping, but that didn't mean that he wouldn't like to try it.

The bar was set at five feet when the track team started its jumping. Five feet was easy. Everyone could

do it. They jumped five feet two and five feet three inches easily, too. It was when the bar was raised to five feet six that the casualties began. There were only four or five who could manage that. There were three who could jump five feet seven without spilling the bar. Only two could go any higher. Then the bar was lifted five feet nine.

First one tried it. He stepped back about ten yards, got up on his toes, took the few strides to the bar and leaped. When he came down, the bar came down with him.

Then the second Indian tried it. The short run, the leap, and down he came—and the bar with him.

They tried it again and again and again. They got up there all right,

156

to five feet nine, but when they came down, the stick was down too. They were about to give up, lower the bar for some more practice jumps, when Jim, who had waited patiently by, asked whether he couldn't try.

"Go ahead," said one of the boys who had managed to clear the bar at five feet eight. "Careful you don't break your neck."

"Thanks," said Jim, all eager to get his feet off the ground. He didn't notice the smiles on the faces of the Carlisle high jumpers.

"If a horse can do it," he announced solemnly, "I guess I can do it, too."

But there was something thoroughly serious about the young Indian, despite his quip. The boys turned to watch him. Among them, unnoticed by Jim, was Coach Warner.

Thorpe took his proper distance, looked at the bar once, made the short run and leaped. It was the most beautiful leap anyone had ever seen at the Indian school.

There was daylight, plenty of daylight between those tailor-shop overalls and the bar set at five feet nine. And when Jim came down on the other side of it, the stick stayed right where it had been placed.

Jim looked back at the bar and grinned.

"It wasn't too hard at that," he said. Nothing would ever be too hard for Jim in any sport, in any athletic competition.

The boys of the track team were struck too dumb to answer, their eyes and mouths wide open as they watched the Indian nonchalantly walk back toward the school grounds.

The next afternoon Jim was called in by Coach Warner.

"Anything wrong?" asked the anxious young Indian.

Warner scratched his head. This innocence was something new for him.

"Are those the overalls you wore when you jumped yesterday?"

"Yes, sir. Is that bad?"

"And you were wearing those tennis shoes?"

"Yes, sir. I haven't gotten into any trouble, have I?"

"Listen, Thorpe," said Warner, poking his finger into Jim's chest. "In a track uniform and with spiked shoes you'll be jumping six feet."

"I can do that now," said Jim. "At least I think I can."

"I'll bet you can," agreed the smiling coach. "You report to the track team."

"I can't, sir."

Warner scowled.

"Why not?"

"I'm playing with the Hotshots." (The scrub team was called the Hotshots by the boys of Carlisle.) "I'd like to finish the season," explained Thorpe.

Warner smiled. "So you play football, too?"

"Yes, sir."

"Funny I haven't noticed you around."

"Perhaps you will now," said the blunt young Indian.

"Perhaps," said Coach Warner. He did. . . .

In the spring of 1912 the greatest American athletes from every section of the country, North, South, East, and West, poured into New York Giants' Polo Grounds. The United States was selecting its top runners, hurdlers, high jumpers, and field men to compete in the greatest sport classic in the world, the spectacular international quadrennial Olympics.

Every four years, except when wars have intervened, in the capital or some other great city of the country fortunate enough to be chosen, a whole populace goes all out to welcome the best-trained, the best-equipped athletes in the world. They prepare an elegant stadium, a gala welcome for the different representatives of the invited countries; they deck out the city, then throng to the arena to witness the greatest rivalries and the toughest competition in the history of sport.

In 1912 the Olympics were to be held in Stockholm, capital of Sweden, the neat little Scandinavian country with its remarkably long list of great track and field men. But it wasn't just Scandinavians the American team would meet. There would be Englishmen, Frenchmen, Russians, Australians, Germans, Italians,—men from all over the globe, men who were champions in their own country, and men with reputations that had traveled beyond the borders of their homelands. If a man was to carry home the laurels in Olympic competition, he had to be more than good; he had to be a world-beater.

Some Americans love competition. The tougher the pace, the better they like it. There isn't a man who runs or leaps or throws a javelin who wouldn't give anything just to compete in the Olympics.

Ralph Craig came from Detroit, Lippincott from Philadelphia, Davenport from the University of Chicago, and Duke Kahanamouka from Hawaii. Meredith came from Mercersburg Academy and Jim Thorpe from Carlisle. There wasn't a college, a club, a city, a YMCA that didn't bend every effort to place a man on the squad which was to represent the United States in the great Stockholm Olympics.

In the high jump trials, Jim Thorpe cleared the bar at a mere six feet five. This was one of the times Jim really tried. He outjumped Alva Richards, the national high-jump champion, and was just five-eighths of an inch short of the world record which was held at the time by Mike Sweeney. The jump was enough, of course, to insure a spot for him on the Olympic team they were assembling at the Polo Grounds.

But there was something new being added to the Olympics this year.

"Only a man," argued the European coaches and track men, "who is an all-round athlete, an all-round competitor, is deserving of the title, World Champion."

The United States agreed.

"Let us revive the pentathlon and the decathlon," suggested the men from Europe.

The pentathlon is a five-event competition; the decathlon consists of ten events. Everyone knew that as far as stamina was concerned, and the ability of one man to compete in runs, hurdles, and field events, the Scandinavian athletes had the edge. Everyone knew, too, that this was an attempt to stop the American domination of the world classic.

Still, no protest came from the United States. They just sat about, watched the competitors in the Giants' ball park, and chose their men.

The Americans had a couple of good sprinters in Craig of Detroit and Meyer of New York City. Mel Sheppard was another great sprinter, and Lippincott and Davenport. For the pentathlon they had Menaul of the University of Chicago. For the pentathlon and the decathlon, both, they had a pretty good prospect in Jim Thorpe, the Carlisle Indian. For the modern pentathlon, another new event for the Olympic classic, the United States had an army man, a young fellow called Patton, Lieutenant George Patton. It was this same Patton who was to be called "Blood and Guts" and who would lead his men, as their general, in a merciless drive against the Nazi "supermen," and level them in World War II.

It was a good team of athletes that the United States had assembled, and in the summer of 1912, to the accompaniment of bugle and drumbeat, with a wildly cheering send-off crowd that had assembled at the pier, they boarded a ship and set sail for Sweden, the land of the Vikings.

A sea voyage is generally the signal for rest and relaxation, but not for the Olympic squad from America. They laid out the broad-jump mats, they set up the high-jump bars, they measured off the sprints and ran around the deck. They were in the pink of condition when they said "So long" to the Statue of Liberty. They were going to be in the pink of condition when they landed in Europe.

There was one exception. If Jim Thorpe took any practice jumps, nobody saw him. If Jim ran around the deck once, there was no witness. He was the most relaxed athlete aboard ship. He gave no sign of any pressure on him and couldn't understand why anyone should be tense about the Stockholm meet.

"Sure, it's the Olympics," he said. "But it's fun, isn't it? What's all the sweating for?"

Craig, Lippincott, and Davenport shook their heads in wonder and continued their stints around the deck. They had heard about Jim's training habits but had never quite believed them.

Certainly Jim didn't train the way a man who wins medals usually trains. He lounged in his steamer chair, found a hammock to swing in, looked out on the green water and the endless blue horizon. He liked to watch the big fish jumping over the surf. . . .

All Jim Thorpe did in that Olympic broad jump was to leap twenty-three feet, two and seven-tenths inches. It was good enough, however, to win first place in the event for the United States. The broad jump was the first competition of athletes from all over the world in the new Olympic Pentathlon—and the American Indian had won it.

The next event in the pentathlon was the two-hundred meter hurdles. Jim looked for his special hurdling shoes.

"I just left them here," he complained to Coach Warner.

"No one is going to walk away with your shoes," snapped back the coach. He was angry. He figured that Jim, in his usual easy way, had just forgotten to bring them along.

"Anybody seen my shoes?" yelled Jim.

Nobody had seen Jim's shoes.

"I just put them down before I did the broad jump," Jim tried to explain.

"That's great," said Warner. "We'll just run down to Spalding's and get you another pair."

"You didn't expect me to jump with them, did you?" asked Thorpe, a little annoyed.

Pop was too angry to answer, but Jim never stayed annoyed too long.

"Maybe I should have jumped with them," he said. "I might have cleared the stadium."

But Pop Warner wasn't interested in what his wild Indian might have done had he carried his hurdling shoes. The hurdles had to be run and his prize protegé needed something to put on his feet. He ran around till he found an extra pair of

161

spikes and a pair of sprinting shoes nobody was using. Hurdling shoes need spikes for the heels as well as for the toes. He hammered those heel spikes into the sprinting shoes and impatiently handed them to his runner.

"Here!" he said. "I hope you don't end by breaking your neck on them."

No manufacturer would have dared to send the shoes Jim Thorpe put on, even to a cellar club team. They were the kind of shoes a boy will bang up for himself just to play at the game of running hurdles. They certainly weren't shoes to wear in a race against the best hurdlers in the world. But Jim didn't complain. He never complained.

"They look pretty good to me," he said, grinning again.

Pop Warner may have been used to Jim's quirks. This was too much for him. He just turned on his heels and walked off.

Jim laughed. He never fussed and he couldn't understand fussing. He laughed and walked to the post.

With the squeezing of the trigger of the starting gun, Jim was off. Regulation shoes or an amateur imitation of them, it didn't matter. Jim was out in front at the first hurdle. And he kept going, gathering momentum, and didn't stop till he cut the tape at the finish line. He was in first. His time was fifteen

and six-tenths seconds. It was a great record—one which was to stand up for thirty-six years until Bob Mathias won the event in the 1948 Olympics held in London. It took thirty-six years and a great deal of new technical knowledge of the event to beat the time Jim Thorpe had set with a pair of shoes Glenn Warner had fixed up for him in the emergency.

"Did you try?" was all Pop Warner asked when the race was over.

"I guess I tried a little," said Jim, and he grinned.

The pride of Carlisle had won the first two events of the pentathlon. He didn't do so well in the third event, the javelin hurl. He tossed the rod 153′ 2 19/20″. Although that's a long way to hurl the javelin, it won only third place for the amazing Thorpe.

"You're slowing down," said Coach Warner.

"I'll win the next two," answered Thorpe.

"Do you think you can?" egged on the knowing coach. Warner knew how to get at his great Indian.

"I know I can!" shot back Jim Thorpe, and he meant it.

He threw the discus 168′ 8 4/10″ to give him first place in that event. In the 1500-meter race he cut the tape in 4 minutes 44.8 seconds to place first again, and to keep his promise to Coach Warner.

"Well?" he demanded of his straight-faced mentor.

"Not bad," said Glenn Warner simply. "How are you going to do in the decathlon?"

It was an astoundingly low score of seven points which Jim Thorpe had come in with for the five-event competition. It was better than twice as good as that of the runner-up R. F. Bie of Norway, who had come in second with fifteen points. Third man in the event was J. A. Menaul from the University of Chicago with twenty-eight points. The United States did well enough in the new event which was supposed to put the Americans at a disadvantage.

It was a great American team in the best tradition of American sport, but the feats of Jim Thorpe were those of a competitor beyond compare. He had been remarkable in the pentathlon. It would be too much to ask any man to duplicate the victory in the decathlon. That is, it would be too much to ask of any man but Jim Thorpe.

In the pentathlon Jim had won four firsts. In the decathlon he won four again. He was first in the high hurdles, coming in at 15.6 seconds; first in the 1500-meter run, coming in at 4:40.1; first again in the high jump with a leap of 6' 1 6/10"; and first in the shot-put with a toss of 42' 5 9/20". He placed third in the 100-meter race, the discus throw, and pole vault and the broad jump. He was fourth in the 400-meter and the javelin events.

Competing in ten such varied events against the best men in the world is to take on a most grueling pace, even for skilled and highly trained athletes. To compete in ten such events, after the five events of the pentathlon, is enough to kill off the heartiest of men. But not Jim Thorpe.

After setting the seemingly impossible score of 7 points in the pentathlon, the Indian had gone on to score an unbelievable 8,412.96 points out of a possible 10,000. And, of course, he was high man again, first. The nearest man to him was Hugo Wieslander of Sweden. The great Swede had scored a very creditable 7,724 points. But he was almost 700 points behind the great Indian from Carlisle.

With 7 points in the pentathlon, 8,412.96 in the decathlon; this was an athletic feat that was never to be repeated.

Before the tremendous crowd of sport enthusiasts who had gathered from all corners of the world to witness the greatest athletes vie against each other, King Gustav of Sweden summoned the grandson of the Indian warrior, Black Hawk, to the victory stand.

"For winning the decathlon . . ."

163

said the king of all Sweden, and Jim took from his hands a bronze bust which had been cast in the likeness of the monarch.

"For winning the pentathlon ..." continued the king, and he handed the boy from Carlisle the prize awarded by the Czar of all the Russias, a silver Viking ship, studded with magnificent jewels.

A laurel wreath was handed King Gustav and he draped it over the shoulders of a triumphant athlete.

"Sir," said His Majesty, "you are the most wonderful athlete in the world."

The return of the American heroes to their native shores was all pomp and splendor. Jim's welcome home was one long string of magnificent celebrations. The American athletes had come back with first place in the Olympics. Jim Thorpe had come home with first place in the heart of every American man, woman, and child.

"Jim Thorpe is the highest type of citizen," said the President of the United States, Howard Taft.

In New York there was a huge parade to welcome the Indian who had shown the world that a native

American was the greatest living athletic competitor. There were parades in Philadelphia and Boston. At Carlisle the school went wild, welcoming the return of its three heroes, Louis Tewanima, winner of the mile and the two-mile races at the Olympics, their great coach, Pop Warner, and the incomparable, smiling, modest Jim Thorpe, grandson of Chief Black Hawk of the Fox and Sac Indians.

It was a memorable moment in the life of the great athlete.

"We'll pay you seven hundred and fifty dollars to do a stage tour," came one offer.

"We'll pay you one thousand dollars a week," came a second.

"We'll pay you one thousand five hundred dollars."

Jim turned them all down.

"They don't understand," he explained. "I just can't talk to people."

Jim should have been able to talk. He might have been able to avert the tragedy which followed so close on the triumphant and happy days of the summer of 1912.

At the end of 1912 Jim Thorpe was the uncrowned king of sports, of every sport. The football season hadn't ended before five of the big-league baseball teams came down to little Carlisle to bid for the mighty Indian.

And then, almost without warning, the sunny skies which had seemed to move wherever Jim moved became clouded over. A noise more ominous than the wind and more destructive than thunder began to come in from the East. At first it was no more than a rumor. Then the storm broke, torrents of abuse came tumbling down on the head of the great warrior and, almost overnight, he was toppled from his throne.

There are many versions of the story. Jim says it was a former pitcher, who had become a newspaper sports writer, who turned the trick. The pitcher had played ball for the Fayetteville ball club in North Carolina the year Jim had been on its roster, and late in 1912 had recognized the Indian on a picture the team had taken on a hunt. It was a snapshot the manager of the ball club had taken, blown up and hung on a wall in his ranch house. Early in January, 1913, the reporter wrote for the Worcester, Massachusetts, paper that hired him:

"Jim Thorpe played professional baseball in 1909–10 for Rocky Mount and Fayetteville in the Eastern Carolina League."

Another version of the story had Francis Albertanti, a rookie sports reporter, as the man who broke the news which rocked the sports world.

However the Amateur Athletic

Union learned of Jim's playing with the Eastern Carolina League, the result was the same. They got in touch with Coach Warner and Warner called in Thorpe. There was no beating around the bush.

"You played ball when you weren't at Carlisle?" said Pop Warner.

"I told you that when I came back," said Jim, still completely unaware of what was in store for him.

"Baseball?" continued Pop Warner.

"Sure. I played for Rocky Mount and Fayetteville and . . ."

"Did you get paid for it?"

"Sure, I got paid for it," said Jim. "Everybody got paid for it."

"Don't you know an amateur isn't supposed to play for money?" exploded Pop. He got up from his chair and began to pace the room. Pacing the room was Jim's trick, but the truth had suddenly dawned on the Indian and he was too stunned to move.

"But everybody plays ball and gets paid for it, Pop," he protested.

"And gives his right name, too?" snapped the coach. "You sure have handed yourself a mess! How do you expect to pull out of it?"

"I didn't know I was doing anything wrong," said Jim simply. "I hope this doesn't give you any trouble, Coach."

"Me!" bellowed Warner. "Don't you worry about me! It's all those medals you brought back from the Olympics. It's the king's head and that Viking ship they want!"

Thorpe was thoroughly beaten. He didn't understand. During July and August the roster of every semi-pro club was jammed with college football and baseball players. True, they played under some assumed name, but Jim didn't see that that made any difference. They must have known that he had played semi-pro ball. There were big-league scouts who had come down to watch him play. Everybody knew that Jim Thorpe had pitched for Rocky Mount, he figured. Why did they wait till now to make a fuss about it?

"It's too much for me to make out," he said quietly. "I sure would hate to give up those trophies," he added in a voice which didn't carry to the other end of the room.

Pop Warner put his hand on the Indian's shoulder. "We've got to do something about it," he said. "The A.A.U. wants to talk to us."

The proud Indian, like his ancestors before him, was forced to lower his colors. He had played ball for a bush club in a bush league, never earned more than sixty dollars a month doing it. That, by itself, hadn't created even a ripple in the big ocean of the sports world. But his name had appeared in the line-up of the club. It was as "Jim Thorpe" that he had pitched or played in the infield or patrolled the garden. He had been too honest, or too simple. All the other boys who had earned the "honest dollar" during their vacations had not been honest and assumed other names, such as Joe Smith, Bill Brown, John Doe. But not Jim Thorpe. That name Jim Thorpe in the Fayetteville roster was enough to whip up as fierce a storm as the ocean of athletics had ever witnessed.

"I did not play for the money that was in it," Jim wrote to the moguls of the Amateur Athletic Union, "but because I like to play ball."

Everybody in the game—football, baseball, track, basketball, lacrosse—knew that Jim only played for the fun of it.

"How many events do you want to get into?" Coach Murphy of the United States Olympic squad had asked the Indian.

"All of them," Jim had answered. "What's the fun of watching when you can play?"

This was Jim Thorpe. He was always an amateur at heart, the greatest of the amateurs, and he never changed. He was first, last, and always a competitor. That fifteen dollars a week would never make him rich, but he got a kick out of swinging a bat, fielding a hot grounder, whipping the old apple down the middle, making it dance around the plate, slamming it past the swinging batter for a *K* in the score book.

"I did not play for the money," Jim wrote. However, it was that money and his name—the fifteen dollars a week to an Indian named Bright Path and called Jim Thorpe —which had upset the equilibrium of the great amateur world of sports and threatened to send all the trophies won by a magnificent athlete back to Sweden.

"I was not very wise in the ways of the world," continued the humble Thorpe in his letter to James I. Sullivan, secretary of the A.A.U., "and did not realize that this was wrong."

The big leagues knew that Jim had played semi-pro ball. There must have been a lot of others who knew that Jim had played in the bush league. The Indian certainly wasn't "wise in the ways of the world" which let him compete in the trials for the Olympic team, allowed him to go abroad with the United States squad, allowed him to receive the plaudits of a king and a czar and accept their magnificent trophies, only to reverse itself and blacken and besmirch his name.

But the Indian people are a stoic people. They can be humble in all their pride, accept punishment

167

without complaining, suffer great pain, even death, without uttering a cry in protest.

"I hope I will be partly excused by the fact that I was simply an Indian schoolboy and did not know that I was doing wrong," he wrote in all simplicity and sincerity, "because I was doing what many other college men had done, except they did not use their own names."

Jim Thorpe was simple enough to speak the plain truth, but college men playing professional ball under assumed names had ever been a source of irritation to the simon-purists of athletics. They might forgive Jim his errors, taking into consideration his great humility. They could never forgive his bringing into the open again the semi-pro excursions of college and school athletes.

"If Thorpe is guilty," declared James Sullivan on the eve of the meeting of the A.A.U., the meeting to decide the fate of the Indian, "we want to find it out as soon as possible. We have no desire to cover up the doings of anyone connected with the A.A.U. who may be charged with having broken the laws of amateur competition. This is a matter in which a delay is dangerous to the best interests of the union, and because of Thorpe's chances to be accredited greatest athlete in America there is no reason why prompt action should not be taken."

The Amateur Athletic Union was on the spot. Jim Sullivan was really one of Thorpe's great admirers.

"It has been said," he told the press, "that sustained charges against Thorpe would not be acted upon with the speed that would prevail in the case of an ordinary athlete. In reply to this I will say that we will act with greater dispatch than would prevail with the action in regard to any other athlete in America."

There was more than Jim Thorpe at stake as far as the A.A.U. was concerned. There was its honor in accepting the Olympic championship with a man who might not be simon-pure.

"While it has never been shown that he has broken the amateur law in any form of track and field competition," explained the secretary, "the fact that he signed a registration blank attesting that he had never in any manner transgressed the amateur rule makes him amenable to discipline by the Amateur Athletic Union. If he is found to have broken the rules," said Mr. Sullivan severely, "he will be stripped of all his records; his name taken from the athletic annals, and he will be compelled to return all the prizes he has won since his infraction of the rules."

"Thorpe won the pentathlon," he said simply. "The head belongs to him."

It was a sharp note. The following day the Amateur Athletic Union held its meeting. It voted Jim Thorpe "Guilty."

Pop Warner wrapped up the sculptured head of the king of all Sweden. He wrapped up the Viking ship which the czar of all the Russias had awarded the great Indian. He wrapped up all Jim's medals and ribbons. With a heavy heart he sent them back to Sweden.

Norway's F. R. Bie was declared the winner of the pentathlon. He was offered the sculptured replica of the head of the monarch which Jim had been forced to return. But the Norwegian would have none of it.

To Sweden and H. Wieslander, who was declared the winner of the Olympic decathlon, went the Viking ship.

"Not for me," said the great Swedish athlete. "I did not win the decathlon. The greatest athlete in the world is Jim Thorpe."

Jim never did get back those trophies. They are kept in a case permanently on display in the little neutral country of Switzerland. No one can find the great, unmatched record of Jim Thorpe's Olympic feats in any official record book, but anybody who wants to can travel to Lucerne in the Alps to see the great trophies he won but could not keep.

Noting Contrasts

No doubt you noticed the two contrasting moods in "The Jim Thorpe Story." On your paper write two headings—*Rise* and *Fall*. In the first column list the events which led Jim to the peak of the sports world, and in the second column list those which led to his downfall.

Noting the Author's Viewpoint

Do you think the author of the story blamed Jim Thorpe? Prove the worth of your opinion by quoting from the story. If you had been appointed to give a decision in the case, what verdict would you have given? Why?

Practicing Syllabication

The following words were selected from "The Jim Thorpe Story." Copy them on your paper and then, recalling the rules of syllabication, divide them into syllables. When you have finished, check with your dictionary to see if you syllabized them correctly. Study the meanings of the words you do not know.

interference	fascinated	nonchalantly	quirks
phenomenal	competition	innocence	momentum
deceptive	possibilities	representatives	incomparable
field	potentiality	international	ominous

Things Past

Tom Barnaby felt tired and nervous. He had twice driven around the block looking for a parking space. When Nell suddenly pointed down an alley and cried, "There's a horse! Look, Julie, see the pretty horse!" he thought at first that she had found a space, and he slacked the car. Then he understood. "A horse, eh?" They were past the alley and there was no use trying to look, but he felt a kind of slow-rising excitement as he groped for a memory. When I was a little boy, he thought, when they took me to Chicago that time, to Grandpa's. "Did you see the horse, Julie?" he asked his small daughter.

By now they were at the corner and Julie was wailing that she hadn't seen the horsy. Barnaby started around the block again. A horse in all this traffic, you didn't often—a little boy, he thought, those horses in Chicago, how many years ago now, there were millions of them and they were all big. I never saw so many big horses, they had those things like horns sticking up from their collars with gold balls on top, the wheels and hoofs thundered on the cobblestones, all horses in that traffic, no gas fumes, we rode in a hack from the station, it squeaked and smelt leathery. "Nell," he said, "we have to show her that horse. Why, the poor kid, she's never seen a horse up close. Think of it, it's got so a horse is a rarity!"

Nell sighed and stared across at him blankly. "When I was little there were always horses," she said. "I remember. Of course the streets were all dirt."

"My father and one of his brothers owned a race horse once," began Barnaby, but Julie bounced over to his side of the seat and interrupted, "Daddy, can I have a popsicle?"

"Later, darling," said Barnaby. "It was a pretty good race horse too —Dolly B. or Daisy B. or something. Of course that was before I was even born."

"A double popsicle," insisted Julie.

"Quiet, darling." Nell drew the child over to her. "You'll disturb Daddy while he's driving. Mr. Dewey over on the other side of our block at home had a horse," she went on. "Once when I was only a little bigger than Julie he gave me a ride in his buggy. It was a brown horse, I think."

Barnaby glanced at her. She was smiling. Suddenly he felt soothed, peaceful, better than he had felt all day. " 'When to the sessions of sweet silent thought,' " he said.

"What?"

"Quotation. 'When to the sessions of sweet silent thought I dum-da-dum remembrance of things past, I dum-da-dum-da-dum a thing I sought.' Horses. I mean it's nice seeing that horse and remembering this way."

"Dum-da-dum," said Nell. "Aren't we intellectual? Quotations and all!"

"No, I just mean—" But by this time they were around the other side of the block and there was a parking space near the alley. Barnaby stopped, cut the wheel sharply, and backed in. "Don't you worry, honey," he told Julie. "We'll show you that horsy!" He jerked the car forward and hit the curb.

"Scraped the tire," said Nell.

It was one of the new tires, too. "Just grazed," murmured Barnaby, wishing he was right.

"You'd better lock the car, Tom." Nell helped Julie out onto the sidewalk, then climbed out of the car herself. "My library books are in back."

"You take her on ahead then. Poor kid," he crooned, bending over Julie, "never seen a horse except in her picture book, has she?"

Julie stared up at him. "Daddy! Is this the horsy in my horse book?"

"No, no, honey, this is a *real* horse. Take her on with you, Nell —I'll catch up." He was trying to get his key into the door lock, but turned to look over his shoulder at his wife. "Did you hear that? 'Is this the horsy in my book?' " He shook his head and sighed.

Nell said rather sharply. "That's the ignition key you're trying."

Barnaby thrust another key at the lock. A policeman stalked up, stopped, and marked the rear tire with chalk; he gave Barnaby a heavy glance, then ponderously shifted his gaze to the fifteen-minute parking sign.

"Okay," said Barnaby, "okay."

But before he got the door locked, Nell and Julie were back. "It's gone," explained Nell. "It turned around. We saw it way down the other end of the alley."

"Could we catch it around the block?"

"Well, we might, but—"

"Come on, then!" cried Barnaby. "Ah, look, she's been crying! Poor little Julie wants to see her horsy, don't you, dear?"

"She wants to see a double popsicle," muttered Nell.

But they all got into the car again and started off. Barnaby felt a little silly chasing the horse this way; he even felt a little angry; but more than anything he wondered what Nell was thinking. As he sneaked out into the line of traffic behind a delivery truck he shook his head impressively. "I remember how I wanted a pony when I was a boy," he said, and then looked carefully over at Nell. But apparently she didn't seriously mind his horse chasing.

"Once a pony tried to bite me," she said. "He was so cute, but as soon as they put me on him the pony turned around and tried to bite me."

"I wanna pony," sniffed Julie; she glanced from her mother to her father and murmured passionately, "I *love* ponies!"

"Listen, honey," said Barnaby, turning a corner. "One time Daddy sold perfume all over the neighborhood trying to win a pony for a prize."

"Bluing," said Nell.

"What?"

"It wasn't perfume. You told me before. It was bluing."

"I guess it was at that," nodded Barnaby.

"Anyhow, you didn't win the prize," said Nell.

Again he looked quickly over at her, but she didn't seem to have meant anything by the remark. She was gazing serenely at the back of the delivery truck. When the truck stopped at a red light Barnaby said tentatively, "I suppose it must seem sort of crazy driving around after a horse this way."

"Well, maybe just mildly," said Nell. "But who ever said we were sane?"

"I *love* perfume!" cried Julie in sudden rapture.

"Just you wait, honey. Daddy'll show you a real horsy!"

173

"Daddy better get moving now that the light's green," said Nell. "Or does Daddy like it here too much to ever leave?"

Barnaby shot the car around the corner. "Now keep watch," he warned. "You take that side and I'll take this when we go by the alley!"

"Old Tom Barnaby, unparalleled hunter of horses!"

"There!" cried Barnaby. "I saw him. He's just about to the end of the alley over in the next block. Say, he's moving along! But we can catch him over there."

"Do you *really* want to, Tom?"

Barnaby tried to look indifferent. "Well, I think we owe it to Julie," he explained. "After all, if a horse is such a rarity that a child can live practically five years without even *seeing* one close up—"

"Julie, do you want to see the horse?"

"Sure, Mamma!" cried Julie. "I wanna horsy. Where's a horsy?"

Nell sighed. Barnaby smiled at the passing traffic.

"You win," Nell told him, "although I must say I never in my life before spent so much time over one horse. Even when it bit me," she said. "I wonder what kind of a horse it is. I mean I wonder what kind of wagon it's hitched to. I remember when there were beer wagons with horses. I used to play with a little girl in our neighborhood at home; she had an uncle who drove a beer wagon. We used to have a butter man, Mr. Steemer; he came every week in the nicest bright yellow wagon, with a horse, of course, and dogs running behind."

"Sure," said Barnaby. "Dalmations, probably."

"What?"

"Dalmations. Black-and-white. Coach dogs, they used to call them. They always used to follow horses."

"Mr. Steemer's dogs were water spaniels," said Nell. "They were brown, and there were two of them, only one died finally. That was King; the other one's name was Curly."

"It's certainly kind of crazy to do this," said Barnaby as he swept around a corner, "but, you know, Nell, it's kind of ironic too, it's really ironic. I mean when you think here we are chasing this horse around just—well, to give Julie a look at it, of course, and to see it ourselves, because we can remember years ago when there were horses everywhere, and—well, I mean when you think how things have changed in our own lifetimes, Nell."

"Sure have changed," said Nell.

"*There's* a horsy!" yelled Julie.

They all saw it at the same time on the cross street ahead. It was a fine, clean brown horse, pulling a tidy black buggy in which sat a white-haired man wearing a black hat and suit and a black bow tie.

"Might be an ad for something," said Nell. "Only there's no sign on it."

Barnaby leaned toward his daughter. "Julie," he said, "I want to tell you something. When I was a little boy my grandpa used to belong to the Green County Horse Thief Protective Association. You don't know what that is, but I'll explain it to you."

"I didn't know that," said Nell. "You never told me that."

"I just remembered it now," explained Barnaby; he felt flattered by her interest. "In those days there were lots of horses everywhere, Julie, and there were men who stole horses that didn't belong to them. Those men were called horse thieves—"

"Like gangsters," interrupted Nell; and Julie nodded knowingly.

"—And one time my grandpa— that's your great-grandfather, Julie —went all the way to North Dakota with the sheriff to catch a horse thief. The sheriff's name was Warberton, and he and your great-grandfather caught the horse thief and brought him back home and put him in jail."

"That's nice!" cried Nell. "I like that!"

"That's nice, Daddy!" proclaimed Julie, mimicking her mother's accents.

"Well," said Barnaby, "it's something you ought to know. My grandpa was mighty proud of it."

They had turned a corner and ahead of them they saw the horse in the middle of the block. It stopped there, and the white-haired old man climbed stiffly out of the buggy.

"We can park here!" cried Barnaby, swinging the car into a parking-lot driveway. "It's worth a quarter this time! I'll take it out of my lunch money for next week. You go on ahead with her, Nell, while I pay the guy."

Nell jumped out and lifted Julie. They started off, hand in hand. Barnaby waited for the parking-lot man, who came up grinning.

"Little girl wants to see the horse, eh?"

"That's right," said Barnaby.

"Well, you don't get a chance to see many of 'em any more."

"No—not many."

The parking-lot man gave Barnaby his change. "You don't hardly get a chance to see one unless in a circus or out on one of them dude ranches!" he answered, and spat on the gravel. "Nothin' but cars!" he snorted.

"That's right!" Barnaby ran after his wife and child. He caught them on the crowded sidewalk. Julie was hanging back, tugging at Nell's arm.

"Come on!" Barnaby told them. "We don't want to miss it again."

"Julie!" said Nell.

"N-n-n-no!" said Julie, stiffening her knees.

"Come on!" Barnaby picked her up. Beyond the people ahead stood the brown horse and the buggy. "See?" he cried, boosting her high. "See it, honey?"

"I don't wanna!" screamed Julie. "It's gonna bite me!" She wriggled in his arms and kicked him in the chest.

"Julie!"

"I wanna go away!" she yelled.

"It's all right, darling, it's all right!" cried Nell. "Give her to me, Tom. Wait! Now, now, now, Mamma's going to take care of you!"

People on the sidewalk were looking at them and smiling. "I wanna go home!" wailed Julie. They were so close to the horse that Barnaby saw the springs go down as the old man climbed into the buggy. He saw the old man's mouth move as he clucked to the horse. "Now, now, now," murmured Nell, cuddling Julie. "I think if we got her a popsicle, Tom—"

She paused abruptly when she saw Barnaby watching the horse go down an alley.

"Oh, Tom! Don't feel that way! It was a grand idea!"

"I don't know why I got so excited," said Barnaby. "It was a crazy idea, anyhow."

Hearing Julie cry, he felt almost like crying himself, but he knew that would be crazy, too. Then Nell set Julie down on the sidewalk. "Now stop it!" she said firmly. She slipped her arm through Barnaby's. "Stop crying!" she warned Julie again, and reached down to take the little girl's hand. Together the three of them started back to the parking lot. Nell walked close to Barnaby, her steps in rhythm with his. When he looked down at her she was looking up at him; then Julie let out a long, tremulous sigh, and Barnaby and Nell, looking at one another, slowly, almost unwillingly, began to smile.

Reading Critically

Analyze the story critically and answer the following questions.

1. Which incidents make the story humorous? Mention three of them.
2. How is Julie's behavior typical of a child?
3. Is Nell a typical mother in the way she deals with the little girl? Give examples.
4. Was Tom Barnaby's primary interest in the horse his desire for Julie to see it? Explain.
5. Was the ending satisfying to you? How would you have ended it?
6. Imagine yourself an older brother or sister with a younger brother or sister who acted as Julie does in the story. What would you do in the same circumstances?

Noting Style

The author of the story used very vivid, meaningful verbs. Some of them are listed below. Write an original sentence using each of them.

slacked	crooned	muttered
groped	grazed	sniffed
bounced	thrust	snorted
scraped	stalked	wailed

177

ELIZABETH COATSWORTH

On a Night of Snow

CAT, if you go outdoors you must walk in the snow.
You will come back with little white shoes on your feet,
Little white slippers of snow that have heels of sleet.
Stay by the fire, my Cat. Lie still, do not go.
See how the flames are leaping and hissing low,
I will bring you a saucer of milk like a marguerite,
So white and so smooth, so spherical and so sweet—
Stay with me, Cat. Outdoors the wild winds blow.

Outdoors the wild winds blow, Mistress, and dark is the night.
Strange voices cry in the trees, intoning strange lore,
And more than cats move, lit by our eyes' green light,
On silent feet where the meadow grasses hang o'er,
Mistress, there are portents abroad of magic and might,
And things that are yet to be done. Open the door!

LOUDON S. WAINWRIGHT

The Disarming of Diablo[1]

IT WAS pitch dark on Yucca Flat. The valley was waiting for the test atomic blast. "Fifteen seconds to zero time," the speakers intoned.

The tense countdown began. "Ten, nine, eight . . . zero"—and nothing happened. The atomic device called Diablo had not gone off. In its 500-foot-high steel eyrie thirteen miles north of the control point, a silent, thwarted envelope of nuclear energy still awaited release.

A new, excited voice replaced the recording on the loud-speakers. "Misfire! Misfire! Hold your positions!"

For only the third time in six years of testing at the Nevada proving grounds, where more than fifty atomic devices have been fired, one of the great weapons had not exploded.

Now it would be somebody's nerve-racking job to see that it did not go off unexpectedly. Five brave men accomplished it. Two, Walter Arnold, 36, and Forrest Fairbrother, 32, were engineers working for the University of California's Radiation Laboratory at

[1]From *Life* Magazine, Sept. 16, 1957. Copyright, Time, Inc.

Livermore. A third, Bernard Rubin, 33, was a chemical engineer at Livermore. These men all worked on Diablo from the time of its inception.

The fourth man, Edmund Tucker, 37, worked for the firm responsible for the instruments that record the effects of most of the weapons fired by the AEC. Tucker's field job was to see that everything was tied in.

The fifth man was Robert Burton, 33, a Colorado electrical engineer. His firm was responsible for the triggering mechanisms, and Burton did the job manually. He surely ranked among the world's most experienced performers of this particular act, for he had already armed about twenty atomic weapons.

Just a few hours earlier Burton had tightened the final connections. Fairbrother, Rubin, and Tucker were there, too, and had checked over the final assembly. (Arnold was back at the control point.) Everything seemed to be in perfect order.

During the final minute, one of the scientists in the control room stared at his instruments in disbelief. Suddenly, voltages which

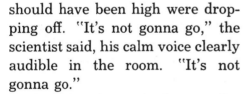

should have been high were dropping off. "It's not gonna go," the scientist said, his calm voice clearly audible in the room. "It's not gonna go."

There in the control room the men huddled around Dr. Gerald Johnson, a bespectacled physicist. Johnson was test director for the series of nuclear detonations.

Johnson's first thought was for the safety of exposed people. He gave orders almost immediately for evacuation of the observers near the control point, but it was decided, temporarily at least, to hold the 2,500 Marines present and

a civil-defense test group of 17 exactly where they were.

Power had failed to reach the device. Now, before anything else was done, Diablo would have to be made completely harmless. One mistake had already been made; the dread possibilities of another were clear.

The disarmers were picked. "The choice was completely logical," reported Rubin flatly. "We just decided how many people we'd need for what functions."

180

Fairbrother had gone to check his instruments, and when he returned Dr. Johnson spoke to him quietly. "Forrest, we've decided that you and Burton and Barney Rubin will have to climb up there and disarm it." Then Johnson asked the three men a question he would never have put unless he felt that his order was extraordinary. "Is that all right with you?"

Fairbrother looked at Johnson. "If I'm going to climb that tower," he said, "I want something to eat first."

The climbers would need support at the tower base for communications and for possible extra help. Tucker and Arnold volunteered and were accepted. There was no difference in danger between their job and the job of the climbers. Most likely nothing would happen. But if the device did go off, with the explosive force of 10,000 tons of TNT, it would make no difference at which end of the tower a man happened to be standing.

After a light breakfast, the disarming party, accompanied by Drs. Johnson and Graves and two other scientists, left the control point in three cars. It was seven o'clock. The three cars, traveling over sixty miles an hour, sped down the single ribbon of asphalt leading toward the distant tower.

Before the men left the control point, they had cut off all power sent from there. Their destination was a timing and relay substation. At this place they would further close off current and confirm their conviction that the removal of an elevator winch had broken a key connection. A blockhouse stood three miles from the tower. The instruments there indicated that a disconnection had prevented the final pulse from ever reaching the device.

The nine men left the blockhouse and squatted in the shade along its west wall. Johnson went over the whole disarming procedure again with the group. Each man's task was very clearly defined. They had the necessary instruments and the rope for slings. It was too bad they would have to climb, but they could not use the elevator. Removing the winch had caused the trouble; putting it back before disarming and then applying power along the troublesome circuit was out of the question.

The men rose. It was time to get started. One man, Dr. Lewis Fussell, was to stay at the blockhouse. Johnson and two others would return to the control point and stand by the telephone.

Dragging rooster tails of dust, the two unmarked sedans sped down the sparsely graveled road, and stopped at the pencil-thin tower.

Before the dust had settled, the five men piled out, three from one car and two from the other. Dressed in shorts and sports shirts, they looked like vacationers. A jack rabbit moved behind an electrical panel at the base of the tower. The men had noticed it the night before, after the arming, and Edmund Tucker now said, "There's the luckiest rabbit in the world."

Rope was cut into three short sections which were attached as slings to three instrument cases. It was seven-thirty. The climbing sun gave little hint of the brutal heat it would throw forth later. On one of the main posts of the tower was a telephone box; Arnold, a bull-necked man with a crew haircut, rapidly dialed a number. He said, "We are at the base of the tower preparing to go through the procedure of disarming. I will report progress."

The tower ladder was built right into the tower; the rungs, a foot apart, were more than wide enough for easy handholds. The tower structure was sheerly vertical, twenty-two feet square at both top and bottom, but the ladder ran upward in twenty-five foot sections, and at the end of each section was a small, indented landing, big enough for a man to stand on before starting for the next level. Encircling the climbing side of the ladder was a welded gridwork which a man falling backward could reach for and hold. In an endless, sharp-edged ripple the ladder stretched up into the sky, almost as tall as the thirty-nine-story United Nations building in New York. Tucker and Arnold nodded brief farewells and Burton started up.

By the time Fairbrother started up, Burton was already fifty feet above him, on the second landing, and Rubin was resting on the landing between. Rubin weighed a hundred and ninety-six pounds; this could be a terrible climb for such a heavy man. And though the climbers had been cautioned that there was no hurry—in fact, they believed this themselves—there was an implicit urgency about the job waiting at the top, an urgency that would keep them straining upward. Arnold checked his watch; it was 7:35. He dialed the control point and reported that all the men were on the ladder.

At 7:40, on about the one hundred and fifty-foot level, the climbers first began to feel fatigue. It was mostly in their arms, which grew taut and trembled slightly. Fairbrother was sharply aware that he had been awake for more than twenty-four hours. Rubin, although he had suffered from asthma as a child, was breathing

easily. In the lead, Burton concentrated on a cautious pace, and rested on each landing while the others did the same on landings below. But he was careful not to rest long enough for the mounting fatigue to lull and stiffen stretched muscles. Tucker and Arnold called up encouragingly from the ground.

After a period of worsening strain, the exertion had become almost mechanical. It seemed to take no effort of will to keep up the rhythm: up twenty-five steps, then rest, then up another twenty-five. The sun had risen perceptibly at their sweating backs and cast westward an elongated tower shadow. Burton tracked the progress of the climb on the shadow.

Fairbrother thought momentarily about his wife. Back at the control point, he had considered calling her, but then decided it would be better to get the job done first. Word of the misfire had probably spread by now, and he hoped she would not hear of the disarming party while she fixed breakfast in Livermore, California, for the two children. Even if his name were not mentioned she might guess his involvement. He looked up past Burton on the next level. Only six more landings to go.

At the four hundred and fifty-foot level was a broad platform with recording instruments on it.

Burton waited there for the others to join him. After the three men had rested silently for a moment, they reviewed the procedure they would follow when they reached the cab, now only fifty feet away. It was almost eight o'clock. All their extensive technical knowledge that nothing could happen did not completely suppress the insistent, ignorant hunch that something might.

Directly beneath the cab floor, at four hundred and ninety-three feet, they took a last, long rest. For the first time they sat and did nothing. They wanted to be in perfect control of themselves when they moved again. Now, the order of climbing would change. Rubin would go up first and open the cab door. He would check the room carefully with his detecting device. If all was well, as they kept reassuring themselves it must be, Burton and Fairbrother would follow.

Rubin's deliberate footsteps clanged softly on steel as he climbed the ladder to the cab door. Finally there, he walked through and looked, not at the cab interior, but at the face of the instrument he had pulled around in front of him. There was no activity out of the ordinary.

The men who had followed him up entered quickly. They all looked around the cab, which was an equipment-cluttered room with a twenty-two foot ceiling. Sunlight poured in through the sides, left open so that ultrahigh-speed, long-lens cameras miles away could record the extraordinary tumult in the cab in the moment between detonation and utter destruction. In the silence, the room looked much as it had looked the night before. Fairbrother picked up the phone and dialed. It was 8:05, just thirty-five minutes after they had started their climb.

"Gerry, we're at the top," Fairbrother said quietly. Rubin had gone to check his apparatus and Burton was ready to detach the cables. "Barney is completing his function," Fairbrother went on, "and Burton's at the patch cables."

This was the decisive act. With these cables detached, the device could not go off. "I looked first to see if they were connected the way I thought they were," says Burton. Then without hesitation, working with bare hands at about waist level, he loosened the screws that held the locking rings about the two cables. This done, he pulled at one cable leading into the device with an even, steady pressure. It came free. Burton reached for the other. At the phone, Fairbrother's view of the device was blocked.

Again the even, steady pull. It

185

was all over, and Burton said, "O.K." While Fairbrother completed his function in the disarming, Burton took the phone and reported to the control point. When he hung up, he was grinning. "They say back there some reporter is calling from London," Burton drawled, "He wants to know all about the heroes."

They remembered Arnold and Tucker, who were waiting anxiously for word down below. Burton phoned to the bottom of the tower and reported their success. "Call for the winch," he said, "we'd like to ride the elevator down."

Then they relaxed and settled down to wait.

Diablo finally exploded on July 15, two and a half weeks after misfire. The tower was demolished, and the fireball's light was visible three hundred and fifty miles away.

Summarizing

Write "The Disarming of Diablo" as a news reporter would. Ask yourself *who*, *what*, *when*, *where*, *why*, and *how*. Report the story as briefly as possible and write a good headline.

Finding Synonyms

From Column II select a synonym for each word in Column I.

1. device _____	*a.* heard
2. inception _____	*b.* implied
3. perceptibly _____	*c.* upright
4. exertion _____	*d.* tense
5. audible _____	*e.* purpose
6. evacuation _____	*f.* crush
7. demolished _____	*g.* strengthen
8. function _____	*h.* appliance
9. confirm _____	*i.* withdrawal
10. vertical _____	*j.* effort
11. implicit _____	*k.* uproar
12. taut _____	*l.* understandably
13. elongated _____	*m.* ruined
14. tumult _____	*n.* beginning
15. suppress _____	*o.* stretched

CALE YOUNG RICE

The Mystic

THERE IS a quest that calls me,
  In nights when I am lone,
The need to ride where the ways divide
  The Known from the Unknown.
I mount what thought is near me
  And soon I reach the place,
The tenuous rim where the seen grows dim
  And the sightless hides its face.

I have ridden the wind,
I have ridden the sea,
I have ridden the moon and stars.
I have set my feet in the stirrup seat
Of a comet coursing Mars.
And everywhere
Through the earth and air
My thought speeds, lighting-shod,
It comes to a place where checking pace
It cries, "Beyond lies God!"

ERNEST POOLE

Cowboys of the Skies

HE WAS STANDING out on a steel girder, with a blueprint map in his hands. He wore brown canvas trousers tucked into his boots, a grimy jumper, a shirt wide open at the throat, buckskin gloves grayed by hard use, and an old slouch hat on the back of his head. His lean, tanned face was set in a puzzled scowl as he glanced now at the map and now downward at the steel frame of the building.

I came cautiously nearer, looked over, and drew quickly back, for there was a sheer drop of five hundred feet between him and the pavement. A gust of wind blew the map up into his face. He leaned slightly out to brace himself and impatiently struck the map open. Then he jammed his hat over his eyes and continued his looking and scowling.

This was on the thirty-fifth floor. The building, the "Metropolitan Life," was to rise fifty stories in all, seven hundred feet. Other Manhattan giants towered around us. From our perch the eye swept a circle some sixty miles across, with Greater New York sprawled in the center. Even through the noise of the wind and the steel you could hear the hum of the city below. And looking straight down through the brisk little puffs of smoke and steam, the whole mighty tangle of Manhattan Island drew close into one vivid picture; Fifth Avenue, crowded with people and automobiles, was apparently only a few yards away from the tenement roofs, which were dotted with clothes out to dry. Police courts, churches, schools, convents hedged

188

close round with strips of green, the Wall Street region, the teeming city lay below; a flat, bewildering mass, streets blackened with human ants. And from the North River a deep shaking bellow rose from the ocean liner that just at this moment was swinging out into the stream.

Down there humanity hurried and hummed. Up here the wind blew fresh and clean and the details of life dropped off into space, and above me on the open steel beams that bristled up into the heavens some two hundred grimy men clambered about. Silent men in the roar of the steel, seemingly careless and unconcerned, in this everyday job of theirs up in the skies.

Between their work and the world below are two connecting links, the blueprint map and the beam of steel.

The map represents long months of labor by scores of engineers. First conceived as a whole by the architect, they are elaborated, enriched by his draftsmen; turned over to the building contractor, to be drawn over and over in ever-increasing detail, first floor by floor, next room by room, and finally beam by beam. There are hundreds of maps and they bear a staggering mass of figures. Here is careful figuring, checked and rechecked by many vigilant eyes. For human lives depend upon its exactness.

Meanwhile the iron ore has been dug from the Lake Superior mines; in the Pittsburgh mills it has been blasted. The white-hot ingots have been rolled out into beams and plates, and, with the blueprints as patterns, the beams and the plates have been shaped and trimmed into columns and girders and trusses. The rivet holes are punched, and the rivets welded in tight—all but those connecting the joints. And when at last the maps and the beams, the brains and the matter, come together up to the skies, the maps show exactly where each mass of steel is to be fitted and riveted into the frame.

"All we do is to put them together," said the man with the blueprint. "Easy as rolling off a log; only rolling off wouldn't be pleasant. Look here," he added, "here's one of the girders just starting up."

There was a creaking and straining over our heads as the ponderous derrick swung round. Its "mast" of steel was lashed by cables to the center of the building's frame. Every week or two, as the building rose, it had been moved farther up. From the base of the mast the steel "boom" reached upward and outward, extending some twenty feet over the canyon below; and from the boom's upper

189

end two cables, looking like mere silken threads but in reality one-inch ropes of woven steel, dropped five hundred feet to the pavement below. Slowly the boom swung out to position; the cables grew taut and began to move. The journey had begun.

Looking over the edge, I could see the girder leave the street—a twenty-ton beam that looked like a straw. Slowly, moment by moment, its size increased. Now you could see it swing slightly, and tilt. It was steadied by a rope that curved out into the wind like a colossal kite string, and far down in the street a tiny man lay on his back with the rope wrapped under his armpits. A crowd stood round with upturned faces. The journey took five minutes in all. At last the beam rose to the rough concrete floor on which we stood. There were no walls around us.

A man beside me gave a sharp jerk to the bell rope. This rope ran thirty-five stories deep into the depth of the building. Down there the engineer jerked a lever; his engine stopped. Up here the great girder stopped and hung motionless. An hour before, I had been down with the engineer; I had been surprised at the strained look on his face as he listened for the stroke of the gong. But I understood now. Up here we could do nothing. He had to do all the moving from below. And lives hung on his promptness.

Another jerk on the bell rope, an instant's pause, then the boom swung in and the girder came toward us. Another sharp jerk, and the girder stopped in mid-air. A man leaned forward, took a tight grip on the cable, and swung out over the street. Still another jerk on the rope, and it started on up with its puny rider. The signals came now in rapid succession, till at last he hung just between the two high columns.

He crept out to one end. He might have been a fly, for all the effect his weight had on the balance. With his left hand clinging tightly to the steel, his eyes fixed steadily straight ahead, suddenly with his right hand he reached out, seized the column, and as the girder slipped into its seat he snatched the long tapered "spud wrench" from his belt and jammed it through two rivet holes. The mass was safely anchored.

Rough pioneers are these men of the steel, pushing each year their frontier line up toward the clouds. Wanderers, living for their jobs alone. Reckless, generous, cool-headed, brave, shaken only by that grim power of Fate, living their lives out fast and free—the cowboys of the skies.

Following the Sequence of Events

Read the statements below carefully, then copy them on your paper in their proper sequence.

_____ Draftsmen elaborate on the plans.

_____ Another signal is given, the girder comes forward, and a man takes hold of the cable and swings out.

_____ Beams are trimmed and shaped into columns, girders, and trusses.

_____ A man gives the signal, the engineer on the pavement stops the engine, and the girder hangs motionless.

_____ The worker takes his wrench and rivets the girder into its place.

_____ The architect conceives the plan for the building as a whole.

_____ Iron ore is dug from the Lake Superior mines.

_____ Two steel cables are dropped to the pavement from the upper end of the boom, and a beam is locked to it.

_____ A building contractor makes detailed sketches of each floor, room, and beam in the structure.

_____ The beam ascends to the thirty-fifth floor.

Using Suffixes

Add a suffix to one word in each sentence below to make the sentence correct.

1. The "cowboys of the sky" perform a danger work.
2. They go about their tasks, seemingly unconcerned and care.
3. Plans must be checked and rechecked by vigil eyes.
4. The mass beam was swung into place by a huge derrick.
5. Skill and co-operation made the labor task seem less burdensome.
6. Thirty-five stories from the ground the girder stopped and hung motion.
7. In order to rivet the girder in its place, each workman had to do his assigned task each success moment.

MICHAEL EARLS, S.J.

The Lights of Worcester Town

FIVE GREAT HILLS with groves and towers
   Stand like a wall round Worcester Town,
Fair are they all days and hours,
   Most of all when the night comes down:
Camped in beauty if winter snows them,
   Royal they wear rich autumn's gown,
Gleaming if dawn or noontime shows them,
   Fairest of all when the night comes down.

Up the hillsides, down the lowlands,
    Jewelled with lights all Worcester glows,
Magical squares like fairy showlands,
    Arbors of lily, or banks of rose:
Some like ghosts with footsteps stealthy
    Pale on the hills where Spencer goes,
Others in windows warm and healthy,
    They of the lily, these of the rose.

Waters in Blackstone's courseway flowing
    Hold in their eyes of pond and stream
Tier on tier, the mill lamps showing
    Arches of light like a land of dream.
Motion of looms is pictured by them,
    Passing of folk in a golden gleam,
Spindle and shuttle and men that ply them,
    Weaving the tapestries fair as a dream.

Out from the deep dark hills come flashing
    Trailing lights when the trains go by,
Eastward, westward, they are dashing
    Quick as meteors cross the sky.
Beacons aloft on tower and steeple
    Signal their words to the watching eye,
Ribbons of light see town and people
    Flash like a comet across the sky.

Five great hills all marked with highways,
    Stand like a wall round Worcester Town,
Lights aglowing in halls and byways,
    Magical look when the night comes down.
Silvery stars of a city gleaming,
    Jewels bedecking its golden gown,
Lily or rose in gardens dreaming,
    Fairest of all when the night comes down.

Headlines and Deadlines

THE AMERICAN NEWSPAPER is the voice of the American people. Its freedom, assured by the Constitution of the United States, has been maintained by vigilance of its reporters, editors, and publishers. Upon this bedrock they have built a tremendous system of communication which spreads from local chronicles to world-wide news coverage.

For many years the news, as reported in American newspapers, was largely local. As time went on, however, and communication facilities increased, news of other communities began to appear in the local press. Most of this was contributed by individual correspondents. From this method, in time, arose the world-covering news agencies.

The first news agency appears to have been organized by Charles Havas in Paris in 1835. Havas began by translating articles for the French press. In 1840 he established news service by carrier pigeons between Paris, London, and Brussels. The Havas agency is now subsidized by the French government. It supplies stories, articles, and news to the French press.

The Reuter News Agency was organized in 1849 by Julius Reuter, a Prussian government messenger. In 1851 he established his headquarters in London, and, in 1865 and 1866, he gained control of several cable lines. Reuter's is now the greatest of European news agencies.

The Wolff Bureau, the most important news agency in Germany, became the organ of the German government after 1917.

In the United States, there are several news service agencies. The Associated Press, which, in its present organization, dates from the year 1900, is a co-operative association of American newspapers. It has contracts for the distribution of copy through Reuter's, the Havas, and the Wolff agency in Europe. The United Press International is an agency which, through its connections in Europe, Asia, and Australia, supplies a world-wide service. It supplies the most extensive news service in South America. The North American Newspaper Alliance provides special articles and reports designed to supplement, with interpretation and explanation, the items of general news reports obtained through other channels. This association features especially a week-end service for Sunday editions.

An influential force in newspapers today is the National Catholic Welfare Conference News Service. This service gathers news, pictures, and other material from all over the world. Its aim is to present a continuous word and photographic record of current events of Catholic importance and interest.

The beginnings of one press association were informal. Joe Alex Morris of the United Press International, in his book, *Deadline Every Minute*, describes a typical scene in a newspaper office of the early twentieth century, where a press association news dispatch was arriving.[1]

"A telegrapher sitting with his ear close to a small wooden box heard the dots and dashes coming over the wire in Morse code and copied them in words on a typewriter at around thirty-five words to the minute. If anybody close to him whistled, it distracted him and he was likely to miss several words, so whistling was taboo in newspaper offices.

[1]From *Deadline Every Minute*, by Joe Alex Morris. Copyright © 1957 by Joe Alex Morris. Reprinted by permission of Doubleday & Co., Inc.

"A couple of times a day the signals would say: "Take ten . . ." and that meant the operator could rest for ten minutes while the wire was silent. Usually he read the sports pages or rushed out for a cup of coffee.

"At the bottom of each page of copy the receiving operator typed his initials, the exact time of day, and indicated whether the story was complete—

more ejm923a

"The operator was and is a vital cog in any press association. In the final accounting, it was what came over the wires, what the operator copied down that meant success or failure. If a reporter had a news story in Miami or Portland or Kansas City and couldn't get it on the wire, the newspaper editor in Pittsburgh or Boston or Denver was out of luck—and so was the press association that sold him the news service.

"The press association was and is almost without physical assets. It is a staff of men scattered around the surface of the globe, a comparatively insignificant amount of office furniture, a vast communications network that is leased but not owned—and confidence. It is the confidence of the staff that it can find and report accurately what is going on all over the world and the

195

confidence of a certain number of newspaper editors in the ability of those men to do their jobs well. If one of them fails, then the value of the property that is called a press association decreases by the importance of his success. If this confidence vanished tomorrow the assets of a press association would be only a jumbled pile of pencils and paper, of typewriters and battered furniture.

"It is the nature of a press association that men and women scattered from St. Louis to Bombay spend their days and nights hunting not only headlines but the small scraps of news that will interest readers in Centerville, Iowa, or Albany, New York, or Santa Barbara, California. There is endless routine and endless drudgery and there are times when a correspondent feels that the press association does possess certain physical assets after all

—it possesses *him*. At other times, when his story skims over the wires for thousands on thousands of miles, carrying his excitement and perhaps his name into hundreds of newspapers around the world, he may feel that he is the press association. But day after day, the wires are always open, always waiting for him to produce. Day and night, on holidays and on days of disaster, the wire is always waiting.

" 'Yes, young man,' a famous statesman said to a reporter who sought to interview him some years ago, 'I'll be glad to prepare a statement for you. Just tell me when is your—what do you newspapermen call it?—your deadline?'

"The reporter sighed. 'I'm from the United Press,' he replied. 'Our deadline is now. Someplace around the world at this instant a newspaper is going to press. We've got a deadline every minute.' "

Recognizing Multiple Meanings of Words

The words listed at the left below have several different meanings. Skim the selection "Headlines and Deadlines" to locate each word and write an original sentence using that word in the same sense in which the author used it in the selection. On the other side of your paper, complete the next part of the exercise.

The words at the right represent meanings for the words at the left other than those used in the selection. In the space provided, write the letter of the word at the right which best matches each word in meaning.

_____ 1. press	a. bar
_____ 2. lines	b. force
_____ 3. organ	c. duct
_____ 4. copy	d. instrument
_____ 5. channel	e. threads
_____ 6. staff	f. detail
_____ 7. skim	g. reproduction
_____ 8. article	h. read

Recognizing Sequence

The news agencies listed below are mentioned in the selection. At the right are the dates when these agencies were organized. Before the names of the agencies, write their correct dates of origin to show the sequence of their development.

_____	The Associated Press	1835
_____	The Havas Agency	1849
_____	The Reuter News Agency	1917
_____	The Wolff Bureau	1900

Conducting Research

Use reference books to find information and prepare a two-minute oral report on the activities of the National Catholic Welfare Conference.

RICHARD J. GEEHERN

I Am America

I am America.
I am her rolling plains,
Whose golden wheat
Bows in rippling waves
To the prairie winds
And rustles and whispers
And breathes.
I am her mountains,
Snow-tipped and purple,
Fading into misty nothingness,
Strong and silent and alive.
I am her lakes,
Beautiful and mighty.
I reach into the very heart
Of earth. I have eyes
That are keen and sharp,
And I have hands
That grasp. But
I am beautiful
And still and calm.
I am the winds of America.
I am cold and blustering,
Full of fury and wrath;
And I am gentle and soothing
And warm and kind.
And I, the rain, am also America.
I am drink to the thirsty,
And I am life to all living things—
I am death, as well,
For I fill the narrowest streams
To raging rivers.
I destroy;
But I am America.

I am the city,
Lifting its arms to the sky
And throbbing with the spirit of men.
I am the concrete
And steel girders,
Arching my mighty back
Over the rivers.
I am the crowded tenement
And lofty penthouse.
I am the human beings,
Black, yellow, white,
All a part of a noisy city.
I am every trial and sorrow,
Joy and happiness,
In every home and every town.
I am America.
I am great;
I am indestructible and fearless.
My blood is the fresh blood
Of new youth.
I am young
And fine and upright;
I turn my face early
To catch
The first glimpse
Of resplendent dawn;
For I am youth,
And youth must live.
I welcome tomorrow so that
I may root out the bad of yesterday.
I must live
And prosper
And grow.

I will persevere
Because I am great—
For I am America.

4. More Stately Mansions

THIS is our spirit:
born in the cities, born on burning plains,
born upon ships and in captivity,
born upon submarines in stormy sea,
born in dim blindness, though the heart still sings
a grateful paean to the King of Kings;
born as men sacrifice their lives for others
knowing that, under God, all men are brothers.
Here, in the land of the eagle who flies,
here, in the land of where the soul of man cries
for honor, not fame; for freedom, not fear,
men live and men die for dreams they hold dear.

This is our spirit:
here men and women lift their humble praise
to God, though danger darken all their days;
here, like swamp lilies, songs of courage rise
and sound His glory in the high-arched skies.
While others plod, courageous souls take wings
and soar beyond the weight of mundane things
to reach the promise of eternity
through deeds that gleam and set the spirit free;
through time, through space, through lonely solitude,
they rush with souls that know the amplitude
of valor that can make decisions grim,
as Simon of Cyrene did for Him.

This is our spirit:
as on and on across the silver night
we strive to win the age-old race with light;
as up and up the streaming golden sky
our man-made planes in close formation fly;
as down the waters of the far-flung world
our ships, flags high, in pathless sunsets swirl,
all symbols of majestic energy
that conquers lands and strives to set men free;
but, neither night nor light nor surging foam
can capture dreams nor bring the vision home
without the fortitude, the strength of men
who give their lives that Christ may live again.

This is our spirit:
we seek not walls against impending pain,
not against darkness, or the falling rain,
though loveliness and squalor, hand in hand,
walk sometimes through the springtime of the land;
Instead, we seek the lessons three
of faith and hope and charity,
that we may face with smiling fortitude
dangers and grief and lonely solitude.
King Arthur and his golden knights are gone
and we are far removed from Avalon,
but, in our own, our native land we crave
the grace of God to keep us strong and brave.

Three Days to See

I HAVE OFTEN THOUGHT it would be a blessing if each human being were stricken blind and deaf for a few days at some time during his early adult life. Darkness would make him more appreciative of sight; silence would teach him the joys of sound.

Now and then I have tested my seeing friends to discover what they see. Recently I asked a friend, who had just returned from a long walk in the woods, what she had observed. "Nothing in particular," she replied.

How was it possible, I asked myself, to walk for an hour through the woods and see nothing worthy of note? I, who cannot see, find hundreds of things to interest me through mere touch. I feel the delicate symmetry of a leaf. I pass my hands lovingly about the smooth skin of a silver birch, or the rough, shaggy bark of a pine. In spring I touch the branches of trees hopefully in search of a bud, the first sign of awakening Nature after her winter's sleep. Occasionally, if I am very fortunate, I place my head gently on a small tree and feel the happy quiver of a bird in full song.

At times my heart cries out with longing to see all these things. If I can get so much pleasure from mere touch, how much more beauty must be revealed by sight. And I have imagined what I should most like to see if I were given the use of my eyes, say, for just three days.

I should divide the period into three parts. On the first day, I should want to see the people whose kindness and companionship have made my life worth living. I do not know what it is to see into the heart of a friend through that "window of the soul," the eye. I can only "see" through my finger tips the outline of a face. I can detect laughter, sorrow, and many other emotions. I know my friends from the feel of their faces.

How much easier, how much more satisfying it is for you who can see to grasp quickly the essential qualities of another person by watching the subtleties of expression, the quiver of a muscle, the flutter of a hand. But does it ever occur to you to use your sight to see into the inner nature of a friend?

Do not most of you seeing people grasp casually the outward features of a face and let it go at that?

For instance, can you describe accurately the faces of five good friends? As an experiment, I have questioned husbands about the color of their wives' eyes, and often they express embarrassed confusion and admit that they do not know.

Oh, the things that I should see if I had the power of sight for just three days!

The first day would be a busy one. I should call to me all my dear friends and look long into their faces, imprinting upon my mind the outward evidences of the beauty that is within them. I should let my eyes rest, too, on the face of a baby, so that I could catch a vision of the eager, innocent beauty which precedes the individual's consciousness of the conflicts which life develops. I should like to see the books which have been read to me, and which have revealed to me the deepest channels of human life. And I should like to look in the loyal, trusting eyes of my dogs, the little Scottie and the stalwart Great Dane.

In the afternoon I should take a long walk in the woods and intoxicate my eyes on the beauties of the world of Nature. And I should pray for the glory of a colorful sunset. That night, I think, I should not be able to sleep.

The next day I should arise with the dawn and see the thrilling miracle by which night is transformed into day. I should behold with awe the magnificent panorama of light with which the sun awakens the sleeping earth.

This day I should devote to a hasty glimpse of the world, past and present. I should want to see the pageant of man's progress, and so I should go to the museums. There my eyes would see the condensed history of the earth—animals and the races of men pictured in their native environment; gigantic carcasses of dinosaurs and mastodons which roamed the earth before man appeared, with his tiny stature and powerful brain, to conquer the animal kingdom.

My next stop would be the Museum of Art. I know well through my hands the sculptured gods and goddesses of the ancient Nile-land. I have felt copies of Parthenon friezes, and I have sensed the rhythmic beauty of charging Athenian warriors. The gnarled, bearded features of Homer are dear to me, for he, too knew blindness. So on this, my second day, I should try to probe into the soul of man through his art. The things I knew through touch I should now see. More splendid still, the whole magnificent world of painting would be opened to me. I should be able to get only a superficial impression. Artists tell me that for a deep and true appreciation of art one must educate the eye. One must learn through experience to weigh the merits of line, of composition, of form and color. If I had eyes, how happily would I embark on so fascinating a study!

The evening of my second day I should spend at a theater or at the movies. How I should like to see the fascinating figure of Hamlet, or the gusty Falstaff amid colorful Elizabethan trappings! I cannot enjoy the beauty of rhythmic movement except in a sphere restricted to the touch of my hands. I can vision only dimly the grace of a ballet dancer, although I know something of the delight of rhythm, for often I can sense the beat of music as it vibrates through the floor. I can well imagine that cadenced motion must be one of the most pleasing sights in the world. I have been able to gather something of this by tracing with my fingers the lines in sculptured marble; if this static grace can be so lovely, how much more acute must be the thrill of seeing grace in motion.

The following morning, I should again greet the dawn, anxious to discover new delights, new revelations of beauty. Today, this third day, I shall spend in the workaday world, amid the haunts of men going about the business of life. The city becomes my destination.

First, I stand at a busy corner, merely looking at people, trying by sight of them to understand something of their daily lives. I see smiles, and I am happy. I see serious determination, and I am proud. I see suffering, and I am compassionate.

I stroll down Fifth Avenue. I throw my eyes out of focus, so that I see no particular object but only a seething kaleidoscope of color. I am certain that the colors of women's dresses moving in a throng must be a gorgeous spectacle of which I should never tire. But perhaps if I had sight I should be like most other women—too interested in styles to give much attention to the splendor of color in the mass.

From Fifth Avenue I make a tour of the city—to the slums, to factories, to parks where children play. I take a stay-at-home trip abroad by visiting the foreign quarters. Always my eyes are open wide to all the sights of both happiness and misery so that I may probe deep and add to my understanding of how people work and live.

My third day of sight is drawing to an end. Perhaps there are many serious pursuits to which I should devote the few remaining hours, but I am afraid that on the evening of that last day I should again run away to the theater, to a hilariously funny play, so that I might appreciate the overtones of comedy in the human spirit.

At midnight permanent night would close in on me again. Naturally in those three short days I should not have seen all I wanted to see. Only when darkness had again descended upon me should I realize how much I had left unseen.

Perhaps this short outline does not agree with the program you might set for yourself if you knew you were about to be stricken blind. I am, however, sure that if you faced that fate you would use your eyes as never before. Everything you saw would become dear to you. Your eyes would touch and embrace every object that came within your range of vision. Then at last, you would really see, and a new world of beauty would open itself before you.

I who am blind can give one hint to those who see: Use your eyes as if tomorrow you would be stricken blind. And the same method can be applied to the other senses. Hear the music of voices, the song of a bird, the strains of an orchestra, as if you would be stricken deaf tomorrow. Touch each object as if tomorrow your tactile sense would fail. Smell the perfume of flowers, taste with relish each morsel, make use of every sense; glory in all the facets of pleasure and beauty which the world reveals to you through the several means of contact which Nature provides. But of all the senses, I am sure that sight must be the most delightful.

Making a Chart

Make a chart which will help you to remember the main points of this selection. Make three headings, *First day*, *Second day*, and *Third day*. Under each heading list the things the author would do on each day if she had the power to see.

Noting Contrasts

Helen Keller, the blind author of "Three Days to See," has used a great number of contrasts in this selection. Skim the story and make notes of the contrasting words and phrases. For example, *darkness . . . sight*; *silence . . . sound*.

Explaining Passages

Explain in your own words what is meant by the following passages:

"But does it ever occur to you to use your sight to see into the inner nature of a friend?"

"I should let my eyes rest, too, on the face of a baby, so that I could catch a vision of the eager, innocent beauty which precedes the individual's consciousness of the conflicts which life develops."

NANCY BYRD TURNER

Courage Has a Crimson Coat

COURAGE has a crimson coat
    Trimmed with trappings bold,
Knowledge dons a dress of note,
    Fame's is cloth of gold.
Far they ride and far they roam,
    Much they do and dare;
Gray-gowned Patience sits at home,
    And weaves the stuff they wear.

Unsung Hero

In the Hall of Fame, memorial to America's heroes, that rises from the heights of the campus of New York University, you will not find inscribed the name of John J. Moran. Neither will you find it in the annals of Americans who fought in great battles. Still, his name calls forth a story of valor, of humility of spirit, and of one man's love for his fellow men.

John J. Moran was, at first, a minor character in a great drama; in a brief span of time he played its leading role. Hostilities had ended in the Spanish-American War but Moran, a civilian clerk in the office of General Fitzhugh Lee, remained at his post in Havana. "We've got to stay and set up some decent living conditions here," he wrote to a friend in the States.

Setting up decent living conditions was easier said than done. A severe epidemic of yellow fever was ravaging Cuba. "Yellow Jack," the Americans called it, as they watched their comrades sicken and die of the dread disease. "More of us have died in this epidemic than were killed by Spanish bullets," cried the men at the Army post at Quemados, outside the Cuban capital.

"Something must be done," said General Fitzhugh Lee.

"Something will be done," thundered General Leonard Wood, the Chief of Staff.

Cablegrams sped to Washington. Letters came in reply. More cablegrams were sent. "The streets of Havana have been scrubbed," ran General Wood's urgent message. "No stone has been left unturned, but our men here in Cuba are dying by the hundreds."

John J. Moran had seen many an American soldier come to the Army Post and, with sorrow in his heart and a prayer on his lips, had watched his body depart, a sheet over his jaundiced face. "There must be a cure for the 'Yellow Jack'," he said to General Lee.

"Pasteur tried," sighed General Lee, "but he failed."

Then, on a June day in the year 1900, John J. Moran watched the arrival of a new major at the base. "Who's he?" he asked a corporal.

"His name's Reed," said the corporal. "He's out from Washington."

"Doctor?" Moran noted the major's medical insignia.

"Supposed to be the best microbe hunter in the Army."

"We can use him," said John J. Moran.

"He's got a title," said the corporal. "Chief of the Yellow Fever Commission."

"Commission!" scoffed Moran. "All they'll do is talk!"

The Commission did more than talk. Three men—Jesse Lazear, a noted European microbe hunter, Dr. James Carroll, and a Cuban named Agramonte went to work under Major Reed's direction, probing case after case of yellow fever. They could find nothing on which they could focus the blame for the dread epidemic.

In Havana there was a Cuban physician who had spent his life studying yellow fever. Ten years before the Yellow Fever Commission arrived in Cuba, Dr. Carlos Juan Finlay had declared that the mosquito was the carrier of the infection. Everyone laughed at him. The mosquito? Don't be funny, Dr. Finlay!

No one knows how Major Walter Reed heard about Dr. Finlay, but a doctor never stops until he has explored every aspect of a medical problem and every suggested cure. The Major called on the Cuban physician, learned Dr. Finlay's theory, and accepted from him some little black eggs shaped like cigars.

"Hatch them," said Dr. Finlay, "then turn them loose."

"Where?" asked the Major.

"On humans," said the Cuban. "We have no suitable animals for the experiment."

Major Reed carried the idea and the little black eggs back to the Army Base. When the eggs had hatched into silver-banded mosquitoes, he spoke to Jesse Lazear. "The mosquito could be the cause of yellow fever," he said.

"What makes you think so?" asked the European-born microbe hunter.

"I've watched the yellow-fever cases in the hospital," said Major Reed, "and I think it's strange that the nurses who've handled dying patients have not contracted the disease."

"Then it is not a bacillus, like cholera or plague," said Lazear.

"I think something is carrying the germ through the air," reflected Reed. "It could be the mosquito."

"Any mosquito?" asked Lazear.

"No, it must be one that has been in contact with a patient who has had yellow fever."

"How can we prove it?" asked Lazear.

"We'll need volunteers, but who would be willing to take the risk of being stabbed by a mosquito that has been inoculated with yellow fever?" said the Major.

Lazear did not hesitate. "I volunteer," he said.

Dr. James Carroll was told of the plan. "You can use me for a guinea pig, too," he said.

The test began in dark secrecy. Men suffering from yellow fever, doomed to die, were bitten by the silver-winged mosquitoes that had been hatched from the little black eggs. Lazear and Dr. Carroll went through the wards, releasing the *Aedes aegypti*, as they called the harbingers of death, watching the mosquitoes stab man after man. Then, carrying their little glass jars, they returned to the laboratory and waited in the belief that it would take twelve days, as in cases of cholera and malaria, for the mosquitoes to become thoroughly infected.

The second stage of the test continued in secrecy. Dr. James Carroll was the first volunteer to be bitten by the yellow-fever infected mosquitoes. An American soldier, known to medical history as "X.Y.," but actually William Dean of Grand Rapids, Michigan, was next. They suffered yellow fever and recovered. "This proves nothing," said Jesse Lazear, "for they did not live in complete isolation during the experiment and could have been infected by hospital bacteria."

The test went on among patients in the hospital. "We have to prove that *our* mosquitoes, infected with the fever, are the culprits," said Major Reed.

One day when Jesse Lazear was working in the hospital ward, he was bitten by a stray mosquito. He dismissed the thought of danger, for he knew that he hadn't been bitten by his own *Aedes aegypti*. Five days later he knew that he had yellow fever. Chills, rising temperature, racing pulse, jaundice told the story; a week later Jesse Lazear was dead, but it again proved nothing.

"Now it's my turn to be bitten," said Major Walter Reed.

General Leonard Wood thundered his protest. "You're fifty years old," he said, "and you have

211

been sent to Cuba to direct this project. You must go ahead with further experiments."

So Major Reed ordered the construction of seven tents and two little houses to isolate men who might volunteer for further attempts to allay the disease. But who in Cuba or anywhere else would offer himself as a sacrifice to a disease that had claimed thousands of victims? "It's suicide," muttered the soldiers, scorning a two-hundred dollar incentive. Lazear was dead; they weren't going to be carried out of Cuba feet first if they could help it.

There were two men at Quemados who volunteered. "You're both crazy!" cried out their friends as Private Kissenger and John J. Moran announced their willingness to be stung by the *Aedes aegypti*.

Kissenger and Moran went straight to Major Walter Reed. "You can try the bugs on us," they said.

"You know the danger?" Reed warned them.

"We know," replied Private Kissenger and John J. Moran.

"You'll receive compensation," said the Major.

"We want no compensation," they said. "We have talked this over. We volunteer for the cause of humanity and in the interest of science."

It isn't often that a private of the Army and a civilian in its ranks receive official salute, but Major Walter Reed, United States Medical Corps, lifted his hand to his cap. "Gentlemen, I salute you!" he said.

Kissenger was bitten and contracted yellow fever. He recovered.

"We'll try again," said Major Reed and, to further his experiment, inmates in the hospital were given the same clothing and the same bedding that had been used by yellow-fever victims. No disinfectants were used to allay the spread of virus, but not one patient came down with yellow fever.

"An airtight test is the only hope that is left," said Major Reed, and selected John J. Moran as the victim.

Into Hut No. 2, which was a model of hygiene, they placed Moran, alone. Major Reed and Dr. James Carroll then opened a glass jar in the sunny, tightly-screened room and released three female mosquitoes that had been fed upon the blood of yellow-fever victims.

In thirty minutes Moran had been stabbed seven times. Late that afternoon he was stabbed again and again. His head ached, his fever mounted, his pulse raced. His skin turned yellow as he lay racked with pain and nausea, nearly dead "in the interests of science and humanity."

"We've found the source of yellow fever!" shouted Major Walter Reed. "Moran has been in contact with nothing but the *Aedes aegypti.*"

Moran only lay on his nice clean cot and moaned in pain. Other volunteers had shown that a dirty house with ordinary mosquitoes was safe, but the civilian clerk, close to death in the cleanliness of Hut No. 2, had proved to medical science that a mosquito that can catch a germ can carry a germ.

John J. Moran lived, but not to tell his story. No one now knows where he came from or where he went when the troops and civilians came back to the United States.

The world gives due credit to Major Walter Reed and Jesse Lazear, to Dr. James Carroll and Dr. Carlos Finlay. We salute the memories of the Cuban Agramonte, of "X.Y.," and Private Kissenger and the nameless volunteers. We praise the concern of General Fitzhugh Lee and the thunderous demands of General Leonard Wood. We must remember, though, the name of the unsung hero of Quemados. John J. Moran, civilian clerk of the United States Army, deserves a wreath of laurel for his help in ending the long, bitter search for the cause of yellow fever.

Determining the Author's Viewpoint

Select the answer that best completes the sentence below.

I think the author of "Unsung Hero" wrote the selection

a. to give us more information about yellow fever.

b. to show that one can be a hero without ever coming into public notice.

c. to discredit the work of Walter Reed and Jesse Lazear.

d. to show the seriousness of the yellow-fever epidemic.

e. to give an example of how the United States helps other nations in time of distress.

Making Comparisons

Read the poem, "Walter Reed," which follows this story. Compare the poem and the story.

1. Which gives more detail?

2. How much of the story is told in the poem?

3. Which emphasizes more the work of Dr. Reed?

4. Which is more exact in giving the location of the yellow fever?

5. Do you think both the poem and the story commemorate the contribution to humanity in detecting the cause of yellow fever? Give reasons for your answer.

Building Adjectives

By adding a suffix to each of the nouns listed below, build them into adjectives and use each in an original sentence. The words were taken from the story.

danger	drama	risk
fever	condition	thought

Walter Reed

"O, Yellow Jack's here,
With his yellow flag flying.
And everywhere, everywhere,
People are dying.
Our doctors and nurses
Work on till they fall,
But he stings us and slays us,
In spite of them all!

"He scourges the tropics
And all the warm South,
But the North has been seared
By the breath of his mouth.
What might shall withstand him?
What skill drive away
The dread yellow fever
That sickens the day?"

It was not a wizard,
With philters and charms,
It was not a champion,
A champion-at-arms,
But a lean army surgeon,
Soft-spoken and slight,
Who read the dark riddle
And broke the dark might.

He found the mosquito
That carried the pest,
He called volunteers
For a terrible test.
They walked in Death's valley,
—And one, to Death's door—
But Yellow Jack, Yellow Jack
Slaughters no more!

There is valor in battle
And statues for those
Who pepper and puncture
Our national foes—
But, if you are looking
For heroes to cheer,
You needn't look farther
Than Reed and Lazear.

An Ordinary Boy

JOHN PATRICK was an ordinary boy. Everyone who knew him—and a great many people knew him in his native city of Newark, New Jersey—says that of him. His family, his neighbors, the Sisters to whom he went to school, all declare, as they recall his boyhood: "There was nothing unusual about him. He was just an ordinary boy, a good boy."

John Patrick was born in 1908, on the Feast of Our Lady of Mount Carmel. He was born in a two-story frame house, one of a row of houses pretty much alike, on South Twelfth Street in Newark. He lived there while he went to grade school, to high school, and to college. Afterward, when his chosen work took him away from the city of his birth, he often returned to the family residence. Through all his lifetime that house was home to him.

His father and mother had both come from Ireland. To American ears their name was so familiar that it did not sound Irish; but the boy's father declared that it was, that for centuries it had been known and respected in and beyond County Roscommon. They were going to keep it respected, too, here in this land of freedom, to which they had already given their love and their loyalty. His father and mother never dreamed, while John Patrick was a boy, of what he, their eldest son, was going to do to add honor to that name.

Even before he could go to school, young John Patrick helped his mother. A sturdy little boy, with rosy cheeks and bright eyes, he saved her steps by running errands to the neighborhood stores. While he was still so small that he had to reach up to the doorknob, he could be trusted to buy and bring home a bag of groceries. He could be trusted to count and return the proper change. He could be trusted, too, not to cross the highway at the corner. In fact, all through his life, John Patrick could always be trusted.

When he was six years old, he went to the St. Rose of Lima parochial school. There are two Sisters of Charity still there who remember him; but they do not remember anything spectacular or exciting which he ever did in school. He was not a brilliant student, but he always knew his lessons. He skipped sixth grade, which was not unusual in those days after World War I. He won no special honors when he graduated from the eighth grade. But already both his elders and his fellow students realized that he had a great deal of the quality called dependability.

From the time when his four brothers and two sisters began to go to school, John Patrick looked after them. He never talked about it, and he never gave them stern orders. He merely saw that they went the way they should go; and he helped them if they got into trouble.

"I don't believe that once in his lifetime he thought of himself first," his sister Anna says of him.

He was no leader in any organization, although old Father McKeever, the pastor of St. Rose of Lima Church, once called him the most valuable member of the St. Aloysius Society. That was because he never failed to attend meetings and did all the work assigned to him. In time his father became the president of the Holy Name Society and his brother Francis became its secretary; but John Patrick did not hold office in any of the parish societies. Always, however, he was the dependable member who helped in the work.

At Seton Hall High School and Seton Hall College, John Patrick kept up the same kind of record. He was a good student, but not the best. There was no better young citizen, however, in either institution; for John Patrick continued to set the welfare of other people ahead of his own interests. He helped his slower fellow students, just as he had helped his brothers and sisters in their homework.

Outside school he did just about what other boys of his age were doing. He played baseball. He went swimming. He went fishing. He went to movies on Friday nights. He went over to New York once in a while and came home to tell his mother that he had seen some of the big liners at their piers. "Someday I'm going out on one of them," he would say. "I'm going to cross the Atlantic to see the places where Dad and you were born."

On Saturday and sometimes on Sunday evenings the young people of the neighborhood came to the house. Then John Patrick played the piano and joined their lively singing. He always liked music. He played, on request, "Honeysuckle Rose" and his mother's favorite, "The Morning Dew." After he had played that, he moved away from the piano. His part of the concert was over.

Because he was quiet, no one knew what he intended to do with his life; yet no one was surprised when he said that he wanted to be a priest. From his childhood he had worn the Miraculous Medal of the Blessed Virgin. He had never failed to be at home for the saying of the family Rosary through the evenings of Lent. He had been a faithful altar boy. He had always been good, so good that his virtue seemed almost commonplace. He had always been unselfish, so unselfish that most people accepted his sacrifices without second thought. There was no amazement in Newark when

John Patrick went from Seton Hall College to the seminary at Darlington.

He was ordained on June 15, 1935, while the world was still at peace. He was curate in one of the churches of the Newark archdiocese when the United States went to war on December 8, 1941. Following his old habit of giving service wherever it was needed, he enlisted as a chaplain of the Army. Like his two brothers and millions of other young men, he was anxious to serve and willing to die for his country.

In late January of 1943, with three other chaplains serving in the Armed Forces, Father John Patrick sailed from American shores on the transport *Dorchester*, bound for Greenland. Because of what happened on that ship, there is a very special star upon a three-starred flag which hangs in the window of his old home in Newark. Within the house John Patrick's mother treasures a decoration, awarded her son after his death. The decoration is one of the highest in the power of the government of the United States to give for bravery. It is the Distinguished Service Cross, given only for "extraordinary heroism."

Father John Patrick Washington was an ordinary, good boy who became one of the most famous heroes of World War II; he was one of the four chaplains on that transport

218

who chose to die so that other men might continue to live.

"If he felt that his act might save one soul," his mother says of him, "I know that he died happy."

The story of Father Washington and the other chaplains, two Protestants and a Jew, who died with him on a February day in 1943, has been written by the Reverend Timothy J. Mulvey, O.M.I., and given as a radio play under the name of

North Atlantic Testament

CAST

THE REVEREND JOHN PATRICK WASHINGTON, *St. Stephen's Church, Arlington, New Jersey*

THE REVEREND CLARK V. POLING, *First Dutch Reformed Church, Schenectady, New York*

THE REVEREND GEORGE L. FOX, *Methodist Church, Gilman, Vermont*

RABBI ALEXANDER D. COODE, *Congregation Beth Israel, York, Pennsylvania*

MRS. MARY WASHINGTON

THE ARCHBISHOP OF NEWARK

CHAPLAIN DIRECTORS

PROFESSOR AT DARLINGTON

EDDIE
FRANK } *boys in Newark*
JACK

THE SKIPPER OF THE TRANSPORT *Dorchester*

JACKSON

JIM, *the orderly*

TOMMY, *boy on transport*

TELEPHONE OPERATOR

SOLDIERS *and* SAILORS

MUSIC. *Violins play 4 bars, "Battle Hymn of the Republic." Lower, then fade*

ANNOUNCER. To the Chaplains of the Armed Forces of the United States . . .

to the young priests who traded the quiet flame of a sanctuary lamp for the raving flames of war . . .

to the priests who walked from a peaceful world of chapel chimes and the Sanctus bell to a world that rocked with the thunder of artillery . . .

to Father Aloysius Schmitt of the Navy, who went down with the battleship *Oklahoma* at Pearl Harbor . . .

to Father Clement Falter of the Army, who fell beneath enemy shells on the shores of North Africa . . .

to Father Thomas Brady of the Army, who crawled with the wounds of death into a foxhole at twilight . . .

to Fathers James Liston and Valmore Savignac, who died under the lashing fury of the North Atlantic . . .

to Father Neil Doyle of the Army . . .

to Fathers Michael Duggan . . .

Lawrence Gough . . .
Eugene Polhemus . . .
James Flynn . . .
to these Chaplains and to the many others who have made the great sacrifice in this Second World War . . .
We offer, this day, the humble tribute of our love and prayers . . .

MUSIC. *Rises into strains of a requiem, then grows soft*

ANNOUNCER. May their souls and the souls of all the faithful departed, through the mercy of God, rest in peace. Amen.
Nor have we forgotten *him*—Father John Patrick Washington of the United States Army.
We shall never forget him, for it was Father Washington who, in the early, black hours of a February morning, gave to the world his . . .
NORTH ATLANTIC TESTAMENT!

MUSIC. *Rises for one bar, holds for one note, then softens into background*

NARRATOR. This is a story about a boy you might have known. It began very quietly one day, not so long ago, when John walked into a kitchen . . .
MRS. WASHINGTON. *Humming distractedly*
JOHN. (*Quietly*) Mom.
MRS. WASHINGTON. Yes, John.

SOUND. *Noise of dishes—fades*

JOHN. (*Not at ease*) Would you —would you mind putting those dishes aside for a minute? I'd like to talk to you about something.
MRS. WASHINGTON. Why . . .
JOHN. Wait a minute. I'll close the door.
MRS. WASHINGTON. Well, what's the trouble, John?
JOHN. Sit down, Mom. There's a—sort of problem that's been—on my mind.
MRS. WASHINGTON. Problem?
JOHN. Yes. It's a—well, I don't know how to begin exactly.
MRS. WASHINGTON. (*Laughing softly*) Why, what's the *matter* with you, John? You look as if . . .
JOHN. It's—it's simply this. I've been a long time in school. You've spent a lot of money educating me, you and Dad. I know the sacrifices you've both had to make. And I know the sacrifices you *still* have to make for the rest of the kids.
MRS. WASHINGTON. (*Laughing*) Sacrifices! Why, the children, John, are nothing at all. Now you take, for instance, that poor Mrs. . . .
JOHN. I understand, Mom. But what I *want* to say is that, being the eldest, I have the responsibility, now, of getting out into the world and helping to pay back some of . . .
MRS. WASHINGTON. (*Cajoling*) Now wait a minute, John.

JOHN. (*Easily*) Oh, I know what you're going to say, Mom. But the fact is I *do* owe you and the rest of the family a debt, (*then seriously*) a debt which I may never be able to pay.

MRS. WASHINGTON. (*Smiling on the words*) John, will you please tell me just *what* is on your mind?

JOHN. Mom, would it make much difference if . . . I mean . . .

MRS. WASHINGTON. You mean you want to become a priest, John?

JOHN. (*Pause*) Yes.

MRS. WASHINGTON. Sure, and didn't I know it all the while?

JOHN. (*Rapidly*) It would mean more years of work and worry for you and Dad. That's what I wanted to talk to you about. It would mean that you . . .

MRS. WASHINGTON. Wait a minute, son. You're talking about work and worry. Sure, and what greater blessing could I work and worry for than the privilege of being the mother of a priest? I used to dream about seeing a son of mine a priest. I dreamed—oh, I guess I dreamed it a thousand times or more, even when you were *that* small, John, even before you were born. And I was thinking that it would be a great day, John, sitting there with your father in the front pew, with the candles lit and the incense floating like a white cloud over your head, with the altar boys in their red cassocks and the grand organ filling the church—I was thinking *that* would be the great day, when I could look up and say, (*trembling on the words*) "There he is! There he is! My *own* Father John!"

MUSIC. *Up and out, then fades into soft background*

NARRATOR. Such was the dreaming of her who once was a young girl playing on the green hills of Kilglass in the County Roscommon. And such was the answer to her dreaming—a young priest-son, who once played on the streets of Newark, New Jersey!

SOUND. *Heavy church bells; accompany with music; then fade*

NARRATOR. (*Talking above music*) And so, on June the fifteenth, nineteen hundred and thirty-five, before the members of his family and at the hands of the Most Reverend Thomas Joseph Walsh, Archbishop of the Archdiocese of Newark, John Patrick Washington was ordained a priest! The bells rang joyously that day at St. Rose's.

SOUND. *One bell rings distantly*

NARRATOR. And for five years, at St. Stephen's in Arlington, a bell rang peacefully. But time can bring strange accents to a peaceful world!

SOUND. *Bell fades with distant thunder*

NARRATOR. (*With intensity*) Pearl Harbor!

SOUND. *Crashing thunder, followed by faint battle call of bugle*

NARRATOR. Pearl Harbor turned bells to bugles!

SOUND. *Thunder crashes again. Bugle tone comes closer, then fades*

NARRATOR. Pearl Harbor was a scream of pain in the afternoon!

SOUND. *Thunder rumbles off; bugle fades*

NARRATOR. Pearl Harbor was a face twisted in surprised agony! And the face was the face of your brother! Pearl Harbor was war!

SOUND. *One last distant rumble of thunder, then heavy marching of feet*

MUSIC. *Martial tune to tempo of feet*

EDDIE. (*Above sound and music*) Just wanted to say "So long" to you, Father Washington. I'm heading for boot camp at Sampson.

JOHN. Good-by, Eddie. Take good care of yourself.

FRANK. Yeah, I'm goin' to join the Marines, Father. Quantico!

JOHN. Good going, Frank!

FRANK. So I guess I'll say good-by. (*Going off mike*) Don't forget to write.

JOHN. (*Calling after him*) I won't, Frank. God bless you.

JACK. (*Above music and sound*) Thought I'd drop over to St. Stephen's before I left.

JOHN. So it's the Army—eh, Jack?

JACK. You bet. There's nothing like the Army, Father. The Marines! Huh! They think they can run the whole show! Boloney! So long, Father!

FRANK. (*Shouting*) We'll be seeing you!

JACK. (*Shouting*) Good-by! (*Almost smothered by sound and music*) Good-by!

JOHN. (*Calling after them above sound and music*) Good-by, fellows! Good . . . (*Then excitedly*) Wait a minute! WAIT A MINUTE, FELLOWS:

SOUND. *Marching feet beat loudly for three seconds, then fade out behind music. An instant of complete silence*

ARCHBISHOP. (*Solemnly*) So you want to become an Army Chaplain, Father Washington?

JOHN. Yes, I do. I've been working with boys for over five years. I *know* boys, know the scrapes they can get into at times. And I know how much they need priests.

ARCHBISHOP. (*Jokingly*) And so you're going to desert your poor old Archbishop, are you? (*Laughing deeply*) Father Washington, I want you to understand that you have my wholehearted approval. I'm proud of you. And I know that wherever you go, you'll be a credit to your country and your God!

MUSIC. *Single note*

NARRATOR. And so Father Washington, curate at St. Stephen's, Arlington, New Jersey, became First Lieutenant Washington, chaplain in the United States Army. First it was the Chaplain School at Fort Benjamin Harrison, Indiana.

CHAPLAIN DIRECTOR. . . . something that every chaplain must bear in mind. For the primary aim of all military life is to prepare men—mentally, morally, physically—so that in time of combat they can bring their flag to victory against every foe. (*Fading*) Therefore the duty of the chaplain lies with the men of his command. You will have to minister to the sick, to the wounded, to the dying, to prisoners . . .

NARRATOR. And from the Chaplain School, Chaplain Washington went next to the 76th Division Artillery, Fort Meade, Maryland. Then came orders!

CHAPLAIN DIRECTOR. Chaplain Washington, you are assigned to overseas duty with a special group. You will proceed immediately to the port of embarkation.

SOUND. *Telephone bell rings during music; rings again when music stops*

MRS. WASHINGTON. Hello.

JOHN. Hello, Mom.

MRS. WASHINGTON. (*Excited*) John—is it—is it—*you?*

JOHN. (*Laughing*) Don't get excited, Mom.

MRS. WASHINGTON. Where *are* you?

JOHN. Take a guess.

MRS. WASHINGTON. What's that?

JOHN. I said—take—a—guess.

MRS. WASHINGTON. Oh—um— (*Eagerly*) Are you coming home?

JOHN. No, I don't think I'll be home, for a while, yet.

MRS. WASHINGTON. (*Deflated*) Oh, I see. Well, I guess . . .

JOHN. Mom.

MRS. WASHINGTON. Yes.

JOHN. Now listen well. Can you hear me?

MRS. WASHINGTON. Yes, dear.

JOHN. Mom, this—this may be the last time you'll hear from me for —well—a little while.

MRS. WASHINGTON. (*Apprehensive*) John, you're not going . . .

JOHN. I can't say anything, Mom. You understand?

MRS. WASHINGTON. Yes, I understand, son.

JOHN. I just thought I'd call you to let you know I'll be thinking about you. Can you hear me?

MRS. WASHINGTON. Yes, John.

JOHN. Mom, I never told you this before, in words. There are so many things I've never said to you, face to face. But *now* I'm going to say it. I want you to know that you're the dearest thing God ever gave me on this earth. I want you to be happy. Do you hear?

MRS. WASHINGTON. (*Close to tears*) Yes, John.

JOHN. Give my love to the folks. And—and—do you know what?

MRS. WASHINGTON. What?

JOHN. (*Trying to joke*) Why, before you know it I'll be back again, and we'll—we'll have our ice-cream sodas together again. O.K.? O.K., Mom?

TELEPHONE OPERATOR. Your three minutes are up, sir!

JOHN. The three minutes are up, Mom.

MRS. WASHINGTON. (*Breaking down*) Yes, the three minutes are up, son.

MUSIC. *Large and sad, then fades*
SOUND. *Breaking waves of ocean*

NARRATOR. Convoy moving in the night. Convoy carrying men and material for the United Nations. Convoy moving up into the cold, black stretches of the North Atlantic. Moving up into the great sea lanes where icebergs thunder loose out of the Greenland fiords and come drifting south like wallowing, white mountains. Convoy stepping cautiously in the night over waters that are treacherous with enemy submarines. Below the deck of a troop transport four chaplains are sitting in Officers' Quarters. Suddenly there's a knock on the door.

JIM. Is this the chaplains' quarters?

JOHN. Step right in, Jimmy.

JIM. Mmm—nice and warm down here.

JOHN. Gentlemen, I want you to meet Jimmy, our new orderly. Jimmy, this is Chaplain Poling.

JIM. Pleased to meet you.

POLING. How do you do, Jimmy?

JOHN. And this is Chaplain Goode, and over here Chaplain Fox.

FOX. How are you?

JIM. Pleased to meet you.

GOODE. Glad to know you, Jimmy.

JIM. Bein' as that I got the altar all fixed up, what I wanta know now is who follows who in the church services?

JOHN. I'm saying Mass at seven o'clock, Jimmy.

JIM. I know that, Father; but what I wanta know is does the Jewish service *follow* you, or does the Protes'ant?

JOHN. (*Slightly puzzled*) Well, perhaps Chaplain Poling will explain.

POLING. If you don't mind, Jimmy, you can arrange the altar for Protestant services after Father Washington says Mass. I believe that was the arrangement. Is that agreeable to you, Rabbi?

GOODE. Perfectly all right with me. I'm holding my services at six if it doesn't make any difference to Chaplain Fox.

FOX. Not at all.

JIM. I gotcha. In other words, first it's the Jewish service, with *no* cross and the altar turned around. Right?

GOODE. Right.

JIM. Then it's the Catholic service, with the cross and the altar turned round the other way. Right?

JOHN. Right.

JIM. Next it's the Protestant service, with—with—the altar turned around again. Right? And then—then—(*flustered*) Whew! Ya know, Chaplains, this would be a heck of a lot easier if you all could only get *together* sometime!

ALL. (*Laughter*)

NARRATOR. The convoy was still moving north in the night. Out on the screening lines the escort destroyers were getting nervous. Right now they knew they were riding deep into Germany's North Atlantic submarine zone.

SOUND. *Two strokes of cabin bell*

SKIPPER. It's black as pitch out there tonight, Jackson.

JACKSON. Yes, sir.

SKIPPER. Any reports yet?

JACKSON. No, sir—except we're running into high seas, sir.

SKIPPER. What did you expect? Zephyrs in the North Atlantic? Let's see the chart.

JACKSON. Here it is, sir.

SKIPPER. Mmmmmmm—5 to 7 Beaufort scale.

JACKSON. 5 to 7? Let me see. That would be, roughly . . .

SKIPPER. Roughly, a 32-knot gale, Jackson.

JACKSON. Yes, sir.

SKIPPER. And we'll be running against it all the way in.

JACKSON. No doubt, sir.

SKIPPER. Mmmmmm—Jackson, what would *you* do if a submarine suddenly pulled up along your port side?

JACKSON. Why, I'd—I'd *run* for it, sir.

SKIPPER. You'd run for it, eh? With a 32-knot gale hitting you in the teeth—you'd run for it, eh?

JACKSON. Yes, sir.

SKIPPER. And *where* would you run, Jackson?

JACKSON. With a submarine patrolling us in a 32-knot gale, sir— I'd run for Kingdom Come!

SOUND. *Wind and waves*

NARRATOR. And these were the sounds that night: the large sounds of wind and wave—and the small, friendly sounds of lifeboats swinging on the davits—the sudden, bright sound of laughter from the galley—and the muffled, gray sound of boots keeping vigil on the bridge —the jesting of boys at games—and the whispering of a boy at Confession. And there was silence too. Silence for thinking. A priest had plenty of time to think, sitting on the edge of his bunk aboard a troop transport.

JOHN. (*Softly*) Seems as though a lot of people were depending on you, John. They're out there talking. And you're in here thinking. And you're thinking how small you are after all. It's only when you close your eyes, like this, in the dark, which makes it doubly dark —it's only when you close your eyes like this and run your fingertips over this small chaplain's cross on your collar—it's only then that you begin to know why people, kids, look at you and bank on you. It's the cross. Strange, when you close your eyes like this and run your fingers over a cross—strange how it seems to grow and grow under your fingertips, in the dark. Just concentrating on this cross, with your eyes closed like this, seems to make it grow bigger and bigger. It's getting bigger than this room. It's getting bigger . . . (*Sighing*) Seems only yesterday that you were standing there. And because you were standing *there*, then, that's why you're sitting *here, now*, on a bunk. You were standing there that morning in a half-circle with the fellows, clothed in white linen and a cincture, with a chasuble over your arm and a candle in your hand. You were waiting nervously, joyously, for the ordination, for the pressure of the Archbishop's hands. And standing there you tried to realize what it all meant. You remembered the Professor telling you . . .

PROFESSOR. (*On slight echo*) And so you are going to be ordained! Ordained for what? To wear a Roman collar? No. To wear a cassock, gold vestments? No. To walk out of a seminary with a trunkful of notes on moral and dogmatic theology? No. You will have to look past the walls of a church to find the answer, past the walls of cities. You will have to look down a long avenue of twenty centuries to find the answer. And the answer? You'll find it on the lips of (*whispering*) the Galilean! "This is my Body," He said. *His* words— and *your* words. The answer is you are ordained to be (*whispering*) another Christ!

MUSIC. *Rises slightly*

JOHN. That was it—another Christ! Another Christ, with a small cross on your shoulder that grows, somehow, in a dark room, grows to be bigger than . . . (*whispering*) Lord—Jesus—You Who walked rough waters—watch over us.

NARRATOR. These were his priest-thoughts. And he had *other* thoughts too, warm, lively memories.

SOUND. *Two bars of "Honeysuckle Rose" whistled distractedly off mike*

NARRATOR. . . . just the smallest bit of "Honeysuckle Rose" from some soldier whistling in a crowd—and he was back again in the little house on South Twelfth Street, playing the piano. He liked a piano. Liked Fats Waller. In fact, he had Fats Waller albums at home right now. Left them in the dining-room before he went away. Of course you *did* have to admit Fats wasn't exactly a nightingale when it came to singing, *but he knew how to use his fingers.* And Frankie Carle. Now you take Frankie Carle's "Sunrise Serenade." Never could get that run quite the way Frankie played it. The tune was there in your head, all right—but—somehow . . . Memories, lying in your bunk aboard a troop transport. That's right, *troop transport.* Almost forgot for a moment where you were.

SOUND. *Wailing sea winds*

NARRATOR. But that night you couldn't forget where you were.

SOUND. *Rhythmic washing of heavy seas*

SKIPPER. (*Impatient*) All right, Jackson—what's the bearing?

JACKSON. We're out of formation, sir.

SKIPPER. Sure we're out of formation. (*Barking*) What do they think we can do? Walk a straight line with high seas running like this? (*Pause*) Where *are* we?

JACKSON. Here's the chart, sir.

SKIPPER. Mmmmmmmmmmm—that leaves us mighty close to Greenland.

JACKSON. Too close for comfort, sir.

SKIPPER. What are we making *now*?

JACKSON. Roughly, three knots, sir.

SKIPPER. (*Exasperated*) Three knots! Running out of formation at three knots! You know what *that* means, Jackson?

JACKSON. I presume it means, sir . . .

SKIPPER. It means we're going to be easy pickin's for any submarine that decides to operate off the mainland tonight.

NARRATOR. They waited that night. They stared into the dark. They listened for sounds. And then, *suddenly, this—this sound.*

VOICE I. (*Excitedly over phone*) Calling all hands. Calling all hands. *Escanaba* to all ships in convoy. We got a contact. It's good. It's good. Acknowledge.

Voice II. Calling *Escanaba—Escanaba*. We got you—5-9-9. Come back.

Voice I. (*Over phone*) *Escanaba* to all ships. Enemy submarines contacted. Enemy submarines bearing down on convoy. Direction 0-3-5. Bearing 0-3-5. Wind velocity 7. Increase speed to maximum.

Sound. *Frantic ringing of electric alarm bell. Hold for three seconds; then fast fade out*

Voice III. (*Over loud-speaker*) All hands alert! Submarines contacted. Gun crews in position. All hands prepare for emergency. Man your battle stations!

Sound. *Excited mob, running feet, high winds and washing of sea*

Narrator. (*Rapidly*) The men came piling out of the cabins, wardrooms. They lined the rails, asked questions, looked out into the night, and waited, waited with the awful tension of men who dread the blow that strikes from the dark.

Tommy. (*From out of the crowd*) Father! Father Washington!

John. (*Calling*) Come over here, Tommy. Hang onto this rail.

Tommy. (*Louder*) I've been looking all over for you.

John. What is it, Tommy?

Tommy. (*Scared*) Do you—do you think there's really *submarines* out there?

John. Could be, Tommy.

Voice I. (*Shouting*) Ready ammunition on deck, sir!

Voice II. (*Shouting*) Gun crews, stand by!

John. They're certainly preparing for *something*, anyway.

Tommy. (*Frightened*) Yeah.

John. (*Startled*) Why, Tommy, where's your life jacket?

Tommy. My life jacket? I guess I must've left it somewhere. (*Suddenly terrified*) Father—I—I gotta see you about something.

John. What's the matter?

Tommy. I got to go to Confession. (*Growing frantic*) I got to go to Confession. Somethin' tells me.

John. Easy, Tommy.

Tommy. If anything happens . . .

John. (*Quieting him*) All right, son. Go ahead.

Tommy. (*Panting*) Bless me, Father, for I have sinned.

Sound. *Wind and waves; hold; then down*

Tommy. . . . to confess my sins . . . to do penance . . . and to amend my life . . . Amen.

John. There you are. Everything better now?

Tommy. Everything's better, Father. Everything.

John. (*Sternly*) All right. Now get your life jacket—and *fast*.

Music. *With depth; hold*

NARRATOR. These were the sounds that night. Wind and wave. Murmuring of anxious men. Whispering of penitent men. Breathing of a priest in absolution. These were the sounds that night as men played a dreadful game of hide-and-seek on the high seas. But the sound they were still waiting for, the sound they dreaded to hear . . .

VOICE I. (*Shouting with terror*) Look out! There it is! TORPEDO!

MUSIC. *Rising to the explosion*
SOUND. *Explosion*
MUSIC. *One piercing discord*

NARRATOR. (*Talking over discord*) Just as quickly as that the torpedo struck!

SOUND. *Mob background, hooting on ship's whistle, running feet*

VOICES. *Confused and frightened*
I. Hey, Freddy! Where are you?

230

II. This way, fellows.

III. Where are you, Jackie? Hey, Newton, where are you?

IV. It's a torpedo. Come on!

V. By the stairway. You left it over there. Go back. Go back and get it.

VI. Sure it's a torpedo. Didn't you hear it? Come on. We got to make those lifeboats.

NARRATOR. The transport shuddered for an instant. The deck was alive with running, shouting men. They didn't know it then, but their ship was gaping with a wound which would never heal.

VOICE. (*Giving order over loudspeaker*) Abandon ship! Abandon ship!

NARRATOR. They *had* to abandon ship. They leaped into lifeboats, jumped over the side. And some— *some* stood terrified at the rail. *Then it happened!*

SOUND. *Wind and waves*

JOHN. (*Calling*) Is that you, Chaplain Fox?

Fox. Yes, Father.

JOHN. I guess there's nothing more we can do. Ship's settling fast.

Fox. Where are the other two chaplains?

JOHN. Wait—I think—Here they come now. (*Calling*) You all right, Chaplain Poling?

POLING. (*Panting*) All right, all right. It's just that we had trouble getting that last batch over the side.

JOHN. How are you, Rabbi?

GOODE. (*Wearily*) So far, so good.

JOHN. Wait a minute! Over there. Look! Those kids along the rail!

Fox. They're going mad.

POLING. No life jackets. *They haven't any life jackets!*

JOHN. Well, gentlemen, there's only one thing left for us to do.

POLING. Yes, you're right. Only one thing left to do.

Fox. Come on!

GOODE. So let's do it!

SOUND. *Wind and waves*

BOY. (*Sobbing hysterically*)

JOHN. All right, son. Stand up. (*Straining as if lifting the boy*) That's it, against the rail.

BOY. (*Hysterical*) I can't die. I can't die. Father, I can't.

JOHN. (*Almost fiercely*) Stop that! (*Panting*) Hold up your arms. Here, you'd better take this life jacket.

BOY. (*Dazed*) Life—jacket— (*Panting heavily*) But what—what are *you* going to do?

JOHN. Tie it on. That's it, tie it on tight. Now you're all set.

BOY. (*Whimpering*) Thanks— thanks.

JOHN. Now jump.

BOY. (*Frightened*) Jump?

JOHN. (*Almost shouting*) Jump quick if you want to get clear of this boat. She's—she's going down fast.

BOY. (*Whimpering*) But I'll be alone.

JOHN. Get up there on the rail. That's it.

BOY. But I'll be alone, Father.

JOHN. You won't be alone. Go ahead. Jump! That's it. JUMP! You won't be alone now, kids, whoever you are. (*Half choked*) Nobody—nobody can *ever* be alone!

SOUND. *Wailing wind*

NARRATOR. In the early hours of a February morning, nineteen hundred and forty-three, four chaplains removed their life jackets and placed them about the shivering bodies of four boys. And then, as the last lifeboats moved away in the night, a rabbi, two ministers, and a priest stood together on a listing deck.

232

SOUND. *Wind and boiling seas fade*

JOHN. (*Tense*) I guess we're all here, gentlemen.

GOODE. All present and accounted for, Washington. Wait!

FOX. (*Quietly*) Just the lights, Rabbi. The lights have gone out.

JOHN. I guess we don't need that kind of light now, Chaplain.

POLING. (*Tired*) No, I guess we don't.

SOUND. *Swirling waters*

GOODE. (*Trying hard to control his voice*) Water's—water's coming over the deck now.

FOX. She's starting to go, Washington.

JOHN. (*Calmly*) Yes, she's starting to go. Well, gentlemen, it was nice knowing you. And now I suppose it's about time we got down on our knees. It's—it's—just about time. MUSIC. *Trembling chord*

NARRATOR. The ship poised for an instant. The ship sank. The ship sank, but in that moment—(*triumphant*) in that moment a miracle of self-sacrificing love converted her slippery deck, once and forever, into a great altar from which four men offered their gallant souls to God!

MUSIC. *Rises majestically, then fades*

Justifying the Title

Why do you think the author called this radio play "North Atlantic Testament"? How was John Patrick Washington "an ordinary boy"? In what ways would you say he was an "extraordinary boy"?

Appreciating Descriptive Phrases

Describe what the following expressions suggest to you.

quiet flame of a sanctuary lamp
raving flames of war
fox hole at twilight
incense floating like a white cloud
icebergs come drifting south like wallowing white mountains

MARY SYNON

Mass before Battle

I will go before the altar of God,
To God Who giveth joy to my youth.
 I never thought, on Sundays back at home,
 That I should hear familiar words like these
 As a gray ship speeds onward through the night
 To a dark island in these southern seas.

Through my fault, through my fault,
Through my most grievous fault.
 I have sinned often, and regretted sin,
 I have done penance both in pain and truth;
 What have I done, O God, to merit this
 Loss of the days of my swift-winging youth?

I believe in one God, the Father Almighty,
Maker of Heaven and earth.
 I believe in God. How often have I said
 These words of the eternal faith of men?
 Now is my time to prove that faith—but, God,
 With all my soul I long for home again!

Lamb of God, Who takest away the sins of the world
Have mercy on us.
 We all may die today. The beach ahead
 Is dark with dangers that we soon shall know.
 There, if I die—O Christ upon Your Cross,
 Be with me in the moment when I go!

Letters Home

Lazarist House—Shanghai, China
Feast of Our Lady of Mount Carmel
July sixteenth

DEAR MOTHER AND DAD,

In a few minutes it's going to be tomorrow, but I just had to sit down and get a line off to you before having my first night's sleep in China. When Father Gallin first told us that we were the volunteers who were to take our last three years in a Chinese seminary and be ordained there, he lined up all the advantages, such as the economic benefit to the Society, a grasp of the language, and a thorough knowledge of the customs. What he never got around to mentioning was how to write a letter home after we had seen more in one day than you could describe within the covers of a mail-order catalogue. So much has happened today that I'm sure I can't recount more than a tenth of it. But there's nothing like trying; so here goes.

At about nine-thirty this morning, Tom Cantwell and George and I were sitting in our stateroom, our bags all packed, playing the card game I told you about, Chinese in Nine Hundred and Seventy-three Not-So-Easy Lessons. I don't know what ever made me think Greek was hard; I'd like to see Homer tackle this stuff. Anyway, just as Tom had me stumped on an elementary little twenty-one-stroke character, George leaped to the porthole, and called us over to see the Saddle Islands. The stir on deck was what had caught his attention. We had heard that these islands are an indication that Shanghai is near, but a steward said that we shouldn't be in port for another four hours or more. So we sailed toward the muddy yellow waters of the Yangtze (do I sound like a movie travelogue?) as we returned to our Chinese. Tom set me straight on the card I'd missed. It was *tu*, the verb for "read" or "study." Can you imagine twenty-one strokes for a word like that? Why, you've practically finished saying it before you've begun.

Of the three of us, I think George Donlon has come along best with the language since we started studying in San Francisco. We have decided that we will ask Father Gallin to teach Chinese at St. Kieran's. That is probably a selfish idea, and traceable only to our all-at-sea feeling. It was a pleasure not to have Chinese last year, with our crowded schedule.

When the ship finally dropped anchor in the Hwang Pu River, we were quite surprised at the sky line. Except for the small Chinese boats cruising around, it might have been any American port. We knew Shanghai was a large city, but weren't prepared for the Western architecture.

A steam launch took us in to the customs, where Father Albert Martin of the Society was waiting for us. He saw us through the fairly easy examination of luggage in fine style, and off we went by ricksha to the French Vincentians' house. (Only they call them Lazarists here, just as in France.) I felt like an old hand at Chinese when I heard Father Martin give his "boy" the address: "*Sapaysa Lu.*" *Lu* means street—that was one of the first cards I printed. The other word, I learned later, is the closest the drivers can come to the French street name *Chapsal.* Their rickshas don't come very close to it either. Mine touched the ground about three times on the whole trip. Tell Grandma one of these rides is just what she needs.

The Lazarists are very open-hearted, and as jolly a group of

Zikawei College—Shanghai, China
Feast of Saint James the Greater
July twenty-fifth

Dear Ed,

How are things at St. Kieran's? I'd hate to hear how well they're going without us; so please don't tell me. Did Mother forward any of the letters I wrote on shipboard? I shall ask her to, for we're pretty busy, and it's hard to get off long, descriptive epics in any great number. China is still very much like New York's Chinatown as far as we're concerned. Shanghai is a large city, as you know, and we haven't been anywhere except the French Vincentian house (or Procure, as they call it).

The Vincentians played hosts to us for three days. Father Martin says they've offered hospitality to more communities new in the work, such as our own, than you could count. It was interesting to hear these men tell of their first days in China, toward the beginning of the century, when their every move was suspect. They gave us some very sound advice on mission activity, such as that of never trying to Westernize China. American missionaries are well thought of, they say, but some of the European priests are handicapped because they come from countries that have, or would like to have, big

priests as I've ever met. Several have been on the Chinese mission for thirty and thirty-five years. We had a five-hour session with them after supper, and learned all sorts of things from stories of their experiences. One of them, a Father Joulon, met our Bishop Dalton in Seattle.

It shouldn't be hard to fall asleep tonight. An ax murderer's conscience wouldn't keep him awake if he felt as tired as I do. Know any?

God bless you all, and please keep me in your prayers. I'll write soon again.

Love,

Joe

P.S. Is my sister Louise going to marry Frank?

empires. The non-Christian Chinese, not knowing their work, sometimes think that these priests may be agents of their countries.

The Lazarists told us how necessary it was to work for the day when China should have only her own sons as priests and bishops. I also learned quite a bit about the characteristics of the Chinese people, and the hold that paganism has on the country. You would have been thrilled to hear of Father Lebbe, the Belgian priest who became a Chinese citizen and founded a native community of "Little Brothers of St. John the Baptist." They won thousands of hearts to Christianity by their heroic deeds of charity during the Japanese hostilities of the twenties.

That's the way we have to move ahead, Ed. For work like this you and I entered the seminary. Through works of charity among the people, and then through Christian education, from the kindergarten to the university. In that way we shall have both leaders and people to lead.

We have been in the Jesuit College at Zikawei only for a few hours; so I can't give you much of a report. The plan is for us to spend the summer here, studying the language, and then start our second year of theology at the Hankow seminary in the fall. Keep praying you'll be sent on the missions, Ed, and don't show too much proficiency in canon law or you'll find yourself teaching it at St. Kieran's, a fate worse than death.

> Sincerely in Christ,
> *Joe*

●

The Seminary—Hankow, China
Feast of the Holy Rosary
October seventh

Dear Ed,

It seems strange to feel homesick for Shanghai, but that's the way it is with all three of us. The French Jesuits on the faculty at the Zikawei couldn't have been any nicer, not to mention their seminarians. We learned quite a bit of the language too; so the bishop's plan was a success all round. It isn't Chinese that's giving me trouble these days, but the holy Latin tongue. Most of the conferences of the opening retreat were given in fine Roman diction by an old and venerable Franciscan father. I missed a good part of it—and hope it was only because of his Italian way of speaking. The Chinese fellows throw the Latin language around at meals like Saint Jerome on one of his good days.

All the seminarians here except

us are seculars from the Hankow area, which includes several vicariates. At my table are Timothy Tchang-Ping, Joseph Lieou, and Paul Ouang. They are fine fellows, and extremely intelligent. The latter two were born Catholic (or at least, became such after a week or two), but Timothy's entire village, including his own parents, is still non-Christian. His father is mayor of the town, and sent him off to a Catholic mission for higher schooling. There, thanks to God's goodness, he received the grace, both of faith and of vocation.

The food is somewhat hard to get used to. We found the daily breakfast of noodles with sauce the strangest of all, but now have coffee and a regular Western breakfast, thanks to the European priests on the faculty. Tom Cantwell is the one who handles chopsticks best, at this stage. Rice is served at every meal, just as we have bread at home. Meat, fish, and vegetables are put on the table in separate bowls. One doesn't see much butter or milk. There is a bean curd that resembles the latter in appearance, but the similarity ends there. It's both stringy and sour. I'm saving it for Lent.

The theology course here promises to keep us stepping. Some of the seminarians can quote Saint Thomas by the yard. Canon-law classes will be interesting, I think, both because the professor is good and because of the many applications to mission problems.

Any little bit of news you send me from St. Kieran's, Ed, will be as welcome as the flowers in May.

Ever yours in Christ,
Joe

●

(*Two years later*)

Hankow, China
Feast of Saint Luke
October eighteenth

Dear Mother and Dad,

Sometimes it seems much longer than two years that we've been here, and at other times, as if we arrived only a few days ago. I know it must be more than a day or so, however, for yesterday somebody in your family preached a sermon in Chinese. It was given from the pulpit, in surplice and stole, and was a real triumph of mind over matter. I know the Holy Spirit was close because I've pulled some awful boners on my own. (Did I ever mention the time I asked for a

chi'tze instead of a *chi tze?* In the higher tone it means "wife," and all I wanted was a wrench for my bike.) If I can memorize twenty basic sermons by ordination, I'll be happy.

This deacon year is a busy one, and I'll need the help of your prayers to get through it well. We have started to practice the Mass already. Something nice happened to me not long ago. We had a Solemn Mass in the Hankow cathedral, and I was on as subdeacon. Joseph Ouang was deacon, and Bishop Massi celebrant. The whole seminary body went into the city in a line of rickshas that attracted everyone's attention. It was a thrill to stand beside the stocky little bishop at the altar and assist him in offering Mass. He is well known for his brave refusal to leave the city when the Russian Communists overran it in the twenties. My throat tightened up a bit when I heard the Chinese congregation give the response to the husky manner in which he chanted the Pater Noster.

Bishop Dalton was here last week on his way to our west-China mission. He says the Society may take over some territory in Inner Mongolia. I hope we can, though storm clouds are rising in China. Communism is spreading everywhere.

Have Louise and Frank set a date for their wedding yet? If they weren't so impatient, I'd be happy to oblige. We're due for a home visit in five years.

Say a big hello to the twins.

Best love,
Joe

◐

Hankow, China
Trinity Sunday
June fourth

Dear Mother and Dad,

For months I have been planning what I should say in the letter that would describe my ordination and first Mass. Now that the time is here and the second of the glorious days almost at an end, I am afraid that the letter will hardly do justice to the events. The enclosed photographs should help to overcome my inability to give a complete account. George, Tom, and I arranged several months ago to have a complete set taken at the Solemn Mass. They were developed only today of course; I hope the blotting paper keeps them dry. As soon as possible, I shall get a copy of the photos taken at the ordination ceremony by the Hankow papers. Some bulbs flashed, I think, as I knelt with my bound hands resting upon the chalice and paten.

I do these things only because I know how happy they will make you. The much greater thing is well known to us all. Yesterday Our Lord did more than raise up sons of Abraham from stones along the road. He made, out of nothing, priests after His own heart. The intention that needs your prayers from now on is that I may ever live up to His expectations for me.

The retreat was fine. An old Austrian missioner gave it, and I cannot recall another week that I have enjoyed as much. We were ordained by Bishop Emmanuel Tsao, a visiting prelate. As I knelt there and received from him the power to offer Masses "for the living and the dead," I knew for a brief moment how very much Christ wants this great people for His Church.

This morning at Mass I was as cool as could be, but there were three other major ministers there. At tomorrow's Low Mass, I'm afraid the Credo may appear where the Gloria should be. It's a good thing there are altar boys.

Let me know if you hear of another family whom God has blessed as much as ours. You have my prayers and I need yours. The Chinese Communists have set up a government at Peiping.

All my love,
Joe

241

(Two years later)

Our Lady's Mission—Yingshang,
   China
Feast of Saint Monica
May fourth

Dear Mother and Dad,

If I've been a little slow to write this spring, blame it on the Church universal. We've been going like a house afire these past two months, for we are only a stone's throw from the Communists. They surround us. When the ground thawed out, as I think I told you, our Catholic farmers got a start on the irrigation ditches, which are so badly needed. The soil is good near the big loop in the Hwang Ho, but this vicinity has always been a wasteland because of the lack of rain. Some of our prospective villagers didn't remain long at the backbreaking work of digging ditches, but went back to their sheep and goats. I made them promise never to lose touch with the mission. They'll be good apostles, if not such good "hewers of wood and carriers of water." Those who persevered have worked wonders.

It was a great day when I was able to assemble the men and distribute the plows, carts, oxen, and seed. Don't ask me how I got hold of all this material, although I want to assure you that the Seventh Commandment remained intact. There were bargainings with the local feudal lords, begging on several continents, and generous help from the Propagation of the Faith. (Those were only a few ways employed.) The mission is playing landlord, so to speak, and the first payment is to be made on all loans at harvest time.

You should have seen our Rogation Day processions to ask God's blessing on the season's yield. The youngsters from the Sisters' school sang some hymns and the litany in Latin, and then we sang others at the close in Chinese. The people have really caught on, I think; it's one for all, and all for Christ.

There is a lad here who seems very strongly attracted to the priest-

hood, and I'm trying to get him ready to enter a minor seminary in the fall. He spilled the lighted charcoal on the sacristy floor last night, so I'm sure he's material. If we were to have a vocation so early in the work, I'd really think that God's blessing was upon us. Please get busy with your prayers, will you? We need them.

Love,
Joe

◑

Our Lady's Mission—Yingshang, China
Feast of Christ the King
October thirty-first

Dear Bishop Dalton,

You were kind enough to mention a home visit next spring. Really, nothing would please me more, but because things are going so ominously here, I think I'll beg off and roll with them for a while. This is a request rather than a mere suggestion, provided, of course, that you have no special work for me in the States. God is good, and I have a notion He will spare my parents at least a few more years. I pray that He will spare me for His work here in Red China.

Sincerely in Christ,
Joseph Rellis

243

(*Six months later*)

Press Dispatch
from Reuter's, Hong Kong

Reverend Joseph Rellis, a Catholic priest, for months a prisoner in the Communist prison in Yingshang, China, died last week, according to information brought here by a group of refugees. Father Rellis was an American missionary, one of those who refused to leave their missions when the Communists gained control of China. It is understood that he was the last of the group to die in the Yingshang prison.

Selecting and Classifying Specific Information

Pretend you were one of Father Joseph Rellis' companions in China. Since his death you have returned to the United States to speak to Catholic students about the missions in China. During the discussion period following your talk, these questions were asked. Base your answers on what you learned in "Letters Home."

1. What religious orders were located in China?
2. What countries sent these missionaries?
3. In what cities were they located?
4. Were there any religious communities for native Chinese? What were they?
5. What type of food do the Chinese eat?
6. What cities had universities and seminaries?
7. Are there any Catholic lay organizations in China?

Write your answers in outline form on your paper in the way in which a speaker would write it on a chalkboard so that the audience will get a brief summary of it. An example is given.

Religious Orders	Native Country	Location
Lazarists	France	Shanghai

244

Saint of France

WIDE, restless, gray, like two bewildered birds
Her eyes were troubled with some nameless quest:
She had heard voices—and she could not rest;
She had heard voices crying without words.
And she rose up, and left her father's herds,
And took the path to the hill's blazing crest,
And stood, a crimson cross against the west
One instant, and her eyes were homing birds.

She had found peace: and when she came to die,
She heard the voices calling her again . . .
The crackling faggots smoldered on the sky,
And she had made a miracle of pain.
But people who were come to see her die
Remembered only flame against the sky.

ALEXANDER WOOLLCOTT

The Fleet and Brother Joseph[1]

THIS IS A STORY of naval action by certain American battleships in the waters of the Pacific just off the Hawaiian Islands—a fleet action involving the American flag and directed by the commander-in-chief of our Armed Forces. The month was July, the year 1908.

The story begins years before that—begins, let us say, on a certain Sunday more than half a century ago in a church at Molokai. That is the gray, lofty, and most desolate Hawaiian island, long ago set aside as a place where lepers might hastily and conveniently be hidden from the sight of healthy men. The church was one built for Father Damien, a laughing and violent peasant from Belgium—a crude little wooden church built for this priest of theirs by parishioners who had fashioned the homely tabernacle with their own rotting hands. On this Sunday came the first tidings of Damien's now historic martyrdom, for then it was that he changed the familiar beginning of his sermon. This time he

did not begin, as so often before, with the salutation "My brethren." Instead, the first words that morning were "We lepers."

One day in 1887, when Damien's malady had so advanced that he could no longer walk and trundled himself about his strange parish in a home-made tricycle, he went down to watch the arrival of the periodic steamer from Honolulu, which usually lingered only long enough to toss the mailbags over the side before hurrying on her way. But this time she was landing a passenger, a lean fellow clad in blue denim and bearded like a prophet. This stranger toted enough luggage to give Damien the wild notion that he had come to stay. He had. He stayed forty-four years. He nursed Damien in his last illness, buried him there on the island, administered his estate, and, until his own death in 1931, carried on the work which the flaming little Belgian had so nobly begun. Back in Vermont, where he was born the son of the village schoolmarm and Ezra Dutton, the shoe-cobbler, he had been christened Ira, but at Molokai they knew him as Brother Joseph.

[1]Originally published in *The Reader's Digest*. Copyright, 1942, by Alexander Woollcott. Reprinted by permission of The Viking Press, Inc., N.Y.

About the uneasy years before this man Dutton sailed for Molokai we have much scattered information, but the crucial periods are blank. We know that after his service in the Union forces and after the wreck of his disastrous marriage, he took his troubled heart to the Church of Rome. We know that even after months of meditation in the Trappist monastery at Gethsemane in Kentucky he had found no peace. Then, when he was adrift in New Orleans, he came one day, through what we have the effrontery to call chance, upon a magazine article about Father Damien. A few months later he was in San Francisco, booking steerage passage for Honolulu.

Brother Joseph never saw his native land again, never would consider even a visit to it. But there was no day in those forty-four years when he was not homesick. The vast litter of letters and diaries left behind him bear witness to his love of his country, and the leper boys who learned about America from Brother Joseph were taught to think of it as an earthly paradise. He set up a flagpole on the Molokai shore at a point so high that the flag snapping in the breeze could be seen from far out at sea, and the old-timers there will tell you that no one else was ever allowed to run it up in the morning or take it in at sundown. They say that in that moment when the red-and-white folds fell tumbling to his shoulder, he would let them rest there just for the space that a breath is held. It was as if the flag caressed him.

Then, in 1908, there came, in letters from the United States and in the news packets from Honolulu, word that our fleet was going around the world. Brother Joseph was beside himself with excitement. Each day, when he ran up the flag in the morning and took it down at night, he used to point out to sea and tell the leper boys that maybe the ships would come near enough for them all to see them. Now someone happened to mention this unworded prayer in a letter to the White House in Washington. When Theodore Roosevelt read that letter, his heart skipped a beat, for *he* knew that the fleet was not scheduled to pass by Molokai at all. There was no time to lose. In another moment he had the Navy Department on the telephone, and in an hour the cable was catching the admiral in Honolulu with a change of sailing orders.

Thus it befell that there came a day on Molokai when Brother Joseph—he was getting on now, and his beard was snow-white, but his back was as straight as ever—a day when Brother Joseph stood on the promontory with the leper boys around him and his heart overflowing as they watched the long file of battleships go by. It is good to remember that to his gay bit of bunting, so bright in the sunlight—was ever a flag dearer or more honored?—each gray ship, as she went by, dipped her own colors in salute.

Recalling Details

Copy the statements below on your paper and fill in the blanks to complete them. Do the exercise without referring to the selection.

1. Molokai is in the . . . Islands.
2. Father Damien, the great apostle of the leper, was born in . . . .
3. Ira Dutton was a native of . . . .
4. Brother Joseph joined Father Damien in the year . . . .
5. When Brother Joseph died in 1931, he had been with the lepers at Molokai for . . . years.
6. The event commemorated in the story took place while . . . was President of the United States.

Proving Statements

In your own words prove the following statements by giving an example from the selection.

1. Leprosy is a dread disease.
2. Brother Joseph's early life was not happy.
3. Brother Joseph's love for his country was very strong and sincere.
4. The commander-in-chief of the Armed Forces was a very kindly, warm-hearted person.

Writing Original Sentences

Show that you understand the meaning of the words listed below by writing original, meaningful sentences using each word.

desolate	crude	salutation	malady
crucial	caressed	effrontery	disastrous

ARTHUR HUGH CLOUGH

Say Not, the Struggle Naught Availeth

SAY NOT, the struggle naught availeth,
  The labor and the wounds are vain,
The enemy faints not, nor faileth,
  And as things have been they remain.

For while the tired waves, vainly breaking,
  Seem here no painful inch to gain,
Far back, through creeks and inlets making,
  Comes silent, flooding in, the main.

And not by eastern windows only,
  When daylight comes, comes in the light,
In front, the sun climbs slow, how slowly,
  But westward, look, the land is bright.

LT. SHEPHERD M. JENKS, U.S.N.
Navigator, U.S.S. *Nautilus*

Under the Ice to the North Pole[1]

In ninety-six historic hours, the atomic submarine *Nautilus* hung up what is probably an all-time record in "blind flying." For 1830 submerged miles, while crossing the polar sea at the top of the world, ninety-eight men, thirteen officers, and five specialists operated the nuclear sub solely on instruments. How this amazing feat of navigation was accomplished is told by the man who had the most to do with it.

OUR ROUTE from Bering Strait across the North Pole lay under an ice canopy of rafted, jumbled blocks and floes with deep-hanging "keels" that sometimes jutted nearly 100 feet down.

We had to steer without benefit of star sights, sun lines, or radio-direction systems, in an area where magnetic compasses are unreliable. Yet, when we finally surfaced near Spitsbergen, in the Greenland Sea, we were within a few miles of where the ship's electronic eyes and ears—and my own dead reckoning—said we should be.

It goes without saying that as ship's navigator I was probably more pleasantly startled than anyone else aboard. For even a one-degree error could have put us

[1]Copyright, 1959, by The Reader's Digest Association, Inc. Reprinted with permission.

hundreds of miles off. But this apparent miracle was no accident.

To nose her safely all this distance—between the irregular bottom and the jagged pack ice—the *Nautilus* was equipped with guidance and detection gear comparable to that of a space ship in a science-fiction movie. In the bustling "attack center"—the sub's operational heart—every inch of space was crowded with glowing light tables, cathode screens, banks of colored lights, meters and dials. These indicators, plus special electronic computers held her on course with unbelievable accuracy. The three "pilots," sitting behind a row of aircraft-type control sticks, did little steering, since the computers were tied in with an automatic steering device which magically nudged our blunt bow along a narrow corridor in the sea.

251

Our complex vehicle carried thirteen echo-sounding devices to aid us. Upside-down sonar, aimed upward from a pressure-proof dome on the outer hull, painted a continuous profile of the rugged ice ceiling above us and told us how much clearance we had. (On a closed-circuit TV screen, crewmen could watch the underside of the ice canopy, illuminated by twenty-four-hour polar sunlight, move swiftly by like scudding clouds.) The fathometer gave us a picture of the soaring sea mounts and deep valleys over which we passed. Automatic depth-control equipment kept the *Nautilus* within inches of whatever depth was ordered.

Nautilus carried three Sperry compass systems, all involving high-precision gyroscope mechanisms and intricate calculators. The fanciest piece of equipment aboard was a North American Aviation inertial-guidance system. Known as the *N6A*, it performed wonders that Jules Verne never

dreamed of. Our faintest roll, pitch, or turn was instantly felt by the *N6A*'s sensory "brain." Electronic messages then flashed to a computer, which in turn was hooked up to dials on the controls console, providing us with a reading of *Nautilus*' exact position at any moment.

All this equipment got a good workout long before we reached the polar sea. En route to the deep Arctic Ocean, a sub must pick its way through the islands of the Bering Strait and the shallow waters of the Chukchi Sea, which run from 100 to 150 feet deep. If there's ice in the Chukchi, a sub like the *Nautilus*, measuring some 50 feet from top of "sail" (superstructure) to hull bottom, has little clearance.

On our first stab at the North Pole, in June, the arctic pack, driven by winds, had piled up like a log jam north of the funnel between Siberia and Alaska. There, in the Chukchi Sea, we found ourselves with only 25 feet of water

above us and 45 below. The ice sonar was painting a jagged picture of the ceiling overhead. Suddenly the ceiling dropped to within ten feet of our sail. Above us was a massive ice block some 30 feet deep!

Comdr. William R. Anderson, our skipper, immediately ordered a turnabout, and we headed back to the Strait to have a try on the Alaskan side.

Again we moved submerged into the Chukchi's shallow waters. Here the ice seemed to run about 20 feet thick. Soon, however, the sonar showed we were creeping under a gigantic floe with rams projecting downward 63 feet! The sonar needle and the location of our sail top were barely parted. Beneath us, the muddy bottom was only a few feet away. Again we slewed into a turn. As we crept around, the needle inched downward. For several breathless moments everyone watched that sonar, expecting momentarily to hear the grinding crunch of ice on steel. The needle came within a scant five feet, hovered ominously, then slowly receded. Back we went to our Pearl Harbor base.

It was a month before we headed north again. Starting on July 29, on the western side of the Strait, the *Nautilus* tried for two days to find a hole in the frozen fence—

without success. Then we turned eastward and headed for the great Barrow Sea Valley running north from Alaska's coast. We made it without incident.

On August 1, off Point Franklin, I took my last fix. Then we dived, and headed for the North Pole. Once we were in the deep trench, the going was easy. The treacherous pack ice above us had rams that jutted down as much as 75 feet, but the *Nautilus* was able to hit a steady pace of about 20 knots some 400 feet below the surface.

Throughout the next 1830 miles I kept two tracks. One represented the constant position reference from inertial-guidance system. The other, our primary navigation, was my own dead-reckoning track, using the master compass, plus our electro-magnetic log, for speed and distance information. Compasses were checked regularly. During the entire trip, both tracks and all the compasses were in complete agreement, so the navigation department felt considerable confidence.

A few miles from the top of the world, our dials indicated that we would pass a hair to the right of the Pole if we kept going on that course. So we made an almost inconsequential three-degree change, and, a few minutes later, at 11:15 P.M. Eastern Daylight Time, on

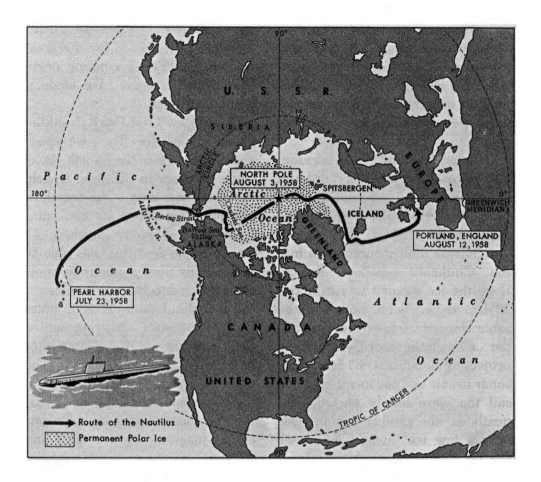

Route of the Nautilus
Permanent Polar Ice

August 3, 1958, Commander Anderson ran a count-down over the public-address system. He ended with a sharp "Mark!" as the *Nautilus* rode across the North Pole in triumph.

This was the first time a seagoing vessel had ever reached the North Pole. And we had made impressive discoveries. Our TV screen and sonar showed that the arctic ice pack is as full of holes as a Swiss cheese, making it entirely feasible for submarines to operate there: they can rise for air, repairs, direction-finding, or target practice almost at will. Our high-precision depth sonar informed us that the sea over the Pole itself is 1927 feet deeper than previously reported, and in some places the Arctic Ocean is 8000 feet deeper than shown on existing charts. A submarine mountain range 9000 feet high crosses near the Pole like a great spine on the back of the world.

254

Our celebration took various forms. One engineer claimed he was the first of the crew to "set foot at the Pole." He'd been lying down, feet first, in the forward torpedo room. Another crewman re-enlisted by raising his hand and taking the oath just as the sub crossed the Pole. A North Pole cake was cut and demolished.

I had little time for taking part in the festivities. Soon after starting down the other side of the world I plotted our course for the Greenwich meridian, and we headed south for open water in the Greenland Sea.

On August 5, at 4 A.M., the TV screen and sonar showed clear water overhead. Commander Anderson brought us up to periscope depth, then surfaced. I took two sun-line fixes through the periscope sextant and was able to report that we were almost exactly where we had thought we were. Our few miles of discrepancy could have been in my sun line as easily as in the navigation systems on board. We'll never know.

Appreciating the Author's Vocabulary

Lieutenant Jenks applies some of the less common meanings to many words to dramatize his story of the *Nautilus*. Column A below lists some of these words and Column B lists their meanings in this story. Write the letter preceding the correct definition before each word in Column A.

Column A	Column B
_____ 1. pack	a. maximum height of visibility
_____ 2. ceiling	b. a projection for piercing or cutting
_____ 3. funnel	c. records
_____ 4. rams	d. rising mass
_____ 5. tracks	e. a large area of floating ice
_____ 6. reading	f. without visual guidance
_____ 7. mount	g. indication
_____ 8. scudding	h. gently pushed
_____ 9. blind	i. driven by the wind
_____ 10. nudged	j. passage

OLIVER WENDELL HOLMES

The Chambered Nautilus

THIS is the ship of pearl, which, poets feign,
　　Sails the unshadowed main,—
　　The venturous bark that flings
On the sweet summer wind its purpled wings
In gulfs enchanted, where the Siren sings,
　　And coral reefs lie bare,
Where the cold sea-maids rise to sun their streaming hair.

Its webs of living gauze no more unfurl;
　　Wrecked is the ship of pearl!
　　And every chambered cell,
Where its dim dreaming life was wont to dwell,
As the frail tenant shaped his growing shell,
　　Before thee lies revealed,—
Its irised ceiling rent, its sunless crypt unsealed!

Year after year beheld the silent toil
    That spread his lustrous coil;
    Still, as the spiral grew,
He left the past year's dwelling for the new,
Stole with soft step its shining archway through,
    Built up its idle door,
Stretched in his last-found home, and knew the old no more.

Thanks for the heavenly message brought by thee,
    Child of the wandering sea,
    Cast from her lap, forlorn!
From thy dead lips a clearer note is born
Then ever Triton blew from wreathèd horn!
    While on mine ear it rings,
Through the deep caves of thought I hear a voice that sings—

Build thee more stately mansions, O my soul,
    As the swift seasons roll!
    Leave thy low-vaulted past!
Let each new temple, nobler than the last,
Shut thee from heaven with a dome more vast,
    Till thou at length art free,
Leaving thine outgrown shell by life's unresting sea.

5. World Brothers

THESE are our brothers:
the people of our friendly neighbor land
where northern lights flash down from Hudson Bay,
the farmers near the wide Saskatchewan,
the fishermen who go out from Grand Pré;
the people of the far antipodes
where in dark skies the Southern Cross hangs low,
the riders of the pampas, and the tribes
within the jungles where wild orchids grow.
Neighbors upon our Western Hemisphere,
we differ much in ways both large and small,
but stand united in a common bond,
children of God, the Father of us all.

These are our brothers:
the goatherds of the gray Moroccan hills,
the Arabs riding over desert sands,
the Kaffirs in the mines and on the veld,
the sweating toilers of the blazing lands;
the patient tillers of an ancient soil
who labor in the delta of the Nile,
farm folk of Egypt. (Many years ago
Christ dwelt among them for a little while.)
The blood of martyrs bought for Africa
her entrance to the great fraternity,
the company of those who die for Christ
that all His living children may be free.

These are our brothers:
the camel-drivers of the caravans
that slowly travel down the desert trail;
the haughty Druses of the Lebanons,
and patient Jews, come back to Israel;
dark Persians weaving rugs of beauty rare,
and Hindus sweltering in the tropic rain,
Formosans planting soggy fields with rice,
and Filipinos cutting sugar cane;
the Aussies of the Never-never Land,
the scattered peoples of the western sea.
With all of them we build a better world
in hope of never-ending unity.

These are our brothers:
people of towns that saw Saint Francis pass
upon the climbing roads of Italy;
men of old faith within the wide Ukraine;
and men who speak the tongue of Romany;
Saxons and Celts, Teutons and Norsemen fair,
kinsfolk of splendid saints of France and Spain,
men who have prayed at Czestochowa's shrine,
children on sunny Fátima's green plain.
These are our brothers, and with them we lift
our voices to proclaim our unity,
one people, under God, Who made us all,
one people, saved by Christ on Calvary.

EDGAR LAYTHA

Flying North to Eldorado[1]

For several hundreds of years the word *Eldorado* has stood for a legendary kingdom abounding with gold and riches. It was the lure of Eldorado that brought many explorers to the New World. They sought for the gold of Eldorado in South America; they searched for it in the Southwest of the United States. But they never found it. Today there is an Eldorado, but its treasure is something the old explorers never dreamed of—it is radium and uranium. This modern Eldorado is far, far north on the Arctic Circle in a bay of Great Bear Lake. Like the Eldorado of old it is the mecca of the adventurous. Today if you should journey north you would find a flourishing settlement at Radium City near the Eldorado radium mines and bustling activity at Fort Norman. The following description of a journey to modern Eldorado gives a vivid picture of the great expanse of country between civilization and this new empire which is being opened to the world.

IT WAS VERY COLD in Edmonton, the "Gateway of the North." It was colder yet out on Cooking Lake, Edmonton's smooth-frozen plane base for northbound planes, thirty miles out of town.

The thermometer registered just twenty degrees below zero. The sun was shining brightly, but there was no warmth in its rays. Humming like great wasps on their wide wooden skis, six or seven planes stood ready to take off from the ice of the forest-bordered lake. The uniform survey-machines of the Royal Canadian Air Force glittered silver gray. *Santa Maria*, the cobalt-blue monoplane of the *Eldorado Radium Silver Express*, the big grass-green Bellanca, which wore its name, replete with promise, daubed in conspicuous gold letters on its side. The big Bellanca was the private plane of the radium mine.

Mechanics swarmed beside, under, and in the machines. Pilots, awaiting the final weather report, were stowing away the freight

[1]From *North Again for Gold*, by Edgar Michael Laytha; copyright 1939, by Edgar Michael Laytha. Published by J. B. Lippincott Company and used with their permission.

and mail. The *Green Bullet*, a smaller sister ship of the *Radium Express*, was to take off first. The passengers, two engineers from Toronto going to inspect the beginnings of a gold mine on Great Slave Lake, were bundled up almost beyond recognition as human beings. Scarcely more of their faces than their noses could be seen, for their fur hoods were tied up below the nose to keep out the air. Large dark glasses protected their eyes from sun and wind. Over their leather trousers and jackets they wore imposing raccoon-skins. Mukluks—high Eskimo boots of caribou hide, hair inward,—worn over thick wool socks, warmed their feet and legs.

But the Finn, Elmar Ketole, a passenger on the *Radium Express*, was walking the ice in black oxfords, a black overcoat over a blue Sunday suit, and a homespun cap that left both ears uncovered. His right hand anxiously clutched a violin wrapped in brown paper. Two fingers of his left hand held the thick cord that kept together a

pasteboard box with his things in it. In the face of such nonchalance I was ashamed to put on the grandiose polar outfit which I had borrowed, although I was well frozen in my blue ski-suit. But the iron-covered soles of my heavy ski-boots skidded dangerously on the ice, and I pulled over them my borrowed moose-hide moccasins, which were as soft as velvet.

We got aboard. The motor roared deafeningly. On its streamlined skis the *Eldorado Radium Silver Express* whipped across the ice.

The skis were drawn upward, like surf-boards. Far below us lay Edmonton. The snow-covered prairie glimmered silver in the sun.

Blue-white sky encircled the horizon. At long intervals the farmhouses of Alberta rose darkly from the snow. The earth was a disc. Not a valley, not a hill, not a mountain disturbed the uniformity. Across the white landscape a line of tracks went as straight as a string. A little branch railway raced us toward Waterways-McMurray, its terminal.

The seats had been taken out of the plane, so that two of us could be very comfortable in the machine, built for twelve passengers. We lay stretched out on the cases of eggs and cigarettes; and the fresh aroma of lettuce, turnips, oranges, and lemons tickled our noses. I was more at ease than in a transcontinental plane, where you do not always have room to stretch out at full length.

Passengers were secondary for our ship. The *Express* was built not merely to fly miners from civilization to the mine and from the mine back to civilization. In the mine's infancy the plane carried important machine parts from Edmonton to the Arctic Circle; and, before the water-transportation lines were developed, it had moved more than a million dollars worth of radium-containing pitchblende from the mine to the nearest railway.

These tasks it had now accomplished. Diesel motors furnish power for the mine and the mill on Great Bear Lake; and a fleet of four steel ships and twelve barges brings the precious ore down the rivers to the radium refinery, four thousand miles to southeastward.

Today the great green bird is flying back and forth the eleven hundred miles between the mine and Edmonton to bring fresh fruit, vegetables, and eggs to the hundred men in Eldorado, winter and summer. Now in winter, when the caribou come down in great herds from the Arctic islands to the Sub-Arctic, the *Express* follows their migration like a great bird of prey. The pilot knows the Indians' temporary hunting-camps. The Indians await the plane on certain agreed days, and the *Express* often comes back to Eldorado with booty amounting to five thousand pounds of game.

After two hours' flight, between the fifty-fifth and sixtieth parallels, the cultivated farms vanished. Pine and spruce climbed from valleys to hills, framed small and larger lakes. Frozen rivers twisted northward like snakes. We skimmed the last railway station, circled over the twin towns Waterways-McMurray, and, landing, with a bold sweep on the ice-covered Athabaska River, whipped the flying, powdery snow into great clouds.

Along with the *Express*, a white-dotted, almost opaque, moist veil descended to the earth. We could hear only the rhythm of human work. The pounding and filing of the mechanics mingled with the noise of many propellers. We waited in the plane, which had landed, for the end of the snow flurry. Within a few minutes the weather was clear and very bright, although the sun did not appear, and we went outside.

High walls of black-green firs lined both sides of the Athabaska River's deep cut. Close under the wall of sheltering firs ice-bound river steamers hibernated. Around the sleeping ships all was life, motley and tumultuous.

A little fleet of planes of various kinds—perhaps a dozen in all—was being worked over by a swarm of mechanics. Gasoline drums, painted red and blue, rolled down with the noise of thunder from the high banks to the frozen surface of the river. Being rolled to the airplanes, they were emptied of their contents and ended on a mountainous funeral pile of empty drums.

The pilots, sitting at the radio table, heard weather reports so discouraging that we, who meant to stay at the Fort only for lunch, had to make up our minds to a whole night. The wings of the *Express* were covered with coarse canvas to protect them from frost, which would make trouble in taking off with a heavy load. Propeller and motor (to prevent trouble in taking off) too had canvas hoods. The ship was muffled beyond recognition. It looked like a huge insect sitting on the ice.

The fur-trading post of Fort McMurray is the first filling-station at the great crossroads of the North. The planes that take the common route from Edmonton to McMurray scatter thence in all directions. Most of them fly straight north to the gold and radium mines on Great Slave and Great Bear lakes, and to Coronation Gulf, the headquarters of the white-fox trappers along the Arctic coast. Others serve the eastern route, the gold mines on Lake Athabaska in northernmost Saskatchewan. The third route, the northwestern, follows the fur-trading posts on the Mackenzie River down to the islands of the Arctic Ocean.

Three miles from McMurray its new sister town, Waterways, is growing—thanks to the industrialization of the North. At Waterways ends the northernmost railway of Alberta, which transports prospectors who cannot afford a plane passage, and a great deal of freight. The wilderness special can make three hundred miles in twenty-four hours.

Here ships are built in spring that in summer will move lumber, machine parts, turbines, nay, whole gold and silver mills, along the chain of rivers and lakes.

At Waterways and Fort McMurray the mineral wealth of the North begins to show itself. From here there stretches out, within a hundred-mile radius, one of the richest tar-sand deposits in the world. A layer of salt two hundred feet thick guards the reserve of thirty million tons. The bitumen and salt mines work winter and summer.

The take-off was announced for nine the next morning, but the fog did not break up. It was almost noon before the *Eldorado Radium Silver Express* rose skyward again.

We have been flying without interruption for six hours—now low, now at five thousand feet. The pilot needs no map; we follow the course of the rivers automatically. The sun is blazing, the plane cabin is heated, yet still it is unbearably cold. The pilot gives the controls to his assistant, pulls off his mukluks, and tosses them to me in the cabin. I change my ski-boots for them. They are as soft as a special featherbed for feet. The hair inside is as warm as if an electric current were passing through it. The silent Ketole, his violin still in hand, is not shivering at all in his black oxfords.

Lake Athabaska is far behind us. Fort Chipewyan, Fort Fitzgerald, Fort Smith, Fort Resolution, trading-posts where we have not stopped, are far behind us. The ice sheet of Great Slave Lake is glimmering far behind us. Behind us crouch the few wooden houses of the tiny town of Yellowknife. Behind us wander terrified herds of caribou that fled as if chased by wolves when the *Express* threw its shadow on their white hunting-grounds.

For eight hours we have been floating between a white disc of sky and a white disc of earth. The closer we get to the higher regions, the more the face of the earth changes from a vast chain of cliffs to a landscape strewn with lakes.

For hours, infinity to the right, infinity to the left, infinity behind us, infinity before us. For hours the motor has been roaring in our ears. For hours ultra-violet reflections have tired our eyes. For hours we have been looking at the same patterns on the flat ground.

Always and always little lakes and bigger lakes. Always and always narrow rivers and broader rivers. Always and always the same dwarf firs on the same hills. We are flying over country where perhaps no man has yet set foot, over lakes no one has swum, over hills no one has climbed. Nowhere a soul; nowhere the trace of man.

Before us on the clear brow of the horizon, a beaming magnet is pulling us—the sun. The myth of the North is now a living reality. The high North goes through us, frightens, rejoices, exalts, inspires us. In its boundlessness it gives us a fragment of eternity.

We are floating more than eleven hundred miles north of Edmonton. The sun reddens on the snow, dyeing it orange. At last the landscape begins to change. The dwarf firs are growing more sparse. White hills are becoming white mountains. White ranges barricade the horizon. We fly at the barricade and sink slowly upon the far-from-smooth ice in a cliff-bound bay of Great Bear Lake.

Thinking It Out

Write your answers to these questions and be prepared to discuss them with the class.

1. The author mentions that it was twenty degrees below zero. He tells how the engineers from Toronto were dressed; that he is frozen in his ski-suit and his heavy ski boots. He mentions in two places that Elmar Ketole, the Finn, wearing oxfords and an overcoat and cap, is not even shivering. How do you account for this?

2. From what you learned in this selection, why do you think that this far northern country is referred to in the title as "Eldorado"?

3. List the minerals found in this "new empire which is being opened to the world."

4. What is another source of wealth in this area?

5. Do you think that the possession of this area is important for military purposes?

6. The unit theme is "World Brothers"; how can the rich mineral deposits of this area be used to make us world brothers?

7. What use does the medical profession make of radium today?

8. Locate on the map the general area described in the selection. Find such places as Edmonton, Alberta, Athabaska River, Fort McMurray, Waterways, and Saskatchewan.

Locating Poetic Expressions

In this selection the author used many poetic expressions, although he was writing prose. Skim the story and list ten poetic phrases. Beside each phrase, name the poetic device used by the author. The following are examples: *humming like great wasps on their wide wooden skis, forest-bordered lake.*

ANNA M. HENDERSON

Parliament Hill, Ottawa

LIKE a departing conqueror, the sun
Goes trailing crimson banners down the sky,
Taking the pointed towers, one by one,
With a grave loveliness in passing by.
The twilight shadows deepen on the snow;
The young moon swings, a slender, golden arc
Above the town; and yellow street lamps glow
Like crocuses against the purple dark.
And something of the life that throngs the street—
The essence of its laughter and its pain,
Of mounting dreams and triumphs and defeat—
Is woven in the carillon's refrain,
And lifted through the starlight, clear and high,
Is flung, transformed, a song against the sky!

ALDEN STEVENS AND PATRICIA KENDALL

The Lion Decides[1]

THEY were very different, the three who set out on this long, perilous journey across East Africa. Simba, the youth with the lithe, honey-brown body and the keen eyes, had never before traveled farther from his village than the nearby hills, where he guarded his father's herd of cattle. Mucheri, the strong young warrior, had wisdom and experience gained through many safaris across plains and into jungles. Kibeti, the aged warrior, was now returning to spend his last years in the village where he had been born. It was to guide him safely there that Simba and Mucheri had undertaken this dangerous mission.

They went on at a steady pace. As the sun moved up the sky, the heat bore more and more heavily on their backs.

They kept to the grass, following the giant circle of the mountain's base in its slow swing to the westward. At their left, where the towering mountain slopes came down to the plain, the dark green robe

[1]From *The Mark of the Leopard*, by Alden Stevens and Patricia Kendall; copyright 1947 by J. B. Lippincott Company, and used with their permission.

of jungle wore a brilliant border of colors. Clusters of lavender flowers drooped from the high-growing acacias. Simba inhaled the perfumed air that vibrated to the drone of bees. There was nothing like this near the village, where the earth was drier. Here a thousand springs on the mountainside fed the edge of the ever thirsty plain. Here, more blue than the sky at dawn, morning-glories as big as his head starred the pale pink and yellow mist of mimosa bloom.

At their right billowed the open plains. For four years, as he watched over his father's cattle from some lofty hilltop near the village, Simba had studied this mighty expanse of veldt. He had seen it veiled with driving rain, brilliant with sunlight, dappled with the racing shadows of clouds.

The hollows and ridges, the little streams, the rocks and gullies, the wandering game trails, the blue mountains that bounded its far horizons—these were printed deep in Simba's mind. But now, walking on its surface, he found it was different. The horizons began to draw in. What had seemed almost boundless was now bounded by the immediate foreground. Unless a man had some well-defined landmark to steer his feet, he would soon be lost out on those grassy wastes. Simba knew this. There had been warriors who never returned to the village. It had been lucky for him that he had studied these landmarks.

Where their way led through a widespread patch of tall acacia bush, Mucheri's warning hiss brought them to a halt. In the sun-dappled pattern of leaves and branches ahead something moved.

There was a sharp crackle of rending twigs, then, high above, came a whisper of movement. Mucheri and Kibeti relaxed, but Simba stood taut. "Raise your eyes," said Mucheri in a low voice.

Simba looked up. His mouth opened, then widened to a broad smile. Towering high above the foliage, two giraffe looked down at them. The long, graceful columns of their necks supported heads that tapered from broad foreheads to narrow nose tips. Between the delicate ears were little knobs of velvet-covered horn. The large brown

eyes were mild. They gazed with fearless curiosity at the three silent humans below. The stirring of branches continued. A third giraffe loomed above the thicket. Simba's laugh of delight broke the spell. The long necks swung in sudden fright. There was the crash of great bodies as the beasts tore through the tall cover. They were gone. Simba whooped and slipped swiftly through the screening trees to the open ground.

In slow, rocking motion that seemed without effort the three giraffe moved off across the plains. Their speed was incredible, for they swept past a herd of startled zebra that had thundered away at the first alarm. Long lines of wildebeest twisted back and forth amid the flying forms of kongoni, eland, and impala. The whole veldt seemed in motion. The vast herds disappeared over a distant rise. On its ridge a single kongoni paused and looked back at the patch of acacia bush.

"Why does he wait?" cried Simba.

"A single kongoni always waits. He is the sentinel of the plains. Were we to move toward him, he would signal a warning with his ears to the herds that are in the valley beyond." Mucheri glanced at the sun. "We had best be on our way," he said.

271

The heat was savage now, and Simba felt the drag of his pack. He glanced at his companions. They had walked a long time, but Kibeti hadn't slackened. The grass swished before the steady cadence of their feet. Simba stopped once more. One more look back at the hills he knew so well. One more look! But he couldn't see them. The great curve of the mountain shut them from view. Not until he returned from this journey would he see them again. It would be a long time.

It was midday, for the sun cast no shadow, when Mucheri grunted with satisfaction. His timing had been good. Before them a double line of green wandered off across the land. They hurried on, and soon came to the bank of a clear, swift stream. Mucheri walked toward the trees where the stream emerged from its forest covering. "Let us rest in the shade," he said.

The waters came from far above, finding their way through the leafy caverns of the forest to a broad, rock-rimmed pool. It was cool here. Kibeti stretched gratefully on a moss-covered boulder, Mucheri beside him. Simba laid aside his pack and weapons. "Here I go," he called. His slim, brown body cut the water. The splash of his dive showered the two men on the flat boulder.

Hardly had Simba's dripping head emerged when Mucheri's bulk hit the surface beside him. Kibeti didn't dive. Cautiously he eased himself into the pool until he stood, chin-deep, shivering.

"It's cold," he growled.

"Of course it's cold. Strike out and you'll soon be warm." Mucheri splashed water on the old man's face.

They swam lazily for a little while, then came out and lay on the deep dry moss. They slept. Outside the screening wall of jungle the hot plains shimmered in the sun.

Lulled by the cries of birds and the soft voice of the water, it was a full hour before Mucheri awoke. With a light pressure of his palm, he touched the foreheads of Kibeti and Simba. They awoke instantly. "Come," he said. "It is time to go. We must reach the first water hole before sunset. Untie your pack, Simba. Fill gourds. We shall need water this afternoon." He picked up his weapons.

With the bulbous gourds gurgling at their hips, they stepped from the cool retreat of their resting place into the furnace of the plain and set out due westward. They faced into open savannah, following a well-marked trail. Under the searing blast of the sun their bodies were soon dried, and they stopped frequently to drink of the tepid water in the gourds.

"Drink sparingly," Mucheri warned Simba. "In heat like this a man's body becomes as ashes. One dies quickly without water. Water is life."

Yes, water was life. Even on the hilltops at home above the cattle where he spent long hours without moving, Simba had no water left in his gourd when the day was done. Now his body was in constant motion. Every hour it dried and cried out for moisture. It was lucky for them that they were people of the plains, thought Simba. Men of the lakes, rivers, or forest would die in country like this.

The three plodded steadily forward, yet they did not seem to progress. Far ahead, blue peaks showed dimly above the veil of distance, peaks that seemed to retreat before their marching feet. The savannahs rolled on and on in changeless succession. Even the trees appeared weary of the endless monotony, for now they were sparse and stunted.

Near a matted patch of thorn Mucheri hissed sharply, "Stand still." He swung abruptly and faced the tangled bush. They stood motionless. Mucheri brought the big oval shield up across his body. His fingers tightened on the heavy spear. Simba's nostrils widened.

Faint, but unmistakable, a sickly sweet odor tainted the air.

The bush gave no whisper of sound. There was only the hint of something huge and stealthy that moved within the screening cover. The thicket parted before the thrust of heavy shoulders, and the lion stalked into the open.

His mane was dark and heavy. Long, flat bands of muscle writhed under the tawny skin of his flanks and mighty forelegs. The long, black-tipped tail twitched gently. The hard stare of his yellow eyes was menacing. He padded forward. A pebble toss from his enemies he came to a stand, glaring a savage challenge.

No less challenging was Mucheri's answering stare. His hard eyes fixed the beast in heavy-lidded arrogance. Slowly he dropped on one knee. Only his head showed above the edge of the heavy shield. The tip of the long-bladed spear slithered forward, its haft gripped firmly, the tapering iron butt clamped between elbow and ribs. Coldly watchful, he awaited the appalling shock of the charge.

"Do not move, Simba," whispered Kibeti. The old man edged cautiously forward and knelt beside Mucheri. No shield covered his body, but his skinny arm supported the weight of his spear. Its gleaming blade lined up, level and

273

steady. The old warrior smiled as he felt Mucheri's elbow press a message of thanks against his ribs.

Three paces behind the kneeling warriors Simba waited, legs braced, body thrust forward from the hips. The Zanzibar knife was clutched in his hand. His father and Kibeti and Mucheri had faced lions before this, and killed them in battle. Every male of his tribe, to warrior grown, had killed a lion, or died under slashing teeth and claws. The blood sang in his ears.

Suddenly, the animal's mighty muscles tensed. Its shaggy head dropped down and forward.

"I do not fear you," said Mucheri, addressing the lion.

At the sound of his voice, the beast's head lifted, and the black lips writhed back in a rasping snarl.

"I understand," continued Mucheri evenly. "You do not fear me. We are in agreement." There was insolence in his steady gaze.

The snarl lowered to a deep rumbling growl. Mucheri stiffened. In heavy silence, the deadly moment hung in balance.

Then, smoothly, the tawny body turned. Deliberately, the lion skirted the edge of tangled bush to a small thorn tree. In its shade he dropped to earth. His decision was made.

"For a moment, I thought he would charge," said Mucheri, drawing a deep breath. He rose with caution. Kibeti regained his feet with equal wariness. Together, they considered the giant cat under the thorn tree.

Mucheri glanced at his long shadow on the grass. "Come," he said, "we have lost time. Let us walk slowly past him. I believe he has made up his mind, but we must not be too sure. We will walk with care until he is well behind us."

"Do not look at him, Simba," cautioned Kibeti. "Pretend you don't even know he is there." With wary alertness they paced by the little blot of shade where the lion lay. Out of the corner of his eye, Mucheri watched the massive head swinging steadily as it followed their movements. When he could no longer see without turning his head, his ears were keyed for the swift rush of padding feet behind them. They came from the growth of bush into the clear. The beast had not charged. They were safe.

The breath whistled from Kibeti's lung. "Your judgment was good," he commended. "I thought surely he would make his rush when he dropped his head."

"That was when I spoke to him," answered Mucheri.

The hard knot in Simba's chest loosened. "He understood you," he murmured wonderingly.

"Perhaps he did." Mucheri's grim mouth relaxed. "Lions are wise beasts. Had he come at us, it is likely that one of us would have died. But he would have died as well, for our spears would have been through his heart. He had sense. The lion is a warrior and he has judgment. This one did not fear us. He had no reason to give battle."

"Why did you halt? How did you know the lion was there?"

"I smelled the taint of rotten meat. No vultures rose when we came near. No hyenas or jackals fled at our approach. It was my guess that some beast, either lion or leopard, was lying there by his last night's kill." Mucheri's voice was grave as he added, "It was lucky for us that he was alone. Had his lioness been with him, she would have charged, and he would have followed."

Kibeti nodded. "Yes," he agreed. "She is ever the first to fight in defense of her mate." He smiled sideways at Simba. "It seems your father named you well," he said quietly, "Simba—the lion. You showed no fear. Your father will be pleased."

Simba smiled in answer. It wasn't easy to smile. Death had been very close. Now that the danger was past, his knees felt strangely weak. So that was the sort of beast he would have to challenge when he became a warrior. He would be alone, armed only with his spear and shield. He would blood his new spear in the lion. When he drove the point home, the thrust must be true and strong. He must not fail or he would die.

Strength flowed again within him and his knees stiffened. A little laugh escaped him. Kibeti was right. Back there, when they had all faced death together, he had not been afraid! He was tense then, to be sure, but cold and watchful. There had been no fear in him. It was only afterward that his stomach shook. He laughed again. He was sure of himself.

"Is there a joke?" inquired Kibeti. "Tell us."

"I was just thinking that the lion too was lucky," replied Simba. "He made a wise decision."

Illustrating the Story

The authors of "The Lion Decides" have given many colorful pen-pictures throughout the exciting story. List ten striking phrases, and illustrate a scene from the story which most appeals to you.

Identifying Local Color Words

Make a list of the local color words that are associated with Africa and which set the scene and the atmosphere for this story.

Enjoying Suspense

These authors knew how to hold the interest of their readers by using suspense in telling the story. List episodes in "The Lion Decides" which interest you because of their suspense.

Writing Original Endings

From any of these points of suspense, use your imagination to write an original ending to the story.

I Wonder What Became
of Rand-McNally

MR. RAND and Mr. McNally,
Arbiters of hill and valley,
Portraitists of sea and land,
Mr. McNally and Mr. Rand,
Two sad cartographic chaps,
Sat in their office surrounded by maps.
Globes and maps around the room,
And on *their* maps a look of gloom.

"Time was when this business of ours was grand,"
Said Mr. McNally to Mr. Rand,
"When our toughest job was to sit and think
Shall France be purple and Britain pink?
Shall Spain be tinted a bright cerise,
And perhaps a dash of green for Greece?"

"But that," said Rand to Mr. McNally,
"Was before Benito got rough with Hallie,
When we didn't fret about changing borders,
And we just sat here receiving orders."

"Remember those days," McNally said,
"When we'd plan a map a month ahead,
And we'd know, if it came out at noon, let's say,
It was up to date the entire day?
Then the countries stayed as fixed by their founders,
And boundaries weren't made by bounders."
"Those days," said Rand, "are gone *totally*."
"You said it, brother," said Mr. McNally.

ERIC P. KELLY

"Lead Not Forth, O Little Shepherd"

ON A DAY in early spring, Jasek had led his sheep high up among the mountains. All day they toiled upwards into the stony pastures where savory and nourishing grass grew in the spaces between rocks. Above them where trees and grass ended suddenly because of thin air, the sun shone on the rugged peaks and was reflected in that deep dark lake, The Eye of the Sea, and down the furrowed slopes swift streamlets of snow water ran in little streaks of white foam against the rocks.

It was time to go higher. Standing on a rock halfway across a huge opening in the mountains where tons of earth and stone slid down every year, the boy raised his pipe and played the age-old melody, "Lead not forth, O little shepherd." It was a lively air, sad too in places, and had in the third set of verses a distinct minor which the shepherd's pipe could reproduce best. It was the story of a shepherd boy, who, centuries ago, had led his flocks upon lands reserved for cattle, and of the ensuing feuds that had made it dangerous for the shepherd to trespass.

And as he began to play the sheep pricked up their ears and the leader moved toward the boy. Now with Jasek leading and playing, the sheep followed in single file across the cleft in the hills, stopping here and there to crop a mouthful of grass. On and on they went across the slopes until they came at length to the Black Lake amidst the clouds; higher than this there was no growth.

What were the thoughts of this fifteen-year-old boy alone all day long amidst the solitary silences of the mountains? In his tight goatskin trousers, with the colored embroideries along the seams, his wool-lined jacket and round blue hat with its border of small shells, he seemed wholly apart from a world. Yet his thoughts were akin to those of the richest Warsaw lad in his academy or of the government-chosen boy at Modlin. For in the winter he went to the new school in the village of Zakopane many miles below. He had completed most of the preliminary work of the school and hoped to finish the high school which led to the University. By a certain talent for playing upon the woodwind instruments he had attracted the attention of local musicians who hoped

to get him a scholarship for his musical education.

Dusk settled over the mountains. Jasek assembled the sheep again and went ahead, playing the pipe, while they followed after him down the slopes and through the ravines until there lay between him and the folds below only one steep slope thickly strewn with loose stones. Looking about before plunging down this incline, he could barely see the white fleeces through the gloom.

"Wanda-Wanda," he called.

Instantly, the leader of the flock was so close that her nose touched his leg. Stooping, he caressed the woolly head. There was plenty of intelligence in that sheep's head, and much affection in her heart. In the midsummer nights when the sheep remained in the hill pastures from dusk to dawn, the boy had often slept with his head upon her soft mass of wool. When it was lonely in the peaks and the stars alone gave light, the beating heart of the leader of the flock served for comradeship The two had shared adventures in those heights and each could trust the other.

But as Jasek stood to resume his playing, Wanda wheeled around his legs and went ahead of him. Surprised, he stopped and called her, then hurried ahead to catch up to her. The next moment he nearly went sprawling. Wanda had come to a stop on the broad stone that marked the beginning of the descent into the last ravine; she stood right across the path, blocking the way entirely.

Wanda had never acted like this before. Must he tease her and push her away before he could get through and start down the descent? As his pipe had ceased its music momentarily the sheep behind him, trained to advance or stand still as he played, had come to a stop. . . .

He pushed at Wanda hard. She refused to budge. He tried to lift her feet out of the way. That didn't work either. Suddenly it dawned on him that she was blocking the path because something was wrong.

It was pitch dark now. The stars were partly clouded and the moon had not risen. All at once he saw lights far below swinging up the ravine and heard voices calling out his name.

"Hallo-hallo-hallo—" he shouted.

His father and brothers answered. He was about to step over Wanda when the words came booming up, "Stay in your place. Don't move. The whole slope has fallen away."

As the three lanterns were massed together he saw what he had escaped. The whole slope, undermined by spring rains, had fallen into the crevice which the torrents had washed out, leaving a muddy, perpendicular wall almost forty feet high from the base where the path had once run up it, with boulders and jagged rocks all about.

Jasek threw himself on his knees and put his arms about the neck of the old sheep. But for her sure mountain instinct he must have plunged over the wall. And when his father and brothers came up by a roundabout path and helped him get the flock home, he did not release his hold upon the wool of her back. That night and for many nights thereafter, the sheep slept at the foot of his cot in the home on the meadow in the intervale.

Late that summer the director of the Warsaw Philharmonic Orchestra, and his friend, a leading actor in the Krakow Municipal Theater, were touring in the mountains with a guide from Zakopane. One misty morning they had come by automobile up to The Eye of the Sea, and with knapsacks and mountain axes were crossing slowly a stone-strewn slope beyond which rose the peak they intended to climb.

"The clouds hang too low," the guide suddenly observed. "If we got up on the height, they might thicken and we would be lost."

The director was impatient. "I am not afraid of fog."

His friend answered, "That is because you come from Warsaw. In Krakow we know better. Too many people have been killed in these mountains."

The director struggled with his feeling. At last he spoke aloud. "Well, have it your own way then. I suppose we can stay in some peasant hut here and go on tomorrow. There's nothing to prevent our walking a little way up the slope now, is there?"

"Not so long as we keep on the path."

They went along toward the stone wall that marked the outer limit of the highest slopes.

All at once the guide stopped. "Do you hear anything?"

The director cupped his ear with his hand. "Why, yes, voices—a great calling and shouting and whistling."

The guide quickened his step. "Someone in trouble!"

The mountain guides, who dress as did their remote ancestors, wear soft alpine shoes, long goatskin trousers, wool-lined jacket, round black shovel hat, and a short hooded cape that falls to the waist. About their bodies they wind a coil of rope, long, and, though fine, very, very strong. Their keen mountain axes are always ready for work, either in cutting a foothold in ice or in clinging to bushes or rocks or trees.

The three men hurried along the path until they got into the sloping ground where tons of broken and almost powdered stone had collected so thickly that their feet sank in the mass almost as if they were walking in feathers. Progress was utterly impossible; their legs went up and down as if they were walking on a treadmill. Yet they were only on the bottom of the slope, which rose in a dizzy slant for several hundred feet above. One would come sliding down with an avalanche of small stone before he had attained one quarter the distance to the nearest rock showing gaunt and grim in the mist.

Suddenly they were aware of shadowy figures about them, of men and boys and some women. All were shouting and pointing toward the place where, upon a projecting rock some hundreds of feet above, yet far below the top, was a continually moving form. The guide mingled with the crowd. He was one of them; of the visitors the mountain folk took no notice.

"It is Wanda," the shepherd Jasek exclaimed. "We were crossing the height above when in the mist she went too near the edge and fell. I brought my sheep down by the other path, but I can't get to her. Can't we lower someone from the top?"

The guide, who had uncurled his rope, shook his head. The wind momentarily cleared away some of the fog, and they saw the helpless sheep clinging to the narrow rock.

"A bad place," the guide exclaimed. "Those sharp rocks above would cut a rope almost immediately. If it were a man, I'd take the chance; seeing that it's only a sheep I wouldn't risk my life or anybody else's."

"But we must do something." The tears surged into Jasek's eyes. "It's my Wanda. Can't you lower me?"

The guide shook his head. "Impossible," he said.

"If I could only climb up from below!" But Jasek, stumbling forward through the mass of sliding stones, came tumbling back in an instant as the treacherous footing gave way.

"There is nothing to do," exclaimed his father.

"I won't leave Wanda," declared

Jasek. "You say there is nothing we can do?" he asked the guide.

"Not a thing."

"Then Wanda will stay there and finally either die of hunger or else lose her balance and fall on the stones directly below?"

The guide nodded.

"Then I will try something." He had thought of the sliding gravel. "At the foot of the cliff the points of the boulders stick out; beyond that the top of the gravel begins. It is very deep there and almost perpendicular, but the slope becomes more and more gentle. If one could leap beyond the boulders one might land in the gravel." This he thought to himself. On the other hand, striking a pile of gravel from a jump of three hundred feet might be little less fatal than striking the hard rocks. But perhaps his idea might work.

Marching out to a place where Wanda could see him occasionally as the wind swept little clear spaces in the fog, he took out his shepherd's pipe. Since he was at a distance, Wanda would, he thought, attempt to get to him as quickly as possible if she did decide to leap. If she jumped directly down, she would strike the rocks; however, she might leap far in the direction of the music, and sheep do leap far when in danger or when they feel the need of hurry.

When he had gone a little distance he put the shepherd's pipe in his mouth and began to play the song of the Little Shepherd. This was no mere signal to the sheep to follow his path. This was to be a signal to Wanda whom he loved, and he knew that he must put heart and soul into that song in order to inspire her to brave the danger of the leap. He must make every tone clear. He must play as never before. He felt as he played that this music was the greatest and most powerful in the world. . . . He remembered tales he had read in school of men of old who had done great deeds in song, one who had reached heaven through the strains of a harp. All this came into his mind as he played.

Far below him two men listened, enraptured by the beauty of the shepherd's music.

"Do you hear that?" ejaculated the director. "And on one of those simple reeds they call shepherd's pipes. Did you ever hear anything like it?"

"No," exclaimed the other. "I never did. Is it this setting, I wonder, this wall of rock and shadowy peaks rising above the clouds, or is it such a wonderful performance as it seems?"

"It is magic," said the first speaker. "But it is real magic. That boy loves that animal. And you have the whole story in that simple piece of music."

"It's the 'Little Shepherd,' isn't it?"

"Yes, they've played it for hundreds of years. Listen now, and follow with these words:

'Now the shepherd leads them gaily,
Though death hovers near;
Holds the pipe in nimble fingers,
Holds the pipe in nimble fingers,
Music trickles through his fingers,
While the people cheer—' "

"What music! There is no player of his age in my school that approaches it. . . ."

"Pity it's all wasted on rocks and sheep."

"I'm going to see that that boy gets a chance in the school of music in Warsaw! But see what he is doing," said the director.

Far up, the helpless Wanda was moving back and forth as much as the narrow rock allowed. From below came the familiar strains of that pipe. When it played there could be but one command—to move ahead. Yet now there was no way of moving in the regular direction. But Jasek was her master—she must do what he summoned her to do.

The order was to come.

Wanda braced herself on the rock. She worked her feet about until they found firm support. He was a long way off over there, commanding her to come, and she must reach him as soon as she could. The peril that lay below was vanished; she had orders from her shepherd and she trusted him.

She leaped as far as she could out into the misty void, her forelegs down and her hind legs up, just as she had taken many a dive over the rocks that often beset her course.

A cry rose from below. The watchers would have pressed forward, but the barricade of sliding rock prevented. Still the notes of the pipe were heard.

There was a crash, and through the cloud of dust the onlookers could see the body of the sheep hurtling down the slope at terrific speed.

Wanda had cleared the rocks successfully and landed with stiffened feet in the mass of sliding debris. There were dozens of feet of this loose material below her, yet it gave way so fast, and the slope was so steep that, like a ski jumper, she fell and fell and fell for a long distance before there was any resistance at all. Dust and small stones got into her mouth, and into her eyes and ears and nose, yet she must keep on.

When the people below realized what was coming, they set up a great shout of joy as they ran from the approaching cyclone of rock and pulverized stone. At the bottom of the slope, the cyclone burst and the rock and dust gathered suddenly in a heap; but a live sheep, bleating and coughing, went rolling over and over along the ground. In a moment her shepherd ran up to her, wiped away the dust, and brought water in a cup. A few minutes later she joined her flock and started grazing as if nothing had happened.

But if there were tears in the eyes of Jasek when he realized that Wanda was safe, there were still more when the director of the Warsaw Philharmonic Orchestra led him aside and suggested the plan of a schooling in Warsaw to perfect his playing, with a chance afterward of joining some great orchestra.

Jasek sang with joy as he danced about the cottage that night, embracing his mother and father and brothers. "I am a lucky boy, and Wanda made me lucky," he said. At this, the sheep, which had lain down at the end of his cot, opened her eyes and looked at him. He could have sworn that there was a twinkle there.

Dividing Words into Syllables

Using the words in the list below, find the word which fits the description given and write it on your paper. Use your dictionary to find the meaning of each word, and write it on your paper. You will not use all the words.

die	perpendicular	ejaculated	enraptured
pipe	occasionally	void	uncurled
crevice	immediate	avalanche	reproduce
collect	savory		

1. A three-syllable word with a prefix and the accent on the last syllable.

2. A three-syllable word whose suffix changes it from a noun to an adjective.

3. A word having two suffixes.

4. A five-syllable word with the accent on the middle syllable.

5. A word that is a homonym.

6. A word with a silent *e*, and the primary accent on the first syllable.

7. A five-syllable word with the accent on the second syllable.

8. A one-syllable word containing a diphthong.

9. A two-syllable word with the accent on the first syllable.

10. A three-syllable word with a prefix and a suffix.

FRANCIS LEDWIDGE

The Homecoming of the Sheep

THE SHEEP are coming home in Greece,
Hark the bells on every hill!
Flock by flock, and fleece by fleece,
Wandering wide a little piece
Through the evening red and still,
Stopping where the pathways cease,
Cropping with a hurried will.

Through the cotton-bushes low
Merry boys with shouldered crooks
Close them in a single row,
Shout among them as they go
With one bell-ring o'er the brooks.
Such delight you never know
Reading it from gilded books.

Before the early stars are bright
Cormorants and sea-gulls call,
And the moon comes large and white
Filling with a lovely light
The ferny curtained waterfall.
Then sleep wraps every bell up tight
And the climbing moon grows small.

Marda's Masterpiece

PICTURE to yourself the group of islands in the northern end of the Adriatic Sea. Around them lies the blue sea; between them are the still lagoons, like silver mirrors; among them, like a great water lily, is Venice with her white houses, red roofs, and more towers than you could count on all your fingers twice over; and above them a sky of milky blue. You rub your eyes, as Aladdin rubbed his wonderful lamp, and there stands Venice, rising out of the sea like a piece of lovely magic. Near Venice lies Murano; farther off, Burano (Wouldn't you think they were twins from their names?); and a bit farther off is Torcello, with its tall campanile pointing like a finger into the sky. Centuries ago these lagoons were dotted with empty islands covered with tangled grass. Then one terrible year the people along the shores of Italy and for some distance inland fled before a horde of savage warriors coming down from the north, over the Alps, destroying all the cities, towns, villages and farms that lay before them. Reaching the Adriatic Sea, these fleeing people crossed in their boats the two miles that we now cross by railway trains, and made new homes for themselves on these islands.

After hundreds of years Venice became the Queen of the Adriatic, Burano set the fashion for lace-making to all of Europe, and Murano became the center of the glass-making of the world.

One hot day in August the sun poured its fiery rays into the open windows of the lace-making school of Burano, a big building standing in the midst of very poor and simple homes. The door stood wide open to the narrow street, and into it, and up a pair of stairs clattered and chattered a stream of girls, big and little. They were all talking in the soft speech of the Burano people, which is like the speech of Venice with most of the consonants left out, or like honey flowing free from the restraining honeycomb. From every pair of young laughing lips poured a soft torrent of *a*'s and *i*'s and *o*'s, all melting into each other as the colors of a rainbow melt together, until it is impossible to say just where you cease to see yellow and are looking at green.

Up the stairway clattered the girls, to the door of the big sewing

room, where they quieted down and went to their seats. It was a long, bare room, with no pictures on the walls save a Madonna and Babe at one end. Across the end of the room ran a long wooden table, scoured to silvery whiteness, upon which lay many pieces of lace, showing an endless variety of lovely patterns. The mistress of the school stood looking these over, and three nuns, in their simple gowns and hoods, moved among the girls when they were all seated, giving to each her piece of work, offering help here, or criticism there. Some of the girls were making needle lace. These had stitched a few threads lightly down along each of the lines of pattern drawn on heavy paper. With a needle and thread they were now binding these lines of threads together with stitches from one to another. Here they made knots, here they buttonholed a tiny hole, here constructed a flower petal in smooth, satin-like stitches; there curving a spray of leaves to form a garland, or filling in an empty space with a groundwork of close stitches. The edges of flower petals were usually buttonholed, sometimes lightly, sometimes heavily, according to the kind of lace they wished to make. These were all called "needle point," or "point lace." No lace has been more famous than the "Venetian point" made by the women and girls of Venice and the neighboring islands.

Other girls were making "pillow lace." Each of these girls had on her lap an oblong cushion or pillow, in shape and size like a rather large muff. A paper pattern of the design was carefully spread out over the pillow. Next, pins were stuck into the cushion all along the lines of the pattern, quite close together. To each pin was attached the loose end of a thread, the other end being wound around a little wooden bobbin about the size of a lead pencil. Now the lace-maker, instead of making stitches—for she uses no needle at all—twists here two threads and there two threads around now one pin and now another, the bobbins interweaving rapidly in her quick fingers, until mesh after mesh of lace is formed.

Some of the older girls were making lace scarfs, or little lace caps and bibs for a baby to wear on fine occasions, such as its christening. Some were making flounces or panels for a dress; others, lace tablecloths. Most of the younger girls who were just beginning to learn were making long strips of narrow lace to be used as trimming.

Among the younger girls there was one who was new at the school, Marda by name. Her big dark eyes were full of excitement, for she had long looked forward to this day. Her clothes were poor but spotlessly clean, her feet were bare, and a faded blue ribbon tied about her head kept her curly hair from tumbling into her eyes. She had a pillow made of scarlet silk upon her lap, which looked almost too splendid against her faded and much-patched gingham apron. Already her pins and bobbins were in order and her pattern begun. She listened carefully to the instructions of the teachers and the stories of the mistress. Although her fingers were yet clumsy and slow, she did her best and was very painstaking. But she was so happy that she could not speak or smile as did the rest, for her rosy visions quite ran away with her. "I will make," she thought, "when I grow up, the most wonderful piece of lace that anybody in the whole world ever saw!"

Marda was an orphan, and had nobody belonging to her, so far as she knew, except her brother Matteo, who was two years older than herself to the very day. It seemed strange that these two should have the same birthday and yet not be twins. Marda got around that difficulty by calling herself and Matteo "twinless twins." When they were both very tiny they had been taken to the orphanage, just a few streets away from the lace-making school, on the edge of one of Burano's canals. When Matteo was twelve a fisherman and his wife took him to live with them, for the fisherman needed a growing boy to help him with his boat and nets.

It was the custom of the orphanage to allow every little girl to go to the lace-making school on her twelfth birthday, to learn a trade by which to earn her living. For a long time Marda had been looking forward to her twelfth birthday, which would also be Matteo's fourteenth. Matteo for a week or two before the day had been hinting at a present Marda was to receive, and the little girl could scarcely give her mind to her simple duties at the orphanage, such as washing three times daily the faces of certain of the little ones.

It seems that the good-hearted fisherman, Giuseppe, and his wife Elena, hearing from Matteo that his sister would soon be twelve and going to the lace-making school, had been planning to do something for the twinless twins on their birthday. Matteo said Marda had nothing to make a pillow with, and no bobbins. Elena and her husband put their heads together to see what they could do. Matteo was a big, strong boy now, helpful and willing. In a year or two he could begin to do a man's work with the boat

and nets, and would then have to be paid wages. Now they would reward him for his faithful work by getting the things he wanted for Marda.

"Why not let Matteo go across to the City and get the things himself?" suggested Elena. The City, of course, meant Venice.

"Oh, well, we'll see," said Giuseppe. In his head he thought it a very excellent idea, but he did not wish to agree too soon. In every kind of thinking Giuseppe was slow, except in thinking about those things that had to do with the fishing. Giuseppe set his nets pretty well out at sea, and when a sudden storm came sweeping up the Adriatic, as often happened in hot weather, no one of all the fishermen out in their little red- or yellow-sailed boats could be more quickly ready for the storm than Giuseppe.

That night Elena did a great deal of thinking while she pretended to be asleep. But Giuseppe slept soundly. He knew he could think better with the feel of the tiller in his hand, and the sight of the curling water at the boat's edge in his eye. So Giuseppe made his plans the next morning as he and Matteo sailed out across three miles of water to where the nets were set. Elena sang as she made tidy her small house of one room below and an attic. She sang, too, while she washed Giuseppe's one white shirt and her best white apron, trimmed with lace her own deft fingers had made. It was not many years before that she herself had been a pupil in the lace-making school, and she now often sat with her lace pillow on her lap and her fingers and bobbins flying. In nearly every doorway in the little narrow streets of Burano, women sat at their lace-making when the housework was done. For lace-making pays well, especially when a group of tourists comes along, and one or more of them admire the lovely pieces and must have them at any price. And if no tourist comes along, the stores will buy. And always they can laugh and gossip and sing together, shouting and gesticulating from door to door as they sit at their thresholds and work.

After supper that night, when Matteo had gone to bed in the attic, tired out from his long day of work in the open air, Elena said, "I have everything arranged in my head, Giuseppe."

"You have yet to hear from me," said Giuseppe.

"Listen!" said Elena.

"Listen yourself," said Giuseppe.

"You will take Matteo with you to the City, in the rowboat, and let him buy the bobbins for Marda," said Elena.

"I will do better than that," said Giuseppe, smiling.

"What then? Hasten and tell me. Men are so slow at the telling! I could have told it three times over, forward and backward—"

"Women are so fast at the telling that a man cannot put in so much as a 'yes' or a 'no,' " interrupted Giuseppe, and at that they both laughed, and Elena sat down quietly on the doorstep to listen.

"Well, then," said Giuseppe, lighting his evening pipe and tilting his stool back against the house wall, and speaking in a low tone so that the entire street might not hear him, "well, then, we will all go to the City, you and Matteo and I, and the little sister. We will buy the bobbins and the pillow, and then we will see the sights, and buy some fruit and cheese at the market at noon, and spend the afternoon in the Public Gardens, and hear some music in the piazza in the evening, and row home when the moon comes up, just as we did on our wedding day three years ago, if you remember."

And at that Elena got up and pinched Giuseppe sharply on both cheeks, and said laughingly, "If I remember!"

Then she ran indoors and took a box from under the bed and opened it, lifting out proudly a lace pillow, and lighting a candle so that Giuseppe might see it. She had made it herself that afternoon, she told him, stuffing it with odds and ends, and covering it with—well, what did he think?

"See," she said, "it is silk, a little old now, but of a beautiful scarlet color. It is the scarf I wore about my neck the day we first met, if you remember! So there will be no need to spend pennies upon a cushion for Marda, and you may thank me for that."

When the day before Marda's and Matteo's birthday dawned, it was of a royal loveliness, the broad lagoons like sheets of silver, and the sky fair and blue. Marda had never been to the City, and Matteo only once. It was early when the four started off in the rowboat, Giuseppe at the oars. Soon they overtook the market boats heavily laden with gleaming piles of red tomatoes, plump green watermelons, green and purple cabbages, and great baskets of white grapes and honey-colored pears. Here and there a few figs were to be seen, some green, some purple; and here and there came boats loaded with baskets of bright flowers as many-colored as the baskets of fruits and vegetables. They left Murano on their right, catching a glimpse of the famous glassworks as they passed by that island.

"I'm not going to be a fisherman always," said Matteo. "I'm going to be a glass worker. First I suppose I'll have to stoke the furnaces, but after a while I shall put a bit of glass on my rod, blow it into a goblet or vase, put it into the furnace, take it out, and presto—as beautiful a thing as ever you saw!"

"I shall make an altar cloth of lace such as no one ever dreamed of!" said Marda, with a happy sigh.

But Giuseppe, letting go his oars and holding up two hard and horny hands, laughed and said, "I shall doubtless catch fish for the rest of my days!"

Then, after the boat had rounded the little island which is one of the City's cemeteries, encircled by its high brick wall above whose top dark cypress trees stand like sentinels, suddenly Venice itself lay before them, rising up out of the silver water like a golden vision.

Many tall towers lifted themselves in all parts of the City, but tallest of all rose the campanile of the great Cathedral of St. Mark's.

They made a landing at one of the stone flights dipping down to the water, fastened the boat, and went first of all to purchase the bobbins. They did not go to the fine shops, but to a little shop near the market place, not far from the great arching bridge that is called the Rialto. Many of the market people had already arrived, and the scene was one of bright confusion. In the little shop, which was dark after the bright sunlight outside, Elena bought, after much bargaining, two dozen wooden bobbins.

"You will need more when you make your wonderful altar cloth," said Elena to Marda, "but these will do for a very simple pattern to learn on." Then she bought a paper with a simple pattern marked on it in blue, and some pins. When the shopwoman had handed Marda the package and Giuseppe had paid for the things, running his horny hand deep down into his pocket for the money, they sauntered forth into the sunshine, Elena with many injunctions to Marda not to lose the precious bundle. And then they wended their way along many little narrow back streets that were more like balconies strung along the dark walls of the houses than like

293

streets; crossed over many small bridges arched like the backs of purring cats; and finally came out upon the broad piazza in front of the Cathedral, where many pigeons circled about in the air and settled upon the pavement like a bright and burnished cloud. Around three sides of the piazza ran an arcade, under whose shade could be seen shop windows full of lovely things to buy—bead necklaces, glass vases, and all sorts of things made of leather. Along the edge of the arcade people sat at little tables drinking coffee. On the fourth side of the piazza was that strange and lovely building, bright and brave and magical, the Cathedral.

They went into the Cathedral, where they knelt quietly for a little while. Elena closed her eyes, but Marda's eyes looked almost everywhere at once—at the tall pillars, at the arched ceiling, at the statues of the twelve apostles on the altar screen; at the wonderful pictures on the walls, which were not painted, but were mosaics made of many tiny bits of colored stone and glass set carefully together. Marda had never dreamed of such a magnificent place, and into her mind came the thought, "I will make my altar cloth for this very altar, and it shall have the twelve apostles on it, and a border of angels all around the edge."

Coming out, they walked down the piazetta, a smaller open square, to the water's edge. It was now nearly noon, and the water was so full of golden sparkles that one's eyes were quite dazzled by it. It was like a great opal, with a heart of fire. In every direction moved boats. There were black gondolas filled with tourists skimming here and there, and darting into the small canals like mice into their holes. There were fishing boats with great patched red and orange and yellow sails and slippery silver cargoes. There were steamers that had come all the way from Constantinople, passing, on their way up the Adriatic Sea, that "rocky Ithaca," the island where lived that Ulysses whose story Homer tells.

And moored down near the eastern point of Venice, there stood a great gray battleship, taken from Austria in the Great War. Peaceable enough it looked now, however, with sailor lads washing their white suits on the decks and hanging them up in long rows, like so many ship's pennants, to dry in the hot sun. At twelve o'clock exactly a cannon boomed, and instantly every clock in the City struck twelve, as though there were nothing on earth they enjoyed so much as telling Venice that noon had come.

At this Giuseppe said they must eat. Finding a shop, they bought some bread and cheese and a big bag of plums and pears. And then they walked to where their boat stood, got into it, and ate their lunch. As they ate Matteo had much to say about all that they had seen, but Marda, unlike her usual self, was very silent. At length, when the last crumb had been eaten, Giuseppe took up his oars.

"And now for the Public Gardens," he said, steering for the thick patch of green at the extreme eastern point of the City.

Then Marda exclaimed, suddenly

and unexpectedly, "Oh, Giuseppe! I do not want to go to the Gardens. Let us go home!"

"What! You want to go home?" asked Giuseppe in an astonished tone.

"Yes," said Marda. "I want to go right home, right now."

And then, in excited tones, the following conversation took place.

"Why, what has gotten into you, Marda?"

"I want to go home."

"And miss the bears and animals at the park?"

"There's something I'd rather do at home."

"And not stay for the concert? Why, Marda!"

"But I tell you there's something I'd rather do!"

"Why, Marda, you're a silly thing! This lovely day is only half finished!"

And then Marda, with everybody taking part against her, burst into tears and said, "Oh, Elena! Oh, Elena! I want to go home to your house to my new lace pillow and have you show me how to set the pins and wind the thread on the bobbins. Because, you see, I am already twelve years old to-morrow, and I want to make the most beautiful lace altar cloth in the world for the Cathedral, and maybe I will be too old to finish it unless I begin in a hurry!"

At that Giuseppe burst into a great roar of laughter, and said, "To be sure we will go home quickly, lest Marda get to be an old woman before we reach Burano!"

So back they went, and at Elena's house the little girl was instructed in the many things she must do to make a perfect piece of lace. When she went back to the orphanage, carrying her gift proudly, you may be sure that all the other girls, especially those who would soon be twelve, were deeply interested in that scarlet lace pillow with its paper pattern stretched upon it, the pins like little regiments along the lines of the pattern, the bobbins dangling down in such a fascinating manner at one end, and around the pins the beginnings of a piece of lace!

Marda proudly told the girls of the altar cloth that was going to be her life work, her masterpiece. The girls looked at her with big round eyes.

"But where will you get your pattern for the angels and the apostles, Marda?" asked one of them. "Old Elisabella's daughter has all sorts of patterns. I look at them when I go there to work on Saturdays. But I never saw any angels or apostles. The patterns are all flowers and leaves and wreaths, and maybe a bird or two, or a few butterflies."

Another little girl giggled and said, "Oh, Marda is so bright she can make an angel from a bird pattern. There will be wings, anyway!"

"I will make the pattern myself," said Marda stoutly.

"But you'll have to have something to copy," said another girl.

True enough. Marda knew very well that she could not go to the City every day and copy the twelve apostles in the Cathedral until she had a pattern. She knew in her heart that no other figures on her lace masterpiece would ever satisfy her. Turning away from the girls to hide her disappointment, she went upstairs to the big dormitory where she slept, wrapped the lace pillow in her one clean apron, and laid it on a chair close beside her bed. Then she went slowly downstairs as the big gong rang for supper.

It was the duty of Marda to wash the hands and faces of all the little boy orphans between the ages of three and four every evening before they were tucked into bed. Usually Marda did this duty in a somewhat hasty manner. She did not find any pleasure in lingering over it, and yet it was done well enough to pass muster with the kindly Sister in charge. But on this night she did it thoroughly. For slowly, during the day, there had grown in her mind the thought that a girl who was going to make an altar cloth for the great Cathedral in the City must not be a slacker in even the small duties of life. If she allowed herself to be careless with small faces and grimy little hands, she might grow careless with the lace—make knots, even! And so she washed Tommaso's round face even behind the ears to his great astonishment; got plenty of soap into Babbo's eyes and polished Cecco's round cheeks until they were like two rosy apples; and so on down the line, until a dozen little boys of four or five had had a scrubbing and cleaning not easily forgotten. As if that were not enough, she kissed each pair of cheeks as she gave them the final polishing. They would have protested from the very beginning only that she gave them no time. The washing completed, she tucked them into their beds. Then, surveying the twelve small, spotless faces upon the pillows, she had an idea!

"Ah!" she exclaimed. "Yours shall be the angel faces I shall work in lace as a border around my wonderful altar cloth, each face with a pair of wings coming out from those clean places behind your ears!"

Twenty-four clean hands came out from under the sheets and felt those places behind the ears.

Then a still more imposing idea seized hold of Marda. Think of having two great ideas within sixty seconds! She clapped her hands, then grew grave. The dozen clean faces grew grave also and gazed at her with blinking eyes.

"Now mind that every one of you grows up to be a good man," she said, shaking her finger at them, "because it may be that it will be many years before I shall make the lace well enough to start on my altar cloth. And as you will then be grown-up men, you shall be"—here she paused before springing the great idea upon them—"you shall be the twelve apostles that I shall put in a line across the length of the most wonderful altar cloth in the wide world! Now think of that and go to sleep, all of you!"

And at once the twelve clean-faced apostles-to-be closed their eyes, and Marda was free to climb the stairs to her own dormitory, creep into her own bed, and dream and dream of the great To-morrow.

Identifying Similes

1. Helen Coale Crew beautified her story by using colorful figurative language. Skim the story to find three similes she used to describe the city of Venice.

2. Column A below lists several items described in "Marda's Masterpiece." Find in Column B the similes which the author wrote to describe these things and write the letter of the correct simile before each item.

Column A	Column B
_____ 1. lagoons	a. ships' pennants
_____ 2. campanile	b. a great opal
_____ 3. cypress trees	c. silver mirrors
_____ 4. back streets	d. sentinels
_____ 5. water near the piazza	e. rosy apples
_____ 6. sailors' suits	f. a finger into the sky
_____ 7. pins	g. little regiments
_____ 8. Cecco's cheeks	h. balconies

JAMES J. DALY, S.J.

Boscobel

NOT FAR from here there is a town
Of which I hear the neighbors tell;
It has no title of renown
Except the name of Boscobel.

A dulcet name that might belong
To some Provencal villanelle,
I'll tune my viol and make a song
About the town of Boscobel.

It sleeps below the wooded hills
Deep in the hollow of a dell,
And philomels and whippoorwills
Chant night and day to Boscobel.

In stately homes on shaded lawns,
Calmly the gentle townsfolk dwell;
And sunset splendors, magic dawns,
Alone mark time in Boscobel.

Its ways are arched with ancient elms,
The haunts of Fairy Ariel,
You could not find in twenty realms
A spot so fair as Boscobel.

The old gray church has Spanish chimes;
Their clear-toned accents rise and swell
On Sabbath winds in clanging rimes
Along the streets of Boscobel.

You'll hardly find a parallel
By Danube, Rhine, or blue Moselle,
Much less a hamlet to excel
The little town of Boscobel.

I've never seen fair Boscobel;
And, what is more, I never will;
For I should fear to break the spell
Of that sweet name of Boscobel.

O music of a silver bell!
O nought but name to me, farewell!
Sleep in thy meads of asphodel,
Unvisited, my Boscobel!

AGNES ROTHERY

The Most Beautiful City in the World[1]

IF you should think of a bright blue harbor dotted with islands; of mountains rising up around it, of wide drives and avenues and beaches edging it; of the prettiest houses—rose and violet and white and yellow—built against the sides of the mountains and each one set in the midst of gardens and terraces and pergolas; this would be something like Rio de Janeiro.

But when your steamer passes through that harbor and comes up to a dock at the end of a wide, gay avenue, right in the center of town, you will find yourself in a place far more beautiful than anything you were even able to imagine.

For it is not only the water and the islands and the mountains and the beaches which nature put there, but the houses and churches and gardens that men have built there that make Rio de Janeiro a fairy spot.

In most cities there is a downtown business section which has a few handsome buildings and many ugly ones, and an uptown section with some attractive houses but many ordinary ones. But the Brazilians have taken all of Rio de Janeiro and made every part of it so delightful that, no matter where you go, you will be amazed and enchanted. Instead of taking the land along the water's edge and using it for railroad tracks, they have turned it into a drive which curves along the harbor and twists past the mountains for fifteen dazzling miles. Instead of making sidewalks of concrete or dull, commonplace paving material, they have made them in designs of colored stones, like the patterns on long Oriental rugs. In the big and little parks, which are scattered everywhere, men sweep the grass every day with palm leaf brooms, as if they were living rooms in a well-cared-for house.

Since it is never cold enough in Rio de Janeiro to need furnaces, there is no smoke to dirty the red-tiled roofs and the white and pink and blue walls. There is plenty of rain to keep them washed clean, and plenty of sun to dry them back into their soft colors. The flowers and shrubs and trees and vines grow so quickly, and with such

[1]Reprinted by permission of Dodd, Mead & Company from *South American Roundabout*, by Agnes Rothery. Copyright © 1940 by Dodd, Mead & Company, Inc.

enormous blossoms and leaves, that there are brightness and fragrance everywhere.

It does not make any difference which part of Rio de Janeiro you visit first, for it is all fascinating.

There is the famous drive along the water front, which passes through suburbs whose houses are like rainbow soap bubbles, and along beaches which fringe the dancing water. On the gateposts in front of some of the houses you will see big pineapples made out of stone, or out of blue or yellow porcelain. These are not just for decoration. They are the Brazilian symbol of hospitality as well. There are other drives which wind up into and between the mountains.

And there is the strangest trip on a basket-car that clings to cables stretched from one mountain to another, so that you rise up over the trees and swing through space. The car comes to its first stop on the top of a steep little mountain, which is not quite seven hundred feet high. There you get out of the car, walk across to the other side and take another car, which again swings out over the tops of the trees and glides over empty space and lands on the top of a bare mountain called Sugar Loaf—a rock that rises straight out of the sea.

From here you can look down and see the ocean, far away; the entrance to the harbor, with vessels steaming in and out; and the way, which holds two hundred islands and is so big it could hold all the navies of the world besides. The city of Rio de Janeiro itself is laid out like a picture puzzle. If you take the trip at night, instead of in the day, you will not see the far-away ocean, for it will be lost in darkness. But the sky is so full of stars, the islands are so pricked out in lights, and the city streets and the harbor's edge so illuminated, that it will be like standing in a great bowl pierced with holes above and below and on all sides, with light coming through every hole.

Corcovado—which means Hunchback—is another mountain you can get to, not by a basket-car swinging through space, but by a cog railway. From here you can look down on Sugar Loaf and down on the flying birds and drifting clouds and see more closely the great statue of Christ with His arms outstretched to form a cross, so high above the city that it seems to guard every house and person, every ship and street.

One of the things which make Rio de Janeiro look different from cities in the United States is the royal palm tree. It is very tall, with a perfectly straight, smooth trunk and a crown of leaves at the top which have given it its name—"the feather duster of the gods."

When the first King of Brazil came over from Portugal, he planted the first palm tree. It still stands in the Botanical Gardens, with a stone tablet near by, telling that it was planted by the king in 1808. He thought he would like this to be the only palm tree in Brazil, so he ordered that every seed that fell from it should be burned. But people found the seeds and planted them, and now "feather dusters of the gods" line and shade the avenues and streets and wave from every mountain terrace. They are one of the first things that you see and one of the last that you remember about Rio de Janeiro.

When you come back from your drive, you will want to go down into the busy, bustling section of the city and see the people. You will see so many that you will wonder whether the entire population is not shopping, sitting in the cafés, taking a drive or a stroll, or going to market.

It is no wonder that so many of the people are in the market squares, for there are so many curious things for sale there that you could spend whole days wandering about and never come to the end of them. There are no doors in the shops, only iron shutters that are pulled in at night, so that as you walk down the narrow, crisscross streets, you can look directly in on the shelves and counters.

Besides the queer-looking fruits and vegetables, there are all sorts of live animals. For instance, in many of the shops they sell live snakes. People buy these to keep in their gardens or in their warehouses to kill rats. These snakes sometimes weigh twenty-five or thirty pounds, and their owners feed them on scraps. There are little live lambs and goats and calves and pigs for sale, and parrots and monkeys and tiny little marmosets—like doll monkeys—and lovebirds and parakeets in cages.

The Brazilians love pets and take good care of them. There is one pretty little bird, about the size of a hen, which is called a police bird. If you have one of these, you let it hop around wherever it pleases, in your yard or garden or even in your house. It loves to be with people and follows the members of the family around like a pet. But if a stranger comes to the door or the gate, it will flap its wings and scream; so it is as good as a watch dog or a private policeman.

There are little shops which sell nothing but jams and jellies and marmalades made out of Brazilian fruits. Some of these fruits are guavas, which look something like lemons; and jacas, a fruit that looks like a Japanese lantern as it hangs in the tree; and papayas, which grow on small trees and taste something like a melon and something like an apricot.

Then there are shops where you can get all sorts of delectable candies and cakes and drinks made out of cocoanut and pineapple and bananas and different kinds of nuts.

There are so many churches in Rio de Janeiro that it seems as if bells were ringing every minute. Although many of them glitter with gold and precious stones, the one which will probably interest you most is the miracle church at Penha, a little way out from the city. It is set on the top of a bare crag of stone, like the golden howdah on top of an elephant's back.

There are three hundred and sixty-five steps—one for every day in the year—cut in the rock which leads up to this dainty, two-spired building. Once upon a time great numbers of pilgrims used to come here twice a year and climb up these steps on their knees. At the bottom of the stairs and at the top are piles of crutches and braces which have been thrown away by the people who have been cured in the church.

They say that three hundred years ago a man was attacked by a scorpion and a snake and called on the Virgin Mary for help. She appeared in a vision and placed one foot on the snake and one on the scorpion. The man was saved. He built this miracle church in gratitude, and in honor of the Mother of Christ.

There are so many things to see in and around Rio de Janeiro that you could spend weeks and weeks there and never see them all. If you notice a goat ambling sedately along a road and then stopping at a house and walking in, you will know that she is following her daily route. Just as the milkman comes to your house every morning to leave milk, she goes to certain houses and stands at the door and waits for someone to come and milk her.

You will discover all sorts of pretty little quays with steps leading down to the water, where boats come in and where sailors, with rings in their ears, are laughing with girls in bright colored dresses. You will hear the sound of music from big boats and little boats anchored near by, where people are singing or dancing.

In some of the parks there is an animal about the size of a muskrat, which sits on its haunches and holds its food in its front paws, like a squirrel, as it nibbles it. These little creatures are never caught or killed, but allowed to live as they please. So are the peacocks that strut over the grass, and the long-legged herons that stand and admire their own reflections in the pools. The children often play *petecca* in these parks—a game a good deal like battledore or shuttlecock.

There is no more beautiful city in all the world than Rio de Janeiro, and there were never people who loved their homes more and liked to decorate them and make them even more beautiful.

The people of Rio de Janeiro build and plant in such a way that the mountain sides look like sliding walls of flowers and terraces. They make roads and avenues along the water's edge that are like necklaces. On the islands they erect such dainty towers and spires that they remind you of castles in fairyland. They are always working to make their city not only more beautiful but more healthful as well. They have drained what were once fever-breeding marshes and made them into land for splendid docks and warehouses. They have cut down hills that shut out the ocean breezes from certain sections, and in other sections, they have built sea walls so substantial that the largest ocean liners can come up to the very edge of the city.

Rio de Janeiro is like a jewel which has been cut and polished and is displayed in the most dazzling setting imaginable, so that not only the Brazilians, but everyone who visits it, looks at it with delight.

Making Judgments

Use these questions as the basis for a class discussion.

1. Do you think that this account of the city of Rio de Janeiro is the type you would find in a reference or geography book? Give a reason.

2. Do you think that it might be the script for a motion-picture travelogue? Give a reason.

3. In what ways does this selection differ from the usual geography book accounts?

4. What information which is not given here would you expect to find in a reference book?

Brighter Horizons

THERE WAS A TIME when the world seemed large. Shanghai was far from San Francisco and Moscow a great distance from New York. Today the lines of communication have been shortened so that the world seems smaller to the people of the United States than the thirteen colonies did to the colonists of 1775.

This cutting down of time and distance has made us more conscious of our world neighbors and what we mean to one another. We have come to learn that in the world of today no nation can exist by itself or for itself alone.

The good that has come from this closer contact cannot be measured. The suffering that has come from it has sometimes been equally great, for the same instruments that carry messages and goods of peace with such speed can also carry the codes and armaments of war.

In all ages of Christendom men of good will have tried to keep peace in the world by setting up standards of justice between nations. National selfishness, working in the same way as individual selfishness, broke down these standards and caused wars.

In our own time leaders of nations have tried to set up principles to guide the countries of the world in their dealings with one another. The leaders have worked together in the League of Nations and, later, in the United Nations.

Few have been better qualified to state the principles of justice which should guide nations than the Holy Father, for no one has a broader, more impartial view of the problems involved than the Vicar of Christ on earth

On Christmas Eve of 1939—before the famous Atlantic Charter had been written—Pope Pius XII gave to the world principles for a just and lasting peace. Each Christmas Eve that followed until 1944, —all before the great San Francisco Conference,—the Holy Father spoke to the world on justice among nations. The principles he gave are these:

1. All nations should be assured their right to life and independence. The will of one nation to live must never mean the death sentence to another nation. Larger and stronger states should respect the rights of smaller and weaker ones

to political freedom, to economic development, and to adequate protection. In time of war, stronger states should recognize the right of weaker states to remain neutral.

2. The race among nations to develop tremendous armies, navies, and tools of warfare has been one of the most powerful causes of wars, and should be discontinued.

3. International courts should be set up to settle difficulties between nations in the way that local courts settle cases between individuals.

4. No minority group in any nation should be oppressed because of its language or culture.

5. There should be no hoarding, by one nation or group of nations, of materials needed by others. Fair arrangements should be made for the exchange of goods so that all the world may benefit from the resources which God has provided for all men.

6. There should be no persecution of religion or of the Church.

7. There should be developed among peoples a deep sense of their responsibility to keep the law of God.

Catholic students have two things necessary to bring about a better world: faith which believes in the unity of mankind, and the grace of God which gives them strength to put this belief into action.

"The diplomas of the Catholic schools," someone once said, "are not merely pieces of parchment. They are marching orders from the Prince of Peace."

These marching orders were stressed in the first Christmas message of Pope John XXIII. In the simple and humble words of a saintly man, Pope John revealed the real trouble of the world today when he made a strong plea for Christian unity. He urged all Christians who profess the revelations of the Prince of Peace, born at Bethlehem, to come together and teach the world the spiritual peace found in the message of the Gospels. This, said the Vicar of Christ, is the only true basis for lasting peace.

Selecting Important Ideas

To ask an intelligent question shows that one has learned something new and has been able to relate this to something which he has already learned. Reread the selection, then write five questions which ask for information which you consider important.

James Russell Lowell

The Fatherland

Where is the true man's fatherland?
   Is it where he by chance is born?
   Doth not the yearning spirit scorn
In such scant borders to be spanned?
Oh yes! his fatherland must be
As the blue heaven, wide and free!

Is it alone where freedom is,
   Where God is God and man is man?
   Doth he not claim a broader span
For the soul's love of home than this?
Oh yes! his fatherland must be
As the blue heaven, wide and free!

Where'er human heart doth wear
   Joy's myrtle-wreath or sorrow's gyves,
   Where'er a human spirit strives
After a life more true and fair,
There is the true man's birthplace grand,
His is the world-wide fatherland!

Where'er a single slave doth pine,
   Where'er one man may help another,—
   Thank God for such a birthright, brother,—
That spot of earth is thine and mine!
There is the true man's birthplace grand,
His is the world-wide fatherland!

6. The Bells Ring Out

WE are the bells:
we ring from belfries of the Western world;
we rise in chorus in the widespread Union,
bells of New England, matins for the nation,
the myriad bells of Brooklyn and New York,
the carillons that sound at Valley Forge,
the bells of Baltimore and Washington,
bells of plantations, and of bayou churches,
bells on the Great Lakes and the Mississippi,
bells of the far-flung chapels on the plains,
bells of the Rockies, sounding in the clouds,
bells on the Cascades, chiming toward the sea.

We are the bells:
we sound Our Lady's praises
in lands below the Gulf of Mexico;
we sing her glory in the many titles
the people give to her: sweet names of places;
dear names of supplication.
Bells of Brazil chime for the gracious Lady;
bells of the Argentine lift high devotion;
"Queen of the Rosary," say the bells of Lima,
"of Charity," say Puerto Rican chimes;
"the Queen of Peace," say Bogotá's high bells,
"of Mercy," say the bells on southern mountains.

We are the bells:
the routing, shouting bells of London Town,
old bells that long have sung in nursery rhymes,
that fell in war, only to rise again.
We are the bells of Canterbury, made
when Stephen Langton was archbishop there;
the bells of Glastonbury, where still blooms the thorn
brought from the land where Christ once gazed upon it.
We are the bells that sound down Irish roads,
pealing a people's living faith in God,
bells that Saint Patrick and Saint Brigid struck,
and Columbcille on far Iona heard.

We are the bells of France:
where Joan of Arc once crowned a king,
where common men, for love of God,
built carven shrines of everlasting beauty;
Notre Dame of Paris and Sacré Cœur,
whose bell still booms upon the Montmartre hill;
Notre Dame of Marseille, sailor's bell
that spoke to men who went on the Crusades
and still speaks to the mariners of France.
I am a little bell; I tinkle softly
as the pilgrims pass toward the grotto.
I am the bell of Lourdes. I think the Lady hears.

We are the bells of churches by the Rhine:
where Charlemagne built Christian schools,
where von Ketteler preached the cause of labor;
bells of the Danube, of St. Stephen's tower,
where men once watched for Sobieski's coming
to save the West from Islam and the sword;
of Prague, and Warsaw, and the wide Ukraine.
  Ruler divine,
  Lord of all power and might,
  Smile on us all;
  Be Thou our constant friend,
  Save, ere we fall.

I am the bell of the Basilica of Peter.
I am the mighty and majestic.
I ring hosannas out to Christendom,
I ring the joy of Christ's Nativity,
I ring the glory of the Resurrection.
I ring the splendor of the Church Triumphant,
but, always, in my ringing I remember
the fisherman who came from Galilee.
As He taught, I ring
the Gospel message that all men are brothers
and sons of God. As He taught, I proclaim,
  Laudate Dominum omnes gentes.

GEORGE KENT

Mr. Imagination

BACK IN THE 1880's a big red-bearded man came to call one day on the French minister of education. The receptionist looked at the card and his face lighted up. Hurrying out from behind his desk, he pushed an armchair toward the visitor. "Monsieur Verne," he said reverently, "pray be seated. With all the traveling you do, you must be tired."

Jules Verne should have been worn out. He had gone around the world one hundred times or more —once in eighty days. He had voyaged 60,000 miles under the sea, whizzed around the moon, hitch-hiked on comets, explored the center of the earth, chatted with cannibals in Africa, Bushmen in Australia, Indians on the Orinoco. There was very little of the world's geography that Jules Verne, the writer, had not visited.

Jules Verne, the man, was a stay-at-home. If he was tired, it was merely writer's cramp. For forty years he sat in a small room of the red-brick tower of his home,

turning out in longhand, year in, year out, one book every six months—more than one hundred altogether. Verne himself had made visits around Europe and North Africa, and one six-week tour of New York State. And that was all. The world's most extraordinary tourist spent less than one of his seventy-seven years en voyage.

His books are crowded with hunting and fishing expeditions, but Jules went hunting only once. Then he raised his gun and—poof! —shot the red cockade off the hat of a game warden. The only fish he ever caught was on a plate at the end of a fork.

Though he never held a test tube in his hand, Jules Verne became a stimulus and inspiration to the scientist in the laboratory. He had TV working before simple radio had been invented: he called it phonotelephoto. He had helicopters a half century before the Wright brothers, dirigibles before Zeppelin. There were, in fact, few twentieth-century wonders that this man of the Victorian era did not foresee: neon lights, moving sidewalks, air conditioning, tanks, skyscrapers, guided missiles, rayon, electrically operated submarines, airplanes.

Beyond any doubt, Verne was the father of science-fiction; he was years ahead of Conan Doyle and the other great visualizers of things to come.

Nor was Jules Verne simply an entertainer. He wrote about the marvels of tomorrow with such precise, indisputable detail that he was taken seriously. Learned societies argued with him. Mathematicians spent weeks checking his figures. When his book about going to the moon was published, five hundred people volunteered for the next expedition.

Those who later were inspired by him gladly gave him credit. Admiral Byrd, returning from his flight across the North Pole, said Jules Verne had been his guide. Simon Lake, father of the modern submarine, wrote in the first sentence in his autobiography: "Jules Verne was the director-general of my life." Juan de la Cierva, inventor of the autogiro (now the helicopter), acknowledged his debt to the author, as did Georges Claude, creator of the neon lamp. Auguste Piccard, balloonist and deep-sea explorer, Marconi, of wireless fame—these and many others agree that Jules Verne was the man who started them thinking. France's famous Marshall Lyautey once told the Chamber of Deputies in Paris that modern science was simply a process of working out in practice what Jules Verne had envisioned in words.

Verne, who lived to see many of his fancies come true, was matter-of-fact about it all. "What one man can imagine," he said, "another man can do."

Jules' father was a lawyer; his mother was descended from one of the great families of France. Their son was born on an island near Nantes in 1828. Napoleon had just died, Wellington was prime minister of England. The first railroad was only five years old. Steamers were crossing the Atlantic, but they still carried sail to supplement their engines.

From the windows of his home the boy Jules could see the masts of sailing ships, watch fishermen's nets drying, smell oakum and hides and spices. At the age of eleven he was playing on the wharves with a childhood sweetheart who said she would like a string of red coral beads like those the sailors brought back from their voyages. Jules solemnly promised she would have one, and that same afternoon was on board the bark *Coralie*, about to sail for India, signed on as a cabin boy. Fortunately for his later admirers, a friend of the family saw him go on board and told the family. His father fetched him home, spanked him, and put him to bed.

At eighteen, Jules was in Paris to study law, but he was more interested in writing poetry and plays. His father, impatient with the boy's neglect of his studies, cut off his allowance. Jules obtained a small job in a theater, but the years that followed were lean ones.

Though his father had deprived him of his allowance, Jules remained the devoted, loving son. He wrote regularly, even when he was a middle-aged, successful man. He discussed his books, his projects, his dreams, and rarely took a step without first seeking parental advice. It was this strong family feeling which kept him a church-goer and a religious, even puritanical, man in gay and pleasure-loving Paris.

His first book was *Five Weeks in a Balloon*. Fifteen publishers looked at it, sniffed, and sent it back. In a rage, Jules flung it into the fire. His wife rescued it and made him promise he would try once more. So Jules tucked the slightly charred manuscript under his arm and went around to show it to Pierre Hetzel.

The publisher read the book through as the fidgeting young author waited. Hetzel said he would publish it if Jules would rewrite it in the form of a novel.

In two weeks Jules was back. *Five Weeks in a Balloon* became a best seller and was translated into every civilized language. In 1862,

at the age of thirty-four, its author was famous and a success. He signed a contract with Hetzel which bound him to the production of two novels a year.

His next book, *Voyage to the Center of the Earth*, started his characters off down the crater of a volcano in Iceland. They went through a thousand adventures and finally came sliding out on a lava stream in Italy. Here was everything science knew or could guess about pepped up with adventure and brought to life by the imagination of a novelist. Readers couldn't get enough of him. Ferdinand de Lesseps, who had just finished the Suez Canal, was so enthusiastic he used his influence to get Jules Verne the Legion of Honor, a distinguished award given by the French government.

Perhaps the best known of Verne's books is *Around the World in 80 Days*. Serialized in *Le Temps*, a newspaper of Paris, the progress of its hero aroused so much interest that New York and London correspondents sent cables daily to their newspapers reporting the imaginary Phileas Fogg's whereabouts.

In every country of Europe people made bets on whether Fogg would arrive in London in time to win his bet. Verne artfully kept this popular interest alive: his hero rescued an Indian widow from death on the suttee pyre, fell in love with her, and almost missed connections on her account; crossing the American plains he was attacked by Red Indians, and arrived in New York to see the ship that was to take him to England only a small speck on the horizon.

Cunard, White Star, and every other transatlantic steamship company offered Verne large sums of money if he would place Phileas Fogg aboard one of their ships. The author refused and had his hero charter a vessel. As the world held its breath, Fogg reached London with only minutes to spare, and won his bet.

A New York newspaper engaged a reporter called Nelly Bly to beat Phileas Fogg's record—she circled the world in seventy-seven days. A few years later she was able to do it in seventy-three. Later, a British paper hired Colonel Burnley-Campbell, who lowered the mark to sixty-eight days. Verne, by then an ailing old man, hobbled to the railroad station to talk between trains to the fourth contender, a Frenchman, for the crown of Phileas Fogg. Thanks to the opening of the Trans-Siberian Railroad, which the author had predicted many years before, the Frenchman had done it in forty-three days.

In *20,000 Leagues under the Sea* Verne developed a submarine, named the *Nautilus*, that was not only double-hulled and propelled by electricity but was able to do what two British scientists have just succeeded in doing experimentally—manufacture electricity from the sea. Simon Lake, father of the modern submarine, credits Verne with giving him virtually a blueprint for his invention.

Jules Verne, an intensely patriotic Frenchman, fell in love with America. He was captivated by the great spaces, the adventurous character of its people, the sweep of its engineering enterprises. Washington and Lincoln were his heroes, and his most prized possession was a letter on White House stationery, signed Kermit Roosevelt, which ended with this sentence: "My father (Theodore Roosevelt) asks me to mention that he has read all your books and enjoyed them immensely."

Reading through Verne's books, one finds it hard to believe that they were written almost a hundred years ago. Verne's "sky-scanner," at least eighty years before Palomar, had a reflector of almost exactly the same dimensions as the great telescope. The people of his fancy made diamonds synthetically, developed an automobile-ship-helicopter-plane which was convertible, and fired glass bullets containing an electric spark instantly fatal.

Of all the thousands of words of praise uttered at his death in 1905, Jules Verne would have liked best these two sentences from a Paris newspaper: "The old story teller is dead. It is like the passing of Santa Claus."

Identifying Definite and Indefinite Ideas

Copy the phrases below on your paper, and beside each phrase write *D* if it conveys a definite idea, and *I* if the idea is indefinite.

_____ eighty days
_____ 60,000 miles
_____ in the 1880's
_____ few wonders
_____ age of eleven
_____ six-weeks tour
_____ half-century

_____ years ahead of Doyle
_____ fifteen publishers
_____ large sum of money
_____ only minutes to spare
_____ a hundred years ago
_____ thousands of words
_____ death in 1905

Evaluating Material

Mark the statements true or false and then correct the word or phrase which makes a statement false.

_____ 1. Jules Verne was born on an island near London in 1828.
_____ 2. He spent about seventy-seven years in traveling.
_____ 3. Jules Verne inspired many scientists through the work he did in his laboratory.
_____ 4. Jules' father was a writer.
_____ 5. The author signed a contract in 1862 to produce two novels a year.
_____ 6. His first book was *Around the World in Eighty Days*.
_____ 7. Simon Lake was the father of the modern submarine.
_____ 8. Jules Verne received a distinguished award from the French government, the Purple Heart.
_____ 9. Phileas I. Fogg was the hero of *Around the World in Eighty Days*.
_____ 10. Verne is, without a doubt, the father of science-fiction.

WILLIAM ROSE BENÉT

Ten Miles High

Dr. Auguste Piccard May 27, 1931—August 18, 1932

WHERE are you faring up so high,
    Professor Piccard?
Where do you hope to go in the sky,
What is that thing in which you fly?
"How?" we ask, and also, "Why?"
Of the big balloon that is mounting, mounting
Up from Augsburg this fine May morning.
Do you hope to traffic with moon and star,
    Professor Piccard?

Swiss physicist with the big domed brow,
    Professor Piccard,
What in the world are you up to now?
Over what instruments do you bow?
"Why?" we ask, and also, "How?"
Of your new round home so light and hollow
That the red globed sun is aloft to follow.
You dwindle. Are you climbing far,
    Professor Piccard?

You are out of sight. Are you still all right,
    Professor Piccard?
In your globular gondola black and white
Will you be back by the fall of night?
We hope the aluminum seams are tight,
We hope that the seven-foot ball's not leaking
Its oxygen, while the sun you're seeking;
We hope you won't fall with an awful jar,
    Professor Piccard!

Aristotle made a mighty guess,
    Professor Piccard,
Of temperatures that may distress.
Will you tell him *No* or answer *Yes*.
You may solve the riddles of Space, unless
You know—as you do—your limitation
And the force of cosmic radiation,
As you soar where the rays find earth no bar,
    Professor Piccard.

The earth dissolved in a copper cloud
    For Professor Piccard.
The moon was bright, and he laughed aloud,
For the sun was too—and both seemed bowed
Like heads to view the swelling shroud
Of the big balloon that the sun expanded
In purple space . . . but at last they landed
On the Austrian Alps with scarcely a scar,
    Professor Piccard.

From Zurich, next, he soared ten miles high,
    Professor Piccard.
The Silberhorn looked small from the sky.
And there was the glacier, by the by,
Where he landed first. But he didn't try
To risk more ballast than he intended.
He valved out gas, and so he descended
To the Lombard Plain, with naught to mar
    Professor Piccard.

Would you like to float in a metal shell
    In the stratosphere
That from fury of Space protects us well
Where Force runs wild with a whoop and a yell
And energy-thunder rolls pellmell
And worse than tons of iron unloading
The expanding Universe's exploding—
Would you care to dare where Nature is queer
    In the stratosphere?

You might be burned by a cosmic ray,
     Or a giant gale
Might swoop you up and toss you away.
You might meet death like Captain Gray
Or the later Russians who they say
To over thirteen miles had risen
When down they dropped in their metal prison . .
Would the fabric burst or the valve-cord fail
     In a giant gale?

Twin brother Jean sent Piccard his word
     He would dare the sky.
With his wife, a pilot, also aboard
To the stratosphere he safely soared.
But Stevens's balloon in explosion roared
When three Americans descended
Over Dakota, their first flight ended
With parachutes unfurled on high,
     Who had dared the sky.

Finally, Stevens and Anderson
     Again essayed
With clever instruments second to none
An altitude none before had done . . .
Up fourteen miles toward the wondering sun,
Over the plains of Nebraska lifting,
They radioed as the balloon went drifting.
Will a braver voyage ever be made
     When again essayed?

But first and last, we hail you Man,
     Professor Piccard,
Who, quietly resolute, began
The search aloft round the barbican
Of Outer Space, where such forces ran,
And energy, as are past our wonder,
Where the Secret of Life rends Space asunder—
But the mind of man may challenge a star,
     Professor Piccard!

THOR HEYERDAHL

Across the Pacific by Raft[1]

WHEN THE SEA was not too rough, we were often out in the little rubber dinghy taking photographs. I shall not forget the first time the sea was so calm that two men felt like putting the balloon-like little thing into the water and going for a row. They had hardly got clear of the raft when they dropped the little oars and sat roaring with laughter. And, as the swell lifted them away and they disappeared and reappeared among the seas, they laughed so loud every time they caught a glimpse of us that their voices rang out over the desolate Pacific. We looked around us with mixed feelings and saw nothing comic but our own hairy faces; but as the two in the dinghy should be accustomed to those by now, we began to have a lurking suspicion that they had suddenly gone mad. Sunstroke, perhaps.

The two fellows could hardly scramble back on board the Kon-

[1]From *Kon-Tiki: Across the Pacific by Raft*, by Thor Heyerdahl. Copyright 1950 by Thor Heyerdahl. Published in the U.S. by Rand McNally & Company. Reprinted by permission of Rand McNally & Company and George Allen & Unwin Ltd. (London).

Tiki for sheer laughter and, gasping, with tears in their eyes they begged us just to go and see for ourselves.

Two of us jumped down into the dancing rubber dinghy and were caught by a sea which lifted us clear. Immediately we sat down with a bump and roared with laughter. We had to scramble back on the raft as quickly as possible and calm the last two, who had not been out yet, for they thought we had all gone stark staring mad.

It was ourselves and our proud vessel which made such a completely hopeless, lunatic impression on us the first time we saw the whole thing at a distance. We had never before had an outside view of ourselves in the open sea. The logs of timber disappeared behind the smallest waves, and, when we saw anything at all, it was the low cabin with the wide doorway and the bristly roof of leaves that bobbed up from among the seas. The raft looked much like an old Norwegian hayloft lying helpless, drifting about in the open sea—a warped hayloft full of sunburned bearded ruffians. If anyone had come paddling after us at sea in a

bathtub, we should have felt the same spontaneous urge to laughter.

Even an ordinary swell rolled halfway up the cabin wall and looked as if it would pour in unhindered through the wide open door in which the bearded fellows lay gaping. But then the crazy craft came up to the surface again, and the vagabonds lay there as dry, shaggy, and intact as before. If a higher sea came racing by, cabin and sail and the whole mast might disappear behind the mountain of water, but just as certainly the cabin with its vagabonds would be there again next moment. The situation looked bad, and we could not realize that things had gone so well on board the zany craft.

Next time we rowed out to have a good laugh at ourselves we nearly had a disaster. The wind and sea were higher than we supposed, and the *Kon-Tiki* was cutting a path for herself over the swell much more quickly than we realized. We in the dinghy had to row for our lives out in the open sea in an attempt to regain the unmanageable raft, which could not stop and wait and could not possibly turn around and come back. Even when the boys on board the *Kon-Tiki* got the sail down, the wind got such a grip on the bamboo cabin that the raft drifted away to westward as fast as we could splash after her in the dancing rubber dinghy with its tiny toy oars.

There was only one thought in the head of every man—we must

not be separated. Those were horrible minutes we spent out on the sea before we got hold of the runaway raft and crawled on board with the others, home again.

From that day it was strictly forbidden to go out in the rubber dinghy without having a long line made fast to the bow, so that those who remained on board could haul the dinghy in if necessary. We never went far away from the raft, thereafter, except when the wind was light and the Pacific curving itself in a gentle swell. But we had these conditions when the raft was halfway to Polynesia, and the ocean, all dominating, arched itself round the globe toward every point of the compass. Then we could safely leave the *Kon-Tiki* and row away into the blue space between sky and sea.

When we saw the silhouette of our craft grow smaller and smaller in the distance, and the big sail at last shrunken to a vague black square on the horizon, a sensation of loneliness sometimes crept over us. The sea curved away under us as blue upon blue as the sky above, and where they met all the blue flowed together and became one. It almost seemed as if we were suspended in space. All our world was empty and blue; there was no fixed point in it but the tropical sun, golden and warm, which burned our necks. Then the distant sail of the lonely raft drew us to it like a magnetic point on the horizon. We rowed back and crept on board with a feeling that we had come home again to our own world—on board and yet on firm, safe ground. And inside the bamboo cabin we found shade and the scent of bamboos and withered palm leaves.

It was most remarkable what a psychological effect the shaky bamboo cabin had on all of us. It measured eight by fourteen feet, and to diminish the pressure of wind and sea it was built low so that we could not stand upright under the ridge of the roof. Walls and roof were made of strong bamboo canes, lashed together and guyed, and covered with a tough wickerwork of split bamboos. The green and yellow bars, with fringes of foliage hanging down from the roof, were restful to the eye as a white cabin wall never could have been. And, despite the fact that the bamboo wall on the starboard side was open for one third of its length, and roof and walls let in sun and moon, this primitive lair gave us a greater feeling of security than white-painted bulkheads and closed portholes would have given in the same circumstances.

The fact that the balsa logs always rode the seas like a gull, and let the water right through aft if a wave broke on board, gave us an unshakable confidence in the dry part in the middle of the raft where the cabin was. The longer the voyage lasted, the safer we felt in our cosy lair. We looked at the white-crested waves that danced past outside our doorway as if they were an impressive movie, carrying no menace to us at all.

Though the gaping wall was only five feet from the unprotected edge of the raft and only a foot and a half above the water line, we felt as if we had traveled many miles away from the sea and occupied a jungle dwelling remote from the sea's perils once we had crawled inside the door. There we could lie on our backs and look up at the curious roof which twisted about like boughs in the wind, enjoying the jungle smell of raw wood, bamboos, and withered palm leaves.

One day Knut had an involuntary swim in company with a shark. No one was ever allowed to swim away from the raft, both on account of the raft's drift and because of sharks. But one day it was extra quiet, and we had just pulled on board such sharks as had been following us, so permission was given for a quick dip in the sea. Knut plunged in and had gone quite a long way before he came up to the surface to crawl back. At that moment we saw from the mast a shadow bigger than Knut coming up behind him, deeper down. We shouted warnings as quietly as we

could so as not to create a panic, and
Knut heaved himself toward the
side of the raft. But the shadow
below belonged to a still better
swimmer, which shot up from the
depths and gained on Knut. They
reached the raft at the same time.
While Knut was clambering on
board the raft, a six-foot shark
glided past right under his stomach
and stopped beside the raft. We
gave it a dainty dolphin's head to
thank it for not having snapped.

Generally it is smell more than
sight which excites the sharks' hunger. We have sat with our legs in
the water to test them, and they
have swum toward us till they were
two or three feet away, only quietly
to turn their tails toward us again.
But, if the water was in the least
bloodstained, as it was when we had
been cleaning fish, sharks would
suddenly collect like blue-bottles
from a long way off. If we flung out
shark's guts, they simply went mad
and dashed about in a blind frenzy.
They savagely devoured the liver of
their own kind and then, if we put
a foot into the sea, they came for
it like rockets and even dug their
teeth into the logs where the foot
had been. The mood of a shark may

vary immensely, the animal being completely at the mercy of its own emotions.

The last stage in our encounter with sharks was that we began to pull their tails. Pulling animals' tails is held to be an inferior form of sport, but that may be because no one before had tried it on a shark. For it was, in truth, a lively form of sport.

To get hold of a shark by the tail, we first had to give it a real tidbit. It was ready to stick its head high out of the water to get it. Usually it had its food served dangling in a bag. For, if one has fed a shark directly by hand once, it is no longer amusing. If one feeds dogs or tame bears by hand, they set their teeth into the meat and tear and worry it till they get a bite off or until they get the whole piece for themselves. But, if one holds out a large dolphin at a safe distance from the shark's head, the shark comes up and smacks his jaws together, and, without one's having felt the slightest tug, half the dolphin is suddenly gone, and one is left sitting with a tail in one's hand. We had found it a hard job to cut the dolphin in two with knives, but in a fraction of a second the shark, moving its triangular saw teeth quickly sideways, had chopped off the backbone and everything else like a sausage machine.

When the shark turned quietly to go under again, its tail flickered up above the surface and was easy to grasp. The shark's skin was just like sandpaper to hold on to, and inside the upper point of its tail there was an indentation which might have been made solely to allow of a good grip. If we once got a firm grasp there, there was no chance of our grip's not holding. Then we had to give a jerk, before the shark could collect itself, and get as much as possible of the tail pulled in tight over the logs.

For a few seconds the shark realized nothing. Then it began to wriggle and struggle in a spiritless manner with the fore part of its body for without the help of its tail a shark cannot get up any speed. The other fins are only apparatus for balancing and steering. After a few desperate jerks, during which we had to keep a tight hold of the tail, the surprised shark became quite crestfallen and dispirited, and, as the loose stomach began to sink down toward the head, the shark at last became completely paralyzed.

When the shark had become quiet and, as it were, hung stiff awaiting developments, it was time for us to haul in with all our might. We seldom got more than half the heavy fish up out of the water; then the shark too woke up and did the rest itself. With violent jerks it

swung its head round and up on to the logs; and then we had to tug with all our might and jump well out of the way, and that pretty quickly, if we wanted to save our legs. For now the shark was in no kindly mood. Jerking itself round in great leaps, it thrashed at the bamboo wall, using its tail as a sledge hammer. The huge jaws were opened wide, and the rows of teeth bit and snapped in the air for anything they could reach. It might happen that the war dance ended in the shark's tumbling overboard and disappearing for good after its shameful humiliation; but most of-

ten the shark flung itself about on the logs aft, till we got a running noose round the root of its tail or till it had ceased to gnash its devilish teeth forever.

The parrot was quite thrilled when we had a shark on deck. It came scurrying out of the bamboo cabin and climbed up the wall at frantic speed till it found itself a good, safe lookout post on the palm-leaf roof, and there it sat shaking its head or fluttered to and fro along the ridge, shrieking with excitement. It had become an excellent sailor at an early date and was always bubbling over with humor and laughter. We reckoned ourselves as seven on board—six of us and the green parrot. At night the parrot crept into its cage under the roof of the bamboo cabin, but in the daytime it strutted about the deck or hung on to guy ropes and stays and did fascinating acrobatic exercises.

At the start of the voyage we had turnbuckles on the stays of the mast but they wore the ropes; so we replaced them by ordinary running knots. When the stays stretched and grew slack from sun and wind, all hands had to turn to and brace up the mast. While we were hauling and pulling, the parrot would call out with its cracked voice: "Haul! Haul! Ho, ho, ho, ho, ha ha ha!" And if it made us laugh, it laughed till it shook at its own cleverness and swung round and round on the stays.

At first the parrot was the bane of our radio operators. They might be sitting happily absorbed in the radio corner with their magic earphones on and perhaps in contact with a radio "ham" in Oklahoma. Then their earphones would suddenly go dead, and they could not get a sound, however much they coaxed the wires and turned the knobs. The parrot had been busy and bitten off the wire of the aerial. This was specially tempting in the early days, when the wire was sent up with a little balloon. But one day the parrot became seriously ill. It sat in its cage and moped and touched no food for two days, while its droppings glittered with golden scraps of aerial. Then the radio operators repented of their angry words and the parrot of its misdeeds, and from that day Torstein and Knut were its chosen friends and the parrot would never sleep anywhere but in the radio corner.

The parrot's mother tongue was Spanish when it first came on board. Bengt declared it took to talking Spanish with a Norwegian accent long before it began to imitate Torstein's favorite ejaculations in full-blooded Norwegian.

We enjoyed the parrot's humor and brilliant colors for two months, till a big sea came on board from astern while it was on its way down the stay from the masthead. When we discovered that the parrot had gone overboard, it was too late. We did not see it. And the *Kon-Tiki* could not be turned or stopped; if anything went overboard from the raft, we had no chance of turning back for it—numerous experiences had shown that.

The loss of the parrot had a depressing effect on our spirits the first evening; we knew that exactly the same thing would happen to us if we fell overboard on a solitary night watch. We tightened up on all the safety regulations, brought into use new life lines for the night watch, and frightened one another out of believing that we were safe because things had gone well in the first two months. One careless step, one thoughtless movement, could send us where the green parrot had gone, even in broad daylight.

On July 21 the wind suddenly died away again. It was oppressive and absolutely still, and we knew from previous experience what this might mean. And, right enough, after a few violent gusts from east and west and south, the wind freshened up to a breeze from southward, where black, threatening clouds had again rushed up over the horizon. Herman was out with his anemometer all the time, measuring already fifty feet and more per second, when suddenly Torstein's sleeping bag went overboard. And what happened in the next few seconds took a much shorter time than it takes to tell it.

Herman tried to catch the bag as it went, took a rash step, and fell overboard. We heard a faint cry for help amid the noise of the waves, and saw Herman's head and a waving arm as well as some vague green object twirling about in the water near him. He was struggling for life to get back to the raft through the high seas which had lifted him out from the port side. Torstein, who was at the steering oar aft, and I myself, up in the bow, were the first to perceive him, and we went cold with fear. We bellowed "Man overboard!" at the top of our lungs as we rushed to the nearest life-saving gear. The others had not heard Herman's cry because of the noise of the sea, but in a trice there was life and bustle on deck. Herman was an excellent swimmer; would he manage to crawl back to the edge of the raft before it was too late?

Torstein seized the bamboo drum round which was the line we used for the lifeboat. It was the only time on the whole voyage that this line got caught up. Herman was now on a level with the stern of the raft but a few yards away, and his last hope was to crawl to the blade of the steering oar and hang on to it. As he missed the end of the logs, he reached out for the oar blade, but it slipped away from him. And there he lay, just where experience had shown we could get nothing back.

While Bengt and I launched the dinghy, Knut and Erik threw out the life belt. Carrying a long line, it hung ready for use on the corner of the cabin roof, but today the wind was so strong that when it was thrown it was simply blown back to the raft. After a few unsuccessful throws Herman was already far astern of the steering oar, swimming desperately to keep up with the raft, while the distance increased with each gust of wind.

He realized that henceforth the gap would go on increasing, but he set a faint hope on the dinghy which we had now got into the water. Without the line, which acted as a brake, it would perhaps be possible to drive the rubber raft to meet the swimming man, but whether the rubber raft would ever get back to the *Kon-Tiki* was another matter.

Nevertheless, three men in a rubber dinghy had some chance; one man in the sea had none.

Then we suddenly saw Knut take off and plunge headfirst into the sea. He had the life belt in one hand and was heaving himself along. Every time Herman's head appeared on a wave back Knut was gone, and every time Knut came up Herman was not there. But then we saw both heads at once; they had swum to meet each other and both were hanging on to the life belt. Knut waved his arm, and, as the rubber raft had meanwhile been hauled on board, all four of us took hold of the line of the life belt and hauled for dear life, with our eyes fixed on the great dark object which was visible just behind the two men.

This same mysterious beast in the water was pushing a big greenish-black triangle up above the wave crests. Only Herman knew then that the triangle did not belong to a shark or any other sea monster. It was an inflated corner of Torstein's watertight sleeping bag. But the sleeping bag did not remain floating for long after we had hauled the two men safe and sound on board. Whatever dragged the sleeping bag down into the depths had just missed a better prey.

"Glad I wasn't in it," said Torstein and took hold of the steering oar where he had let it go.

But otherwise there were not many wisecracks that evening. We all felt a chill running through nerve and bone for a long time afterward. But the cold shivers were mingled with a warm thankfulness that there were still six of us on board.

For five days the weather varied between full storm and light gale. Then on the fifth day the heavens split to show a glimpse of blue, and the malignant, black cloud cover gave place to the ever victorious blue sky as the storm passed on. We had come through the gale.

Expressing Opinions

This episode is taken from Thor Heyerdahl's *Kon-Tiki*, a true account of the one hundred and one days which six men spent on the Pacific until they reached a South Sea island. They set out from Peru with the intention of proving it was possible to make such a trip and that perhaps such trips from east to west across the Pacific Ocean had been made in the past.

1. Do you think it is justifiable to take such risks? Why?
2. From what you read in this selection, do you think these men benefited mankind by their expedition? Explain your answer.
3. Would you like to read the book *Kon-Tiki*? Give two reasons.

Drawing Inferences

These statements are gleaned from the selection. Copy the sentences, then skim the story to locate the paragraph from which each inference was taken. Beside each sentence write the page number and the first and last words of the paragraph which expresses the thought.

1. These adventurers became so familiar with their strange appearance that they scarcely noticed it after a while.
2. *Kon-Tiki* and its passengers did present an amusing sight.
3. A shark could easily devour a human being.
4. The raft was so much at the mercy of the wind that it was not safe for anyone to go far from it even in the dinghy.
5. Knut proved his bravery and the fact that he could swim.
6. Herman's near-drowning had a sobering effect on *Kon-Tiki's* party.

John Gillespie McGee, Jr.

High Flight

OH! I have slipped the surly bonds of earth
And danced the skies on laughter-silvered wings;
Sunward I've climbed, and joined the tumbling mirth
Of sun-split clouds—and done a hundred things
You have not dreamed of—wheeled and soared and swung
High in the sunlit silence. Hov'ring there
I've chased the shouting wind along, and flung
My eager craft through footless halls of air.

Up, up the long, delirious, burning blue
I've topped the wind-swept heights with easy grace
Where never lark, not even eagle flew—
And, while with silent lifting mind I've trod
The high untrespassed sanctity of space,
Put out my hand and touched the face of God.

ANTOINE DE SAINT-EXUPÉRY

Prisoner of the Sand[1]

I BEGAN a slow descent, intending to slip under the mass of clouds. Meanwhile I had had a look at my map. One thing was sure—the land below me lay at sea level, and there was no risk of conking against a hill. Down I went, flying due north so that the lights of the cities would strike square into my windows. I must have overflown them, and should therefore see them on my left.

Now I was flying below the cumulus. But alongside was another cloud hanging lower down on the left. I swerved so as not to be caught in its net, and headed north-northeast. This second cloud-bank certainly went down a long way, for it blocked my view of the horizon. I dared not give up any more altitude. My altimeter registered 1200 feet, but I had no notion of the atmospheric pressure here. Prévot leaned toward me and I shouted to him, "I'm going out to sea. I'd rather come down on it than risk a crash here."

[1]From *Wind, Sand and Stars*, copyright, 1939, by Antoine de Saint-Exupéry. Slightly abridged and reprinted by special permission of the publishers, Harcourt, Brace and Company, Inc.

As a matter of fact, there was nothing to prove that we had not drifted over the sea already. Below that cloud-bank visibility was exactly nil. I hugged my window, trying to read below me, to discover flares, signs of life. I was a man raking dead ashes, trying in vain to retrieve the flame of life in a hearth.

"A lighthouse!"

Both of us spied it at the same moment, that winking decoy! What madness! Where was that phantom light, that invention of the night? For at the very second when Prévot and I leaned forward to pick it out of the air where it had glittered nine hundred feet below our wings, suddenly, at that very instant . . .

"Oh!"

I am quite sure that this was all I said. I am quite sure that all I felt was a terrific crash that rocked our world to its foundations. We had crashed against the earth at a hundred and seventy miles an hour. I am quite sure that in the split second that followed, all I expected was the great flash of ruddy light of the explosion in which Prévot and I were to be blown up together. Neither he nor I had felt the least emotion of any kind. . . .

One second, two seconds passed, and the plane still quivered while I waited with a grotesque impatience for the forces within it to burst it like a bomb. . . . Five seconds passed; six seconds. Suddenly we were seized by a spinning motion, a shock that jerked our cigarettes out of the window and pulverized the starboard wing—and then nothing, nothing but a frozen immobility.

I shouted to Prévot: "Jump!"

And in that instant he cried out: "Fire!"

We dove together through the wrecked window and found ourselves standing side by side, sixty feet from the plane.

I said: "Are you hurt?"

He answered: "Not a bit."

But he was rubbing his knee.

"Better run your hands over yourself," I said; "move about a bit. Sure no bones are broken?"

He answered: "I'm all right. It's that emergency pump." . . .

Finally he stopped staring at the plane—which had not gone up in flames—and stared at me instead. And he said again: "I'm all right. It's that emergency pump. It got me in the knee."

Why we were not blown up, I do not know. I switched on my electric torch and went back over the furrow in the ground traced by the plane. . . . At the point of impact there was a hole in the sand that looked as if it had been made by a plow. . . . We owed our lives to the fact that this desert was surfaced with round black pebbles which had rolled over and over like ball-bearings beneath us. They must have rained upward to the heavens as we shot through them.

Prévot disconnected the batteries for fear of fire by short circuit. I leaned against the motor and turned the situation over in my mind. . . . All I could make out was that we had crashed in an empty square two hundred and fifty miles on each side.

Prévot came up and sat down beside me. "I can't believe that we're alive," he said.

I said nothing. Even that thought could not cheer me. A germ of an idea was at work in my mind and was already bothering me. Telling Prévot to switch on his torch as a landmark, I walked straight out, scrutinizing the ground in the light of my own torch as I went.

I went forward slowly, swung round in a wide arc, and changed direction a number of times. I kept my eyes fixed on the ground like a man hunting a lost ring.

Only a little while before I had been straining just as hard to see a gleam of light from the air. Through the darkness I went, bowed over the traveling disk of white light. "Just as I thought," I said to myself, and I went slowly back to the plane. I sat down beside the cabin and ruminated. I had been looking for a reason to hope and had failed to find it. I had been looking for a sign of life, and no sign of life had appeared.

"Prévot, I couldn't find a single blade of grass."

Prévot said nothing, and I was not sure he had understood. Well, we could talk about it again when the curtain rose at dawn. Meanwhile I was dead tired and all I could think was, "Two hundred and fifty miles more or less in the desert."

Suddenly I jumped to my feet. "Water!" I said.

Gas tanks and oil tanks were smashed in. So was our supply of drinking-water. The sand had drunk everything. We found a pint of coffee in a battered thermos flask and half a pint of white wine in another. We filtered both, and poured them into one flask. There were some grapes, too, and a single orange. Meanwhile I was computing: "All this will last us five hours of tramping in the sun."

We crawled into the cabin and waited for dawn. I stretched out, and as I settled down to sleep I took stock of our situation. We didn't know where we were; we had less than a quart of liquid between us;

if we were not too far off the Bengasi-Cairo lane, we should be found in a week, and that would be too late. Yet it was the best we could hope for. If, on the other hand, we had drifted off our course, we shouldn't be found in six months. One thing was sure—we could not count on being picked up by a plane; the men who came out for us would have two thousand miles to cover. . . .

. . . Prévot and I pulled ourselves together. There was still a chance, slender as it was, that we might be saved miraculously by a plane. On the other hand, we couldn't stay here and perhaps miss a near-by oasis. We would walk all day and

come back to the plane before dark. And before going off we would write our plan in huge letters in the sand.

With this I curled up and settled down to sleep. I was happy to go to sleep. . . . I was not yet thirsty; I felt strong; and I surrendered myself to sleep as to an aimless journey. Reality lost ground before the advance of dreams.

Ah, but things were different when I awoke!

In times past I have loved the Sahara. I have spent nights alone in the path of marauding tribes and have waked up with untroubled mind in the golden emptiness of the desert where the wind like a sea had raised sandwaves upon its surface. Asleep under the wing of my plane I have looked forward with confidence to being rescued next day. But this was not the Sahara!

Prévot and I walked along the slopes of rolling mounds. The ground was sand covered over with a single layer of shining black pebbles. They gleamed like metal scales and all the domes about us shone like coats of mail. We had dropped down into a mineral world and were hemmed in by iron hills.

When we reached the top of the first crest we saw in the distance another just like it, black and gleaming. As we walked we scraped the

ground with our boots, marking a trail over which to return to the plane. We went forward with the sun in our eyes. It was not logical to go due east like this, for everything—the weather reports, the duration of the flight—had made it plain that we had crossed the Nile. But I had started tentatively towards the west and had felt a vague foreboding I could not explain to myself. So I had put off the west till tomorrow. In the same way, provisionally, I had given up going north, though that led to the sea. . . .

We walked on for five hours and then the landscape changed. A river of sand seemed to be running through a valley, and we followed this river-bed, taking long strides in order to cover as much ground as possible and get back to the plane before night fell, if our march was in vain. Suddenly I stopped.

"Prévot!"

"What's up?"

"Our tracks!"

How long was it since we had forgotten to leave a wake behind us? We had to find it or die.

We went back, bearing to the right. When we had gone back far enough, we would make a right angle to the left and eventually intersect our tracks where we had still remembered to mark them.

This we did and were off again. The heat rose and with it came the mirages. But these were still the commonplace kind—sheets of water that materialized and then vanished as we neared them. We decided to cross the valley of sand and climb the highest dome in order to look round the horizon. . . .

When we had struggled up to the top of the black hump we sat down and looked at each other. At our feet lay our valley of sand, opening into a desert of sand whose dazzling brightness seared our eyes. As far as the eye could see lay empty space. But in that space the play of light created mirages which, this time, were of a disturbing kind, fortresses and minarets, angular geometric hulks. I could see also a black mass that pretended to be vegetation, overhung by the last of those clouds that dissolve during the day only to return at night. . . .

It was no good going on. The experiment was a failure. We would have to go back to our plane, to that red and white beacon which, perhaps, would be picked out by a flier. I was not staking great hopes on a rescue party, but it did seem to me our last chance of salvation. In any case, we had to get back to our few drops of liquid, for our throats were parched. We were imprisoned in this iron circle, captives of the curt dictatorship of thirst.

And yet, how hard it was to turn back when there was a chance that we might be on the road to life! . . . I knew I was doing the right thing by returning to the plane, and yet as I swung round and started back I was filled with portents of disaster.

We were resting on the ground beside the plane. Nearly forty miles of wandering this day. The last drop of liquid had been drained. No sign of life had appeared to the east. No plane had soared overhead. How long could we hold out? Already our thirst was terrible.

We had built up a great pyre out of bits of the splintered wing. Our gasoline was ready, and we had flung on the heap sheets of metal whose magnesium coating would burn with a hard white flame. We were waiting now for night to come down before we lighted our conflagration. But where were there men to see it?

Night fell and the flames rose. Prayerfully we watched our mute and radiant fanion mount resplendent into the night. As I looked I said to myself that this message was not only a cry for help, it was fraught also with a great deal of love. We were begging water, but we were also begging the communion of human society. Only man can create fire: let another flame light up the night; let man answer man!

I was haunted by a vision of my wife's eyes under the halo of her hair. Of her face I could see only the eyes, questioning me, looking at me yearningly. I am answering with all my strength! . . .

What I could do, I have done. What we could do, we have done. Nearly forty miles, almost without a drop to drink. Now there was no water left. Was it our fault that we could wait no longer? Suppose we had sat quietly by the plane, taking sips at the mouths of our water-bottles? But from the moment I had breathed in the moist bottom of the tin cup, a clock had started up in me. From the second when I had sucked up the last drop, I had begun to slip downhill. Could I help it if time like a river was carrying me away? Prévot was weeping. I tapped him on the shoulder and said, to console him: "If we're done for, we're done for, and that's all there is to it."

He said: "Do you think it's me I'm bawling about?" . . .

"Do you think it's me . . ." There you have what is truly unbearable! Every time I saw those yearning eyes it was as if a flame were searing me. They were like a scream for help, like the flares of a sinking ship. I felt that I should not sit idly by: I should jump up and run—anywhere! straight ahead of me! . . .

341

The magnesium had been licked off and the metal was glowing red. There was left only a heap of embers round which we crouched to warm ourselves. Our flaming call had spent itself. Had it set anything in the world in motion? I knew well enough that it hadn't. Here was a prayer that had of necessity gone unheard.

That was that.

I ought to get some sleep.

At daybreak I took a rag and mopped up a little dew on the wings. The mixture of water and paint and oil yielded a spoonful of nauseating liquid which we sipped because it would at least moisten our lips. . . .

There was still no sign that we were being sought; or rather they were doubtless hunting for us elsewhere, probably in Arabia. . . . When searchers have to cover two thousand miles of territory, it takes them a good two weeks to spot a plane in the desert from the sky.

They were probably looking for us all along the line from Tripoli to Persia. And still, with all this, I clung to the slim chance that they might pick us out. Was that not our only chance of being saved? I changed my tactics, determining to go reconnoitering by myself. Prévot would get another bonfire together and kindle it in the event that visitors showed up. But we were to have no callers that day.

So off I went without knowing whether or not I should have the stamina to come back. I remembered what I knew about this Libyan Desert. When, in the Sahara, humidity is still at 40 per cent of saturation, it is only 18 here in Libya. Life here evaporates like a vapor. Bedouins, explorers, and colonial officers all tell us that a man may go nineteen hours without water. Thereafter his eyes fill with light, and that marks the beginning of the end. The progress made by thirst is swift and terrible. But this northeast wind, this abnormal wind that had blown us out of our course and had marooned us on this plateau, was now prolonging our lives. What was the length of the reprieve it would grant us before our eyes began to fill with light? I went forward with the feeling of a man canoeing in mid-ocean.

I will admit that at daybreak this landscape seemed to me less infernal, and that I began my walk with my hands in my pockets, like a tramp on a highroad. The evening before we had set snares at the mouths of certain mysterious burrows in the ground, and the poacher in me was on the alert. I went first to have a look at our traps. They were empty.

Well, this meant that I should not be drinking blood today; and indeed I hadn't expected to. But though I was not disappointed, my curiosity was aroused. What was there in the desert for these animals to live on? These were certainly the holes of fennecs, a long-eared carnivorous sand-fox the size of a rabbit. . . .

I could imagine my little friend trotting blithely along at dawn and licking the dew off the rocks. Here the tracks were wider apart: my fennec had broken into a run. And now I see that a companion has joined him, and they have trotted on side by side. These signs of a morning stroll gave me a strange thrill. They were signs of life, and I loved them for that. I almost forgot that I was thirsty. . . .

I went on, finally, and the time came when, along with my weariness, something in me began to change. If those were not mirages, I was inventing them.

"Hi! Hi, there!"

I shouted and waved my arms, but the man I had seen waving at me turned out to be a black rock. Everything in the desert had grown animate. I stooped to waken a sleeping Bedouin and he turned into the trunk of a black tree. A

tree-trunk? Here in the desert? I was amazed and bent over to lift a broken bough. It was solid marble. . . .

Since yesterday I had walked nearly fifty miles. This dizziness that I felt came doubtless from my thirst. Or from the sun. It glittered on these hulks until they shone as if smeared with oil. . . . This world was a gigantic anvil upon which the sun beat down. I strode across this anvil and at my temples I could feel the hammer-strokes of the sun.

"Hi! Hi, there!" I called out.

"There is nothing there," I told myself. "Take it easy. You are delirious."

I had to talk to myself aloud, had to bring myself to reason. It was hard for me to reject what I was seeing, hard not to run towards that caravan plodding on the horizon. There! Do you see it?

"Fool! You know very well that you are inventing it."

"You mean that nothing in the world is real?"

Nothing in the world is real if that cross which I see ten miles off on the top of a hill is not real. Or is it a lighthouse? No, the sea does not lie in that direction. Then it must be a cross.

I had spent the night studying my map—but uselessly, since I did not know my position. Still, I had scrutinized all the signs that marked the marvelous presence of man. And somewhere on the map I had seen a little circle surmounted by just such a cross. I had glanced down at the legend to get an explanation of the symbol and had read: "Religious institution."

Close to the cross there had been a black dot. Again I had run my finger down the legend and had read: "Permanent well." My heart had jumped and I had repeated the legend aloud: "Permanent well, permanent well." What were all of Ali Baba's treasures compared with a permanent well? A little farther on were two white circles. "Temporary wells," the legend said. Not quite so exciting. And round about them was nothing . . . unless it was the blankness of despair.

But this must be my "religious institution"! The monks must certainly have planted a great cross on the hill expressly for men in our plight! All I had to do was to walk across to them. I should be taken in by those Dominicans. . . .

"But there are only Coptic monasteries in Libya!" I told myself.

. . . by those learned Dominicans. They have a great cool kitchen with red tiles, and out in the courtward a marvelous rusted pump. Beneath the rusted pump; beneath the rusted pump . . . you've guessed it! . . . beneath the rusted pump is dug the permanent well! Ah, what rejoicing when I ring at their gate, when I get my hands on the rope of the great bell.

"Madman! You are describing a house in Provence; and what's more, the house has no bell!"

. . . on the rope of the great bell. The porter will raise his arms to Heaven and cry out, "You are the messenger of the Lord!" and he will call aloud to all the monks. They will pour out of the monastery. They will welcome me with a great feast, as if I were the Prodigal Son. They will lead me to the kitchen and will say to me, "One moment, my son, one moment. We'll just be off to the permanent well." And I shall be trembling with happiness.

No, no! I will *not* weep just because there happens to be no cross on the hill.

The treasures of the west turned out to be mere illusion. I have veered due north. At least the north is filled with the sound of the sea.

Over the hilltop! Look over the hilltop at the horizon! There lies the most beautiful city in the whole world!

"You know perfectly well that is a mirage."

Of course I know it is a mirage! Am I the sort of man who can be fooled? But what if I *want* to go after that mirage? Suppose I enjoy indulging my hope? . . . What if I choose to walk straight ahead on light feet—for you must know that I have dropped my weariness behind me, I am happy now. . . .

345

It took the twilight to sober me. Suddenly I stopped, appalled to think how far I was from our base. In the twilight the mirage was dying. . . .

"A fine day's work you've done! Night will overtake you. You won't be able to go on before daybreak, and by that time your tracks will have been blown away and you'll be properly nowhere." . . .

Very good. I'll go back. But first I want to call out for help.

"Hi! Hi!"

. . . You can't tell me this planet is not inhabited. Where are its men?

"Hi! Hi!"

I was hoarse. My voice was gone. I knew it was ridiculous to croak like this, but—one more try: "Hi! Hi!"

And I turned back.

I had been walking two hours when I saw the flames of the bonfire that Prévot, frightened by my long absence, had sent up. They mattered very little to me now.

Another hour of trudging. Five hundred yards away. A hundred yards. Fifty yards. . . .

Amazement stopped me in my tracks. Joy surged up and filled my heart with its violence. In the firelight stood Prévot, talking to two Arabs who were leaning against the motor. He had not noticed me, for he was too full of his own joy. If only I had sat still and waited with him! I should have been saved already. Exultantly I called out: "Hi! Hi!"

The two Bedouins gave a start and stared at me. Prévot left them standing and came forward to meet me. I opened my arms to him. He caught me by the elbow. Did he think I was keeling over? I said: "At last, eh?"

"What do you mean?"

"The Arabs!"

"What Arabs?"

"Those Arabs there, with you."

Prévot looked at me queerly, and when he spoke I felt as if he were very reluctantly confiding a great secret to me: "There are no Arabs here."

Now I know I am going to cry.

A man can go nineteen hours without water; and what have we drunk since last night? A few drops of dew at dawn. But the northeast wind is still blowing, still slowing up the process of our evaporation. . . .

Well, it was broad daylight and time we were on our way. This time we should strike out as fast as we could, leave this cursed plateau, and tramp till we dropped in our tracks. . . .

"If I were alone in the world," Prévot said, "I'd lie down right here." . . .

East-northeast we tramped. If we had in fact crossed the Nile, each step was leading us deeper and deeper into the desert.

I don't remember anything about that day. I remember only my haste. . . . Of what happened when the chill of evening came, I remember more. But during the day I had simply turned to sand and was a being without mind.

When the sun set we decided to make camp. Oh, I knew as well as anybody that we should push on, that this one waterless night would finish us off. . . .

. . . Suppose I walked on: at the best I could do five or six miles more. Remember that in three days I had covered one hundred miles, practically without water.

Just as we stopped, Prévot said: "I swear to you I see a lake!"

"You're crazy."

"Have you ever heard of a mirage after sunset?" he challenged.

I didn't seem able to answer him. I had long ago given up believing my own eyes. Perhaps it was not a mirage; but in that case it was a hallucination. How could Prévot go on believing? But he was stubborn about it.

"It's only twenty minutes off. I'll go have a look."

His mulishness got on my nerves.

"Go ahead!" I shouted. "Take your little constitutional. Nothing better for a man. But let me tell you, if your lake exists it is salt. And whether it's salt or not, it's a devil of a way off." . . .

Prévot was already on his way, his eyes glassy. I knew the strength of these irresistible obsessions. I was thinking: "There are somnambulists who walk straight into locomotives." And I knew that Prévot would not come back. He would be seized by the vertigo of empty space and would be unable to turn back. And then he would keel over. He somewhere, and I somewhere else. Not that it was important.

. . . Lying now flat on my face on the stony ground, I took this occasion to write a letter for posthumous delivery. It gave me a chance, also, to take stock of myself again. I tried to bring up a little saliva . . . No saliva. If I kept my mouth closed, a kind of glue sealed my lips together. . . . However, I found I was still able to swallow, and I bethought me that I was still not seeing a blinding light in my eyes. . . .

Night fell. The moon had swollen since I last saw it. . . .

I thought of Prévot who was still not back. Not once had I heard him complain. That was a good thing. To hear him whine would have been unbearable. Prévot was a man.

What was that! Five hundred yards ahead of me I could see the light of his lamp. He had lost his way. I had no lamp with which to signal back. I stood up and shouted, but he could not hear me.

A second lamp, and then a third! God in Heaven! It was a search party and it was me they were hunting!

"Hi! Hi!" I shouted.

But they had not heard me. The three lamps were still signaling me.

"Tonight I am sane," I said to myself. "I am relaxed. I am not out of my head. Those are certainly three lamps and they are about five hundred yards off." I stared at them and shouted again, and again I gathered that they could not hear me.

Then, for the first and only time, I was really seized with panic. I could still run, I thought. "Wait! Wait!" I screamed. They seemed to be turning away from me, going off, hunting me elsewhere! And I stood tottering on the brink of life when there were arms out there ready to catch me! I shouted and screamed again and again.

They had heard me! An answering shout had come. I was strangling, suffocating, but I ran on, shouting as I ran, until I saw Prévot and keeled over.

When I could speak again I said: "Whew! When I saw all those lights . . ."

"What lights?"

God in Heaven, it was true! He was alone!

This time I was beyond despair. I was filled with a sort of dumb fury.

"What about your lake?" I rasped.

"As fast as I moved towards it, it moved back. I walked after it for about half an hour. Then it seemed still too far away, so I came back. But I am positive now, that it is a lake."

"You're crazy. Absolutely crazy. Why did you do it? Tell me. Why?"

What had he done? Why had he done it? I was ready to weep with indignation, yet I scarcely knew why I was so indignant.

Prévot mumbled his excuse: "I felt I had to find some water. You . . . your lips were awfully pale."

Well! My anger died within me. I passed my hand over my forehead as if I were waking out of sleep. I was suddenly sad. I said: "There was no mistake about it. I saw them as clearly as I see you now. Three lights there were. I tell you, Prévot, I saw them!"

Prévot made no comment. "Well," he said finally. "I guess we're in a bad way."

In this air devoid of moisture the soil is swift to give off its temperature. It was already very cold. I stood up and stamped about. But soon a violent fit of trembling came over me. My dehydrated blood was moving sluggishly and I was pierced by a freezing chill which was not merely the chill of night. My teeth were chattering and my whole body had begun to twitch. My hands shook so that I could not hold an electric torch. I who had never been sensitive to cold was about to die of cold. What a strange effect thirst can have! . . .

. . . To myself I said: "It isn't the cold. It's something else. It's the end." The simple fact was that I hadn't enough water in me. I had tramped too far yesterday and the day before when I was off by myself, and I was dehydrated. . . .

Confound it! Down on my knees again! We had with us a little store of medicines—a hundred grams of 90 per cent alcohol, the same of pure ether, and a small bottle of iodine. I tried to swallow a little of the ether: it was like swallowing a knife. Then I tried the alcohol: it contracted my gullet. I dug a pit in the sand, lay down in it, and flung handfuls of sand over me until all but my face was buried in it.

Prévot was able to collect a few twigs, and he lit a fire which soon burnt itself out. He wouldn't bury himself in the sand, but preferred to stamp round and round in a circle. That was foolish. . . .

So long as I lay absolutely motionless, I no longer felt the cold.

This allowed me to forget my body buried in the sand. I said to myself that I would not budge an inch, and would therefore never suffer again. . . .

Farewell, eyes that I loved! Do not blame me if the human body cannot go three days without water. I should never have believed that man was so truly the prisoner of the springs and freshets. . . . We take it for granted that a man is able to stride straight out into the world. We believe that man is free We never see the cord that binds him to wells and fountains. . . . Let man take but one step too many . . . and the cord snaps. . . .

. . . My mind was befuddled and I heard myself say: "There is a dry heart here, a dry heart that cannot know the relief of tears."

I scrambled to my feet. "We're off, Prévot," I said. "Our throats are still open. Get along, man!"

The wind that shrivels up a man in nineteen hours was now blowing out of the west. My gullet was not yet shut, but it was hard and painful and I could feel that there was a rasp in it. Soon that cough would begin that I had been told about and was now expecting. My tongue was becoming a nuisance. But most serious of all, I was beginning to see shining spots before my eyes. When those spots changed into flames, I should simply lie down. . . .

Our first day's nourishment had been a few grapes. In the next three days each of us ate half an orange and a bit of cake. If there had been anything left now, we could not have eaten it because we had no saliva with which to masticate it. I was not hungry. Thirsty I was, yes, and it seemed that I was suffering less from thirst than from the effects of thirst. Gullet hard. Tongue like plaster-of-Paris. A rasping in the throat. A horrible taste in the mouth. . . .

The previous day I had tramped without hope. Today the word "hope" had grown meaningless. Today we were tramping simply because we were tramping. Probably oxen work for the same reason. Yesterday I had dreamed of a paradise of orange trees. Today I would not give a button for paradise; I did not believe oranges existed. When I thought about myself I found in me nothing but a heart squeezed dry. . . . I felt no sorrow. . . . The sun had dried up the springs of tears in me.

And yet, what was that? A ripple of hope went through me like a faint breeze over a lake. . . . I looked at Prévot. The same astonishing thing had happened to him as to me, but he was as far from guessing its significance as I was.

350

I swear to you that something is about to happen. I swear that life has sprung in this desert. I swear that this emptiness, this stillness, has suddenly become more stirring than a tumult on a public square.

"Prévot! Footprints! We are saved!"

We had wandered from the trail of the human species . . . we had found ourselves alone on earth . . . and here, imprinted in the sand, were the divine and naked feet of man!

"Look, Prévot, here two men stood together and then separated."

"Here a camel knelt."

"Here . . ."

But it was not true that we were already saved. It was not enough to squat down and wait. Before long we should be past saving. Once the cough has begun, the progress made by thirst is swift.

Still, I believed in that caravan swaying somewhere in the desert, heavy with its cargo of treasure.

We went on. Suddenly . . . Prévot grabbed my arm: "Did you hear that?"

"What?"

"The cock."

"Why . . . why, yes, I did."

To myself I said: "Fool! Get it through your head! This means life!"

I had one last hallucination—three dogs chasing one another. Prévot looked, but could not see them. However, both of us waved our arms at a Bedouin. Both of us shouted with all the breath in our bodies, and laughed for happiness.

But our voices could not carry thirty yards. The Bedouin on his slow-moving camel had come into view from behind a dune and now he was moving slowly out of sight. The man was probably the only Arab in this desert, sent by a demon to materialize and vanish before the eyes of us who could not run.

We saw in profile on the dune another Arab. We shouted, but our shouts were whispers. We waved our arms and it seemed to us that they must fill the sky with monstrous signals. Still the Bedouin stared with averted face away from us.

At last, slowly, slowly he began a right angle turn in our direction. . . .

The miracle had come to pass. He was walking towards us over the sand like a god over the waves.

The Arab looked at us without a word. He placed his hands upon our shoulders and we obeyed him: we stretched out upon the sand. Race, language, religion were forgotten. There was only this humble nomad with the hands of an archangel on our shoulders.

Face to the sand, we waited. And when the water came, we drank like calves with our faces in the basin, and with a greediness which alarmed the Bedouin so that from

352

time to time he pulled us back. But as soon as his hand fell away from us we plunged our faces anew into the water. . . .

You, Bedouin of Libya who saved our lives, though you will dwell for ever in my memory, yet I shall never be able to recapture your features. You are Humanity and your face comes into my mind simply as man incarnate. You, our beloved fellow man, did not know who we might be, and yet you recognized us without fail. And I, in my turn, shall recognize you in the faces of all mankind. . . .

This is the end of my story. Lifted on to a camel, we went on for three hours. Then, broken with weariness, we asked to be set down at a camp while the cameleers went on ahead for help. Towards six in the evening a car manned by armed Bedouins came to fetch us. A half-hour later we were set down at the house of a Swiss engineer named Raccaud who was operating a soda factory beside saline deposits in the desert. He was unforgettably kind to us. By midnight we were in Cairo.

I awoke between white sheets. Through the curtains came the rays of a sun that was no longer an enemy. I spread butter and honey on my bread. I smiled. I recaptured the savor of my childhood and all its marvels. And I read and reread the telegram from those dearest to me in all the world whose three words had shattered me:

"So terribly happy!"

Writing a Character Sketch

Think of the events of the story and the two men involved. Write a brief character sketch of either man from what you learned in the story.

Comparing Two Stories

Recall the story "Across the Pacific by Raft." Which of the two stories did you like better? Why? Both of these accounts are actual happenings. If you didn't know this, would you think they were fictional? Explain.

What would you have done if you found yourself in the circumstances in which Prévot and Saint-Exupéry found themselves?

JOYCE KILMER

Citizen of the World

No LONGER of Him be it said,
"He hath no place to lay His head."

In every land a constant lamp
Flames by His small and mighty camp.

There is no strange and distant place
That is not gladdened by His face.

And every nation kneels to hail
The Splendour shining through Its veil.

Cloistered beside the shouting street,
Silent, He calls me to His feet.

Imprisoned for His love of me,
He makes my spirit greatly free.

And through my lips that uttered sin
The King of Glory enters in.

A Letter to Mary

Many nuns who never listened to a radio heard Pope Pius XII make his first broadcast to cloistered communities of nuns around the world.

The address was the first in a program called "Invisible Audiences" for the Contemplative Orders who devote their lives to prayer and meditation. One hundred thousand cloistered nuns—Cistercians, Benedictines, Dominicans, Visitation Nuns, and Poor Clares listened to the broadcast from the Vatican.

In Italy, France, and Spain the nuns heard the Pontiff's praise of them. In Latin countries, too, they found "spiritual union" with his message. In America, where many hundreds of young women seek to become novices each year, they listened as Pope Pius lauded their "contemplation of God and divine truths," but warned them not to despise human learning and advancement.

In a monastery in Connecticut, appropriately set in a town called Bethlehem, a young nun listened to the far-off Roman broadcast. Not long before, she had relinquished worldly achievement and the closeness of family ties to join this contemplative, cloistered community.

To Regina Laudis, in lasting affection and with a spirit of pilgrimage, come her parents and old family friends for infrequent visits permitted in the hospitality offered by the Rule of St. Benedict. Thinking only of the young nun behind the grille by her childhood name, two old friends wrote their impressions of her life, which now carries out the Benedictine motto, Ora et Labora, pray and work.

DEAR MARY,

Beyond the turnpikes lies Regina Laudis and an experience etched indelibly in these old minds. We shall forever feel indebted to your Dad and Mother for allowing us to tag along. It was a privilege indeed to make the pilgrimage. For now, first-hand, we know the splendor of simplicity and selflessness.

We caught a glimpse of this splendor as we approached. Here was stuff to stun the senses—Connecticut, the charmer, with October opulence, splashing its liquid sunlight across roadsides ablaze with scarlet and gold.

Simplicity and selflessness may be the keys to your citadel. But the stranger within your gates senses much, much more. It's a bit eerie —something like suddenly meeting up with humans who have found that "perfect happiness" which some say is unattainable in this life. Maybe the theologians might say it's happiness born of humility. But, whatever it is, all you cloistered nuns seem to have it. And it's the most inspiring phenomenon these old eyes have gazed upon.

We saw it in action beside the grille when we visited with you and other inspiring members of your community. It shone in the faces and was eloquent in the voices of those enraptured charmers you call the oblates. It graced the grounds, the gardens, the art shop, the chapel . . . talent, beauty, station, fortune . . . all the exquisites of earth . . . signed, sealed and delivered joyously *ad majorem Dei gloriam*. It recalls the final stanza from an old poem penned by Gerald Griffin:

Behold her, ye worldly! Behold her, ye vain!
Who shrink from the pathway of virtue and pain;
Who yield up to pleasure your nights and your days,
Forgetful of service, forgetful of praise.
Ye lazy philosophers, self-seeking men;
Ye fireside philanthropists, great at the pen;
How stands in the balance your eloquence, weighed
With the life and the deeds of that high-born maid?

We'll long recall our attending Mass and receiving Communion in the chapel at Regina Laudis. Never before—and in sixty-eight years I've been in many chapels and churches—have I known a similar experience. The ritual wherein the receiver selects with his own hands in advance of consecration the Host he will receive at Communion is distinctively different and wholly in keeping with the uniqueness of your cloister.

It is indeed a holy and a wholesome thought to know that we, the sinners, the sleepless, have living saints to plead our cause. So, here's to you, joyous Shepherdesses of the Sleepless . . . and to your prayers, works and sacrifices . . . all done in the deathless ceramics of humility . . . and all-powerful at the throne of God!

With admiration and devotion,

Lou and Laura Pryor

357

Using the Glossary

Locate the following words in the Glossary and write them, with their meanings, on your paper.

relinquished eerie phenomenon
citadel   oblates

Answering Specific Questions

If you read this brief selection carefully, you should be able to answer these questions without referring to the text.

1. Who is Mary?
2. To which Order did she belong?
3. Where is Regina Laudis located?
4. What ritual concerning Holy Communion impressed the authors?
5. Who is referred to as "that high-born maid" in the poem by Gerald Griffin which is quoted in the letter?

Sister M. Madeleva, C.S.C.

Gates

The oranges at Jaffa gate
Are heaped in hills; men sell and buy
Or sit and watch the twisted road
Or David's tower against the sky.

The Golden Gate is walled with stone.
No king can pass nor prophet see
The valley of Jehoshaphat,
The olives of Gethsemane.

St. Stephen's is a quiet gate,
A simple door that lets in dawn.
Its hill, its walls, its ancient stones,
What strange things they have looked upon

Asses, belabored, stumble past;
Traffickers clamor; priests debate;
A child begs alms; a blind man gropes
To sunshine at Damascus gate.

The world has narrow gates and wide;
Men seek their loves through all of them
And I have come here, seeking mine,
Jerusalem, Jerusalem!

BURKE WALSH

The Vatican and the Nations

IN TIME OF PEACE and in time of war I have seen the Vatican. From the summit of a Roman hill I have watched the gleam of Italian sunshine upon streets filled with civilians or soldiers, all of them going in pilgrimage toward St. Peter's Basilica and the Vatican Palace. Men and women from nearly every country in the world, they moved forward with one purpose, the desire to see the capital of Christendom, and the Vicar of Christ on earth.

What were they seeing, these pilgrims from afar, as they moved across the bridges of the yellow Tiber and through the broad Via della Conciliazione, the avenue created to mark the settlement of differences between the Church and the government of Italy?

The dome of St. Peter's is what the pilgrim sees first and remembers longest. In time, however, he grows to a fuller appreciation of the famous Bernini Colonnade, those two semicircular arcades, stretching out like loving arms from either side of the Basilica and almost completely encircling St. Peter's Square. They are masterpieces of architecture, but they are also symbols of the loving care and protection of Holy Mother Church, nowhere better shown than here— the center of Christendom.

Vatican City is the world's smallest independent state. It lies entirely within the city of Rome, and its territory covers less than one square mile. Here are the world-famous Basilica of St. Peter and the Vatican Palace and Gardens. The structure which houses the Vatican radio station is in the Vatican gardens. The Vatican observatory, formerly here, is now at Castel Gandolfo, the Pope's summer residence near Rome. Sundry other buildings, found within the limits of the tiny state, are the Belvedere Palace, which affords a place of residence for members of the clergy who work at the Vatican; a mosaic works, a printing establishment which produces books and papers in many languages, a modern electric bakery, quarters for the members of the various Vatican armed forces, the Ethiopian Seminary, the office building for the government of Vatican City, and some other edifices.

It comes as a surprise to some that St. Peter's, the most famous church in the world, is not "the mother church of Christendom," and that the Vatican, long recognized as the home of the Holy Father, has not always been the place of residence of the Popes.

The Supreme Head of the Catholic Church, as successor of Saint Peter, is Bishop of Rome. The Pope's cathedral is St. John Lateran, situated in the city of Rome. To this edifice belongs the title "Mother Church of Christendom." Likewise, the Popes originally made their residence in the adjoining Lateran Palace. In time the Pontiff came to live nearer to St. Peter's Basilica, in the Vatican Palace. The greater part of the structure known as the Vatican Palace, which is really a number of buildings erected at different times, is given over to museums, picture galleries, and libraries, which house some of the world's finest collections.

The parish church of the State of Vatican City is not St. Peter's Basilica, as many might suppose, but a tiny edifice named in honor of Saint Anna. It is located almost on the limits of Vatican City, near

the Gate of Saint Anna, which leads into the Vatican from the Via di Porta Angelica, a street on the eastern boundary of the Vatican State.

In this church the residents of Vatican City have their marriages solemnized. Here children born in Vatican City are baptized. Here the Mass of Requiem is said at the funeral of any citizen of Vatican City.

The St. Peter's Basilica that one

The Pietà by Michelangelo

Photo Alinari

sees today—the result of the genius of such artistic giants as Bramante, Michelangelo, Maderno, and Bernini—is the second large church to stand on this site, the burial place of the Prince of the Apostles. The first Basilica of St. Peter was begun by the Emperor Constantine at the beginning of the fourth century. The present structure was begun in the fifteenth century.

One hundred and seventy-six years (1450–1626) were required for the construction of St. Peter's Basilica. The original design of Bramante was that of a Greek cross, with four equal wings. After Bramante's death, Raphael, assisted by Fra Giocondo and da Sangallo, decided to give the temple the form of a Latin cross. Finally the work was put in the hands of Michelangelo, then seventy years old, who returned to the idea of the Greek cross and undertook the building of the magnificent cupola.

St. Peter's is the largest church in the world, covering six acres and allowing 80,000 people to stand in it. The floor of the nave is inlaid marble, the ceiling is of gold. Rising over the tomb of St. Peter is the pope's magnificent altar. Soaring over all is Michelangelo's dome.

The Basilica of St. Peter contains many rare treasures, including the *Pietà* by Michelangelo, the world-famous statue of Saint Peter, and other renowned sculptures. But these are few compared with the rich treasures housed in the Palace of the Vatican. They include the famous Vatican Library, the Sistine Chapel, with its ceiling frescoes by Michelangelo, the Raphael Rooms, the Borgia Apartment, and the Gallery of Statues, and such supreme individual pieces as Raphael's *Transfiguration*, the Laocoön group, and the Apollo Belvedere.

And yet it is not in the size of the massive church, the richness of its decorations, the artistic treasures of the Vatican Palace, the beauty of the Vatican Gardens, that the importance of this tiny State of Vatican City—smaller even than Monaco, which covers 5337 acres, or San Marino, which has a population of 10,000—is to be sought. We, and the world, look to Vatican City because it is truly the center of Christendom, the home of the Vicar of Christ, the hub of the Catholic Church.

What is the influence in the world, one might ask, of this tiniest of states, whose armed forces consist of three companies of ceremonial guards and a small gendarmery, whose total number is but a few hundred and whose "weapons" are more colorful than useful? The State of Vatican City, the answer might be, has two aspects: it is an independent, sovereign state among other nations, and it is the center of the Universal Church. As a purely political unit, its influence is not great. As a moral and spiritual force, its influence is certainly enormous. It is, by all odds, the greatest in the world.

The Church, as Pontiff after Pontiff has emphasized, is supranational. That is, it is above any nation and all nations, above their individual and collective disagreements, their bickerings, their contentions, and their ambitions. This has been shown time and again in the letters, statements, and actions of the Popes. His Holiness receives his visitors with "full consciousness" that "Catholic" embraces all nations and that "the love and care of the Vicar of Christ—though he himself necessarily by nature belongs to one particular people—do not exclude anyone, but belong equally to all," and that he loves "all in the charity of Christ."

But it is not alone, or even chiefly, by impressing those who come personally to the Vatican that the Holy See has its influence upon all peoples.

The efforts of Popes Pius XI and Pius XII to prevent the outbreak of World War II are known throughout the world. It is true that these efforts, however great and unceasing, were unsuccessful. But the world knows that this was not through any fault of the Popes. The world also knows, now, that the Vatican had then a better appreciation than was to be found elsewhere of the scope of World War II and of the horror, the suffering, and the ruin that it would entail.

In connection with the efforts of the Supreme Pontiffs to prevent the outbreak of war should be considered the strivings of Pope Pius XII to lessen suffering and bring about a just and lasting peace, once war had broken out.

Each year at Christmas time, beginning in 1939, the Pope spoke to the world on the problem of peace, outlining systematically, step by step, the foundation that had to be laid for lasting harmony among nations. Each of these discourses, and particularly that of 1944, with its insistence on true democracy, received world-wide attention. For the most part, the program of the Vatican was warmly applauded. Some who did not applaud received the words of the Sovereign Pontiff respectfully and with attention. In godless countries the messages were berated. But the important thing is that the words of the Pope received attention round the world. The influence of the Vatican was felt in all corners of the earth.

And, what is more important, though the pleas of the Popes seeking to prevent the war were not heeded by the rulers of nations, and Pius XII's blueprints for a just and lasting peace have not been formally adopted by the leaders of

the world, the principles handed down by His Holiness have become known among an amazing number of the rank and file in many countries, and are being accepted in many influential, if unofficial, quarters. Some of the points brought to public attention by the Papal messages have been incorporated in important international plans for a better world.

The Christianizing influence that has spread from the Vatican through the centuries has likewise been a civilizing influence. This is no less true of missionary activities, directed from the Vatican, which are going on today in all parts of the world. The missions have brought not only the Word of God, but education and medicine and health and fuller lives to the people of countless lands. In carrying out and directing the teaching mission of the Universal Church, the Vatican has projected itself into all corners of the world.

No one will deny the influence that the Vatican has exerted, first, over Europe, and then over the rest of the world, in the field of art and learning. Few people, however, realize how enormous this influence has been. They know that the Vatican saved Europe from the barbarians of the North and the Moslems of the East. But it is difficult to estimate what Europe—and through it the world—owes to the Vatican for having saved and fostered art and literature and science when their lights burned dim indeed and their tiny flames flickered and sputtered in a hostile world.

Leadership in meeting the problems of social action and economics has come from the Vatican in generous measure. The voice of Leo XIII was a lonely one when he first raised it in vigorous defense of the rights of the common man. Now, strengthened and brought up to date by Pius XI, and spoken again by Pius XII, the social teachings of the Holy See are known and respected throughout the world.

The influence of the Vatican throughout the world may be said to be due to many things. First and foremost is the fact that the Holy See has God's own promise that He will preserve it from all error in its teaching on faith and morals. Men can be sure that they have from it the very truth of God. Moreover, in keeping with His divine promise, God has always raised up great figures in the Church, especially in times of great trial.

Men do not always follow the bright banners or rally to the cause of truth, even when its champions are great leaders. Truth is not always popular. Men who stand firmly for truth are frequently unpopular. But truth is powerful, even while shaming those who will not recognize it. It will not die. And so it is not amazing that the citadel of truth in this world—though it is the smallest of the world's states—should constantly make itself and its messages heard throughout the world.

Recalling Details

To show how well you recall the details of what you have read, copy the statements below. Include the phrase which correctly completes each statement.

1. Vatican City is located (near Rome, just outside Rome, entirely within Rome).

2. The area covered by Vatican City is (less than one square mile, ten square miles, one hundred square miles).

3. St. Peter's Basilica is (the Pope's cathedral in Rome, a magnificent church in Vatican City, the parish church for residents of Vatican City).

4. St. Peter's Basilica is (the first, the second, the third) large church to stand on this site.

5. The Pope lives in a portion of (Belvedere Palace, Vatican Palace, Lateran Palace).

6. The Basilica of St. John Lateran in Rome is famous as (the largest and most beautiful church in Italy, the first great church built by the Emperor Constantine, the Pope's cathedral and the Mother Church of Christendom).

7. Castel Gandolfo is (the home of the Papal Secretary of State, the living quarters of the Swiss Guard, the Holy Father's summer residence near Rome).

8. The Sistine Chapel, a world-famous library, and numerous art museums are housed in the buildings that comprise (Castel Gandolfo, the Vatican Palace, the Lateran Palace).

FRANCIS THOMPSON

Envoi

Go, SONGS, for ended is our brief, sweet play;
　　Go, children of swift joy and tardy sorrow:
And some are sung, and that was yesterday,
　　And some unsung, and that may be tomorrow.

Go forth; and if it be o'er stony way,
　　Old joy can lend what newer grief must borrow:
And it was sweet, and that was yesterday,
　　And sweet is sweet, though purchased with sorrow.

Go, songs, and come not back from your far way:
　　And if men ask you why ye smile and sorrow,
Tell them ye grieve, for your hearts know Today,
　　Tell them ye smile, for your eyes know Tomorrow.

Glossary

This glossary, or little dictionary, on the following pages will help you to pronounce and understand the meanings of the new or unusual words used in *These Are Our Horizons.*

The following list shows you how each marked letter is pronounced by giving as an example the same sound in a word that you know. This is called a *pronunciation key.*

ā *as in* lāte
å *as in* al'wåys
ă *as in* ăm
ă *as in* ăp·pear'
ä *as in* ärm
à *as in* àsk
â *as in* câre
à *as in* sofà

ē *as in* hē
ê *as in* ê·nough'
ĕ *as in* nĕt
ĕ *as in* si'lĕnt
ē *as in* mak'ēr
ę *as in* hęre

ī *as in* rīde
ĭ *as in* ĭn
ĭ *as in* pos'sĭ·ble

ō *as in* ōld
ô *as in* ô·bey'
ŏ *as in* nŏt
ŏ *as in* cŏn·nect'
ŏ *as in* sŏft
ô *as in* hôrse

ū *as in* ūse
û *as in* û·nite'
ŭ *as in* ŭs
ŭ *as in* cir'cŭs
û *as in* bûrn

ōō *as in* mōōn
ŏŏ *as in* tŏŏk
oi *as in* oil
ou *as in* out

th *as in* that
th *as in* thin
tû *as in* na'tûre
N *as in* boN

a·beam' (*à*·bēm'), *adv.* Off to one side of a ship, and at a line at right angles to her keel.

Ab'er·deen' (ăb'ēr·dēn'; āb'ēr·dēn). A county in the northeastern part of Scotland.

a·ca'cia (*à*·kā'sh*à*), *n.* A thorny bush or tree, belonging to the mimosa family, with flowers that grow in clusters.

ad ma·jor'em De'i glo·ri·am (ăd mà·jōr'ĕm dā'ē glō'rĭ·àm). Latin words, meaning "For the greater glory of God."

A·ë'des ae'gyp·ti (à·ē'dēz ē'jĭp·tī). A type of mosquito which transmits yellow fever.

A'gra·mon'te, Ig·na'cio (ä'grä·môn'tä, ĕg·nä'syō).

ai (ī), *interj.* An exclamation of pain or surprise.

A'li Ba'ba (ä'lĕ bä'bä). In the *Arabian Nights,* a woodcutter who entered the treasure cave of the Forty Thieves.

al·tim'e·ter (ăl·tĭm'ê·tēr), *n.* An instrument used for measuring altitude, especially one used in aircraft to show the height at which the machine is flying.

a·me'na·ble (*à*·mē'n*à* b'l), *adj.* Liable to be called to account; answerable; also, easily influenced.

am'pli·tude (ăm'plĭ·tūd), *n.* State of being ample; abundance; extent.

an'e·mom'e·ter (ăn'ê·mŏm'ê·tēr), *n.* An instrument for measuring the force or speed of the wind; a wind gauge.

an·tip'o·des (ăn·tĭp'ô·dēz), *n. pl.* Regions on the opposite side of the globe; for example, Americans say Australians live in the *antipodes.*

An·to'nio, Don (än·tō'nyō, dŏn).

A·pol'lo Bel've·dere' (*à*·pŏl'ô bĕl'vê·dēr'). Apollo was a Greek god of manly youth and beauty, of many virtues and accomplishments. The most remarkable of the statues of Apollo is that in the Belvedere Gallery of the Vatican; hence the name *Apollo Belvedere.*

ap·pall' (ă·pôl'), *v.* To fill with horror; to alarm; to dismay.

ap·prais'al (ă·prāz'ăl), *n.* The act of estimating or settling the worth or value of something.

ar'bi·ter (är'bĭ·tēr), *n.* A person chosen to settle a dispute; also, a person having authority to decide what is right and proper.

Ar'i·el (âr'ĭ·ĕl). In Shakespeare's play *The Tempest,* an airy, playful spirit, changing shape at will.

Ar'is·tot'le (ăr'ĭs·tŏt''l). A philosopher of ancient Greece.

ar'ma·ture (är'ma·tūr), *n.* In sculpturing, a framework used to support the clay in molding.

Ar'ti·cles of Con·fed'er·a'tion (är'tĭ·k'ls ŏv kŏn·fĕd'ĕr·ā'shŭn). The first compact passed (November 15, 1777) by the congress of the thirteen original states. They remained the supreme law from 1781 until the Constitution went into effect.

as'pho·del (ăs'fō·dĕl), *n.* A lilylike plant with narrow leaves and white or yellow flowers. In poetic use, the narcissus and daffodil are given this name.

As·to'ri·a (ăs·tōr'ĭ·a). A city in Oregon, founded as a trading post by John Jacob Astor in 1811.

Ath'a·bas'ka (ăth'a·băs'ka) **River.** A river in the province of Alberta, Canada, which flows into Athabaska Lake.

Atlantic Charter. A joint statement made in 1941 by President Franklin D. Roosevelt and Prime Minister Winston Churchill, giving eight points which should serve as a basis for world reorganization at the close of World War II. Their countries pledged support of the eight points. Twenty-four other nations did likewise.

a·tom'ic (a·tŏm'ĭk), *adj.* Operating by means of energy liberated by changes in the nucleus of an atom.

Aus'sie (ôs'ĭ). A nickname for a native of Australia.

a·vert' (a·vûrt'), *v.* To prevent a thing from happening; to ward off; as, to *avert* an accident.

bail'iff (bāl'ĭf), *n.* An officer of a court, having charge of prisoners.

bal'da·chin (băl'da·kĭn), *n.* A canopy of a rich fabric erected over an altar.

bal'sa (bôl'sa), *n.* A tropical American tree with light strong wood used for floats, etc.

Bal·tha'zar (băl·thā'zĕr). One of the three magi who came to Bethlehem to present gifts to the infant Jesus.

bark (bärk), *n.* A sailing vessel or boat.

bar'rens (băr'ĕnz), *n. pl.* Level tracts of land having little vegetation and usually with light, sandy soil.

ba·sil'i·ca (ba·sĭl'ĭ·ka), *n.* A title given to certain churches and carrying special liturgical privileges. A basilica takes precedence over all churches except cathedrals.

Ba·sil'i·ca (ba·sĭl'ĭ·ka) **of St. Peter.** The largest church in Christendom, situated in the Vatican City in Rome.

bat'tle·dore (băt''l·dōr) **and shut'tle·cock'** (shŭt''l·kŏk'), *n.* A game in which the battledore (a light, flat racket) is used to strike the shuttlecock, a cork stuck with feathers.

Beau'fort (bō'fĕrt) **scale.** A scale in which the strength of the wind is indicated by numbers from 0 to 12.

be·deck' (bē·dĕk'), *v.* To deck out; to adorn.

Bed'ou·in (bĕd'ōō·ĭn), *n.* A wandering Arab of the desert.

be·la'bor (bē·lā'bĕr), *v.* To beat soundly with a stick or cudgel.

Bel've·de're' (bĕl'vē·dēr') **Palace.** A place of residence for members of the clergy who work at the Vatican.

bench (bĕnch), *n.* A narrow, raised surface of level ground, rock, etc.; a shelf of land.

Ben·ga'si (bĕn·gä'zē). A city in Libya, in northern Africa, the site of a large air base.

Bengt (bĕngt).

Benito. *See* Mussolini.

Be'ring (bēr'ĭng) **Sea.** Sea between the Aleutian Islands and Bering Strait.

Ber·ni'ni (bãr·nē'nē), **Gio·van'ni** (jō·vän'nē) **Lorenzo** (lō·rĕn'zō). Italian painter, sculptor, and architect.

be·smirch' (bē·smûrch'), *v.* To blacken, as one's good name; to soil or smirch.

bi·tu'men (bĭ·tū'mĕn), *n.* Any of a number of inflammable mineral substances, including asphalts, mineral tars, petroleum, and naphtha.

bob'bin (bŏb'ĭn), *n.* A small pin or cylinder which is stuck in a pillow to form a design around which threads are pleated to make bobbin lace.

Bo'go·tá' (bō'gō·tä'). The capital of Colombia, South America.

boom (bōōm), *n.* A long spar or beam projecting from the mast of a derrick, to support or guide the body to be lifted.

bore (bōr), *v.* Moved or lay in a certain direction.

Bor'gia (bôr'jä) **Apartment.** A part of the Palace of the Vatican.

bound'er (boun'dĕr), *n.* One who determines bounds.

boun'ty (boun'tĭ), *n.* That which is given in abundance; also, generosity.

Bra·man'te, Do·na'to (brä·män'tä, dō·nä'tō). An Italian architect and painter.

bulk'head' (bŭlk'hĕd'), *n.* An upright partition which separates compartments or sections, as on a vessel.

bull'-tongued' (bōōl'tŭngd') **plow,** *n.* A single-shovel plow or cultivator.

bur'geon (bûr'jŭn), *v.* To send forth buds, branches, or any new growth; to put forth.

bush (bōōsh), *n.* Uncleared country; brush.

ca'dence (kā'dĕns), *n.* Rhythm; the measure, or beat, of any rhythmical motion.

cairn (kârn), *n.* A heap of stones piled up as a landmark or a memorial.

ca·jole′ (ka·jōl′), v. To influence or urge on by gentle words.

cal′cu·la′tor (kăl′kŭ·lā′tĕr), n. A machine which performs mathematical computations.

cam′pa·ni′le (kăm′pa·nē′lĕ) n. A bell tower.

can′did (kăn′dĭd), adj. Frank, outspoken, straightforward; without prejudice.

can′on law (kăn′ŭn lô), n. Church law; the body of laws by which the Roman Catholic Church is governed.

Can′ter·bur′y (kăn′tĕr·bĕr′ĭ). A city of England and site of a great cathedral, formerly Catholic, but now held by the Church of England.

Car·de′no (kär·dē′nô).

car′il·lon (kăr′ĭ·lŏn), n. A set of bells played by machinery or from a keyboard.

Car·lisle′ (kär·līl′) School. A Government school for Indians, located at Carlisle, Pennsylvania.

car′pet·bag′ (kär′pĕt·băg′), n. A traveling bag, formerly one often made of carpet.

car′to·graph′ic (kär′tô·grăf′ĭk), adj. Having to do with the drawing or making of charts or maps.

Cas·tel′ Gan·dol′fo (käs·tĕl′ găn·dôl′fô). Place of the Pope's summer residence, twelve miles southeast of Rome.

cat′e·go′ry (kăt′ê·gō′rĭ), n. A class, kind, or division of things.

cath′ode (kăth′ōd) n. The negative pole or electrode; opposite to anode.

cav′ern·ous (kăv′ĕr·nŭs), adj. Of the nature of or like a cavern; hollow.

Celt (sĕlt). One of any Celtic-speaking people, including the Irish, Scots, Welsh, and Bretons.

Chap·sal′ (shăp·sàl′).

Char′le·magne (shär′lĕ·mān). Emperor of the West and king of the Franks.

chas′u·ble (chăz′û·b'l), n. The outer garment of a priest at Mass.

chi′tze (chē′zē), n. Chinese word for wife.

chol′er·a (kŏl′ĕr·a), n. An epidemic disease that causes many deaths.

Cier′va, Juan de la (thyĕr′vä, hwän dē là).

cinc′ture (sĭngk′tûr), n. A belt; the long cord that a priest wears about his waist when vested for Mass.

cit′a·del (sĭt′a·dĕl), n. A fortress that commands a city; hence, a stronghold.

cock·ade′ (kŏk·ād′), n. A knot or ornament worn on the hat as a badge.

cock′pit′ (kŏk′pĭt′), n. In small vessels, a sheltered place lower than the rest of the deck.

co′de·in (kō′dē·ĭn), n. A crystalline drug obtained from opium, not as strong as morphine. It is used to deaden intense pain.

Col′umb·cille (kŭl′ŭm·kĭl), Saint. Known also as Saint Columba; an Irish monk who, with twelve followers, established a monastery on the island of Iona.

com′pa·ra·ble (kŏm′pa·ra·b'l), adj. Capable of being compared with.

con′clave (kŏn′klāv), n. A private meeting or assembly.

con·strain′ (kŏn·strān′), v. To compel; to force; to restrain.

con′tour (kŏn′tōōr) line. An imaginary line connecting the points on a land surface that have the same elevation.

con′tour map. A map showing the configuration of a surface by means of contour lines drawn at regular intervals of elevation.

con′voy (kŏn′voi), n. A ship, fleet, etc., accompanied by an armed escort for protection.

Cop′tic (kŏp′tĭk), adj. Of, or pertaining to, the Copts, Egyptians who are Christians.

Cor′co·va′do (kôr′kô·vä′dō). A mountain peak near Rio de Janeiro.

cor′mo·rant (kôr′mô·rănt), n. A large dark-colored sea bird with a long neck and hooked beak. It is a greedy eater of fish.

cos′mic (kŏz′mĭk), adj. Of, or relating to, the universe, or cosmos.

course′way (kōrs′wā), n. A course or channel, as of a river.

cro′zier (krō′zhĕr), n. The staff, shaped like a shepherd's crook, of a bishop, abbot, or abbess, carried as a symbol of office.

cru′cial (krōō′shăl), adj. Decisive; having to do with a supreme trial or final choice.

crypt (krĭpt), n. A vault or cell wholly or partly underground, as under a church.

crys′tal·line (krĭs′tăl·ĭn), adj. Of, or like, crystal; transparent.

crys′tal·lize (krĭs′tăl·īz), v. To become, or cause to become, settled and fixed in form.

cu′mu·lus (kū′mŭ·lŭs), n. A massy cloud with a flat base and rounded outlines.

cu′rate (kū′rāt), n. A priest who assists the pastor of a parish; an assistant pastor.

Czar′ist (zär′ĭst), adj. Of, or pertaining to, a Czar. The former emperors of Russia were called Czars.

Cze′sto·cho′wa (chĕN′stô·kô′và). A city of southwestern Poland, in which a miraculous picture of Our Lady is kept and venerated.

Dag′mar (dăg′mär).

Da·mas′cus (da·măs′kŭs) gate. An opening on the northern side of the long irregular wall that surrounds the city of Jerusalem.

---

lāte, alwåys, ăm, ăppear, ärm, àsk, câre, sofà, hē, ĕnough, nĕt, sĭlĕnt, makĕr, hēre, rīde, ĭn, possĭble, ōld, ôbey, nŏt, cônnect, sôft, hôrse, ūse, ûnite, ŭs, circŭs, bûrn, mōōn, tŏŏk, oil, out, that, thin, natûre, boN.

Da'mien' (dà'myăN'), **Joseph.**

David's tower. A structure near Jaffa gate, erected on the foundations of one of the ancient towers built in Jerusalem by Herod.

dead (dĕd), *adv.* Directly; exactly; as, to run *dead* away from a place.

de'but (dā'bū; då bū'), *n.* Entrance upon a career or form of entrance into society; a first public appearance, as of an actress.

de·cath'lon (dĕ·kăth'lŏn), *n.* A contest that consists of ten athletic events which take place on the track and field.

de·nounce' (dĕ·nouns'), *v.* To point out a person or thing as deserving of blame or punishment.

det'o·na'tion (dĕt'ō·nā'shŭn), *n.* A sudden and violent explosion.

din'ghy (dĭng'gĭ), *n.* A light rowboat or skiff.

dis·crep'an·cy (dĭs·krĕp'ăn·sĭ), *n.* Stage of being at variance or disagreement.

dog·mat'ic (dŏg·măt'ĭk), *adj.* Pertaining to the truths found in the Word of God, either written or unwritten. These truths are proclaimed by the Catholic Church for the belief of the faithful.

do'ry (dō'rĭ), *n.* A flat-bottomed boat with high sides curving upward and outward, and a sharp bow. It is used mainly for fishing.

dou'ble-reef (dŭb''l rēf), *v.* To lessen the area of a sail by rolling or folding it up to the second reef, thus lessening the heeling or "tipping" of the boat.

Doyle, Sir Arthur Conan. A British fiction writer.

dray'man (drā'măn), *n.* One whose work is carrying or driving a dray, a strong, low wagon used for hauling heavy loads.

Druse (drōoz). One of the people of a religious sect, living chiefly in the Lebanon Mountains of Syria.

dus'ter (dŭs'tẽr), *n.* A light garment worn over a person's clothes to protect them from dust.

dy·nam'ic (dī·năm'ĭk), *adj.* Powerful; energetic; forceful.

Ec'ce Sa·cer'dos Mag'nus (ĕk'sē să·chẽr'dōs măg'nŭs). Latin words, meaning "Behold the Great Priest."

ee'rie (ē'rĭ), *adj.* Weird; uncanny; causing fear.

ef·fron'ter·y (ĕ·frŭn'tẽr·ĭ), *n.* Shameless boldness; presumptuousness.

e·lab'o·rate (ē·lăb'ō·rāt), *v.* To work out in detail; to develop fully.

e'land (ē'lănd), *n.* A large African antelope with twisted horns.

El'do·ra'do (ĕl'dō·rä'dō). Any place of fabulous richness; an imaginary place abounding in gold.

E·liz'a·be'than (ē·lĭz'à·bē'thăn), *adj.* Pertaining to or characteristic of Queen Elizabeth I or her times.

en·com'pass (ĕn·kŭm'pás), *v.* To surround; to encircle; to enclose or contain.

en·cy'cli·cal (ĕn·sĭk'lĭ·kăl), *n.* A papal letter addressed to the bishops of the world.

e'qui·lib'ri·um (ē'kwĭ·lĭb'rĭ·ŭm), *n.* A state of balance between opposing weights, forces, etc.

e·ro'sion (ē·rō'zhŭn), *n.* A gradual destruction by eating or wearing away.

etch (ĕch), *v.* To produce designs or figures on metal, glass, etc., by lines eaten into the substance by acid; hence, as a figure of speech, to make a deep impression on.

E·thi·o'pi·an (ē'thĭ·ō'pĭ·ăn), *adj.* Of or relating to Ethiopia or its inhabitants.

e·vince' (ē·vĭns'), *v.* To make evident; to show clearly; to display.

ey'rie (âr'ĭ), *n.* The nest of a bird high on a crag. As a figure of speech, a dwelling place on a height.

Fal'staff (fôl'stàf), **Sir John.** A character in Shakespeare's play *Merry Wives of Windsor.*

fa·nat'ic (fà·năt'ĭk), *n.* A person who is excessively enthusiastic about something, especially religion.

fan'ion (făn'yŭn), *n.* A small flag used by soldiers and surveyors to mark positions.

fare (fâr), *v.* To go; especially, to go on a journey.

fa·thom'e·ter (fă·thŏm'ê·tẽr), *n.* A direct-reading sonic depth finder.

Fá'ti·ma (fä'tĭ·má). A village in central Portugal where, in 1913, the Blessed Virgin appeared to three children, urging them to pray the Rosary that war might cease.

Feast of Lights. A Jewish festival, the ceremonies of which call for the use of an additional light on each of the eight days' celebration.

fed'er·al (fĕd'ẽr·ăl), *adj.* Of or pertaining to a state or a nation formed by the union of several smaller states or nations which retain limited powers.

Fed'er·al·ist (fĕd'ẽr·ăl·ĭst), *n.* A member of the party most prominent in urging the formation and adoption of the Constitution of the United States.

feign (fān), *v.* To imagine; to form and relate as if true; to make believe; to sham.

fies'ta (fyĕs'tä), *n.* A holiday or festivity.

floe (flō), *n.* A large sheet of floating ice.

For·mo'san (fôr·mō'săn), *adj. and n.* Of or pertaining to the island of Formosa; also, a native of Formosa.

fraught (frôt), *adj.* Filled; laden.

frieze (frēz), *n.* An ornamental band or stripe extending around a building or the wall of a room.

fur'tive (fûr'tǐv), *adj.* Sly; secret; stealthy.

Gas'par (găs'pēr). One of the three magi who came to Bethlehem to present gifts to the infant Jesus.

gauge (gāj), *v.* To find the exact measurement of; also, to estimate, as to *gauge* the height of a room.

gen·darm'er·y (zhän·där'mĕr·ĭ), *n.* A body of policemen organized, armed, and drilled as soldiers, as those in France and some other European countries.

ges·tic'u·late (jĕs·tĭk' û·lāt), *v.* To make gestures when speaking.

gin'ger·ly (jĭn'jēr·lĭ), *adv.* Very carefully; cautiously.

Gio·con'do, Fra (jō·kōn'dō, frä). An Italian architect.

Glas'ton·bur'y (glăs'tŭn·bĕr'ĭ). A city in southern England, the site of an ancient abbey.

gnarled (närld), *adj.* Knotty; having hard, irregular lumps like those where branches of a tree join the trunk.

Golden Age Club. A social club whose members are all elderly persons, especially persons aged eighty years or over.

Golden Gate. A portal on the eastern side of the wall that surrounds Jerusalem. This gate is now closed up. *See also* Damascus gate.

gra'ci as (grä'sê äs), *n. pl.* A Spanish word, meaning "Thanks" or "Thank you." *Gracias a Dios* means "Thanks be to God."

gran'di·ose (grăn'dĭ·ōs), *adj.* Displaying grandeur or splendor; impressive.

Grand' Pré' (gräN' prā'). A village in Nova Scotia.

gro·tesque' (grô·tĕsk'), *adj.* Strange and fantastic in shape, appearance, etc.; also, not in accordance with what is reasonable or right.

gua'va (gwä'và), *n.* A tropical fruit.

gy'ro·scope (jī'rô·skōp), *n.* A wheel or disk mounted to spin rapidly about an axis and free to rotate about a perpendicular axis; a stabilizer to resist the rolling of a ship.

gyves (jīvz), *n.* Shackles.

hack (hăk), *n.* A coach or carriage let out for hire.

haft (hàft), *n.* A handle; the hilt of a knife, sword, spear. *v.* To furnish with a haft.

Hai'le Se·las'sie (hī'lê sĕ·läs'ĭ). Emperor of Ethiopia.

Hallie. *See* Haile Selassie.

hal·lu'ci·na'tion (hă·lū·sĭ·nā'shŭn), *n.* The seeing, usually because of a nervous disorder, of objects which do not exist.

Hamlet. The title and hero of a tragedy by Shakespeare.

Han'kow' (hăng'kou'). A large industrial city in China.

helm (hĕlm), *n.* The apparatus by which a ship is steered; commonly, the tiller or wheel alone.

her'e·tic (hĕr'ĕ·tĭk), *n.* A person who teaches, or holds, opinions contrary to the doctrines of a church.

hewers of wood and drawers of water, *n. pl.* Laborers who do the lowliest tasks—an expression from the Old Testament.

Homer. An ancient Greek poet.

horn'y (hôr'nĭ), *adj.* Hard; calloused.

how'dah (hou'dà), *n.* A seat, usually covered, on the back of an elephant.

hus'band (hŭz'bănd), *v.* To manage in a thrifty way; to use carefully.

Hwang' Pu' (hwäng' pōō'). A large river in China.

im·mo·bil'i·ty (ĭm'ô·bĭl'ĭ·tĭ), *n.* The state or condition of being motionless; fixedness.

im pa'la (ĭm·pä'là), *n.* A large African antelope.

im·plic'it (ĭm·plĭs'ĭt), *adj.* Understood though not directly stated; implied.

im·pute' (ĭm·pūt'), *v.* To ascribe (to one) as author, originator, or possessor; to attribute.

in·an'i·mate (ĭn·ăn'ĭ·mât), *adj.* Without life or spirit; dead; lifeless.

in·car'nate (ĭn·kär'nàt), *adj.* In bodily form. **Man incarnate:** the whole human race, man, represented by the body of one person.

in·con'gru·ous (ĭn·kŏng'grōō·ŭs), *adj.* Not in accordance with what is proper, reasonable, or right; not suitable to or in harmony with.

in·cred'i·ble (ĭn·krĕd'ĭ·b'l), *adj.* Unbelievable; almost beyond belief.

in·er'tia (ĭn·ûr'shà), *n.* The property by which matter will remain at rest or in motion in the same directional line unless acted upon by some external force.

in·ev'i·ta·ble (ĭn·ĕv'ĭ·tà·b'l), *adj.* Bound to happen; not to be avoided; certain.

in·junc'tion (ĭn·jŭngt'shŭn), *n.* An act of directing, commanding, or prohibiting.

in'stal·la'tion (ĭn'stô·lā'shŭn), *n.* The act of being formally placed in an office, rank, or order.

in'ter·mit'tent (ĭn'tēr·mĭt'ĕnt), *adj.* Coming and going at intervals.

in'ter·vene' (ĭn'tēr·vēn'), *v.* To occur or come in between points of time or events.

---

lāte, alwàys, ăm, ăppear, ärm, àsk, câre, sofà, hē, ênough, nĕt, silĕnt, makēr, hĕre, rīde, ĭn, possĭble, ōld, ôbey, nŏt, cônnect, sôft, hôrse, ūse, ûnite, ŭs, circŭs, bûrn, mōōn, tŏŏk, oil, out, ŧhat, thin, natŭre, boN.

in·tone' (ĭn·tōn'), *v.* To recite in musical tones; to chant.

I·o'na (ī·ō'nȧ). One of the Hebrides, islands near Scotland. *See also* Columbcille.

i'rised (ī'rĭst), *adj.* Made iridescent; formed into a rainbow; having a rainbowlike play of colors.

i·ron'ic (ī·rŏn'ĭk), *adj.* Humorous or sarcastic in a way that expresses a meaning opposite to what a person says.

Is'lam (ĭs'lȧm), *n.* The religion of the Moslems; hence the Moslems.

ja'ca (zhä'kȧ), *n.* A tropical tree.

Jaf'fa (jăf'ȧ) **gate.** A portal on the western side of the wall that surrounds Jerusalem. It opens on the road used by the fishermen from Jaffa. *See also* Damascus gate.

jaun'diced (jôn'dĭst), *adj.* Affected with jaundice; made yellow as if with jaundice.

jave'lin (jăv'lĭn), *n.* A kind of light spear used as a weapon or in sports.

Je·hosh'a·phat (jē·hŏsh'ȧ·făt), **Valley of.** The low area which separates Jerusalem from the Mount of Olives.

Je·rome' (jē·rōm'), **Saint.** A translator of the Bible who made the Vulgate, or approved Latin version.

jib (jĭb), *n.* A three-cornered sail extending forward from the head of the foremast to the bowsprit, or jib boom.

John'son (jŏn's'n), **Andrew.** President of the United States (1865–1869). As vice-president, he became President after the death of Lincoln.

Jo·sé' (hō·sā'). A Spanish name, meaning *Joseph.*

Juan (hwän). A Spanish name, meaning *John.*

ju·di'ci·ar·y (jo͞o·dĭsh'ĭ·ĕr·ĭ; jo͞o·dĭsh'ĭ·ĕr·ĭ), *n.* The branch of the government which has to do with courts of justice; the system of courts of justice.

K. A symbol used in scoring to indicate a strike-out.

Kaf'fir (kăf'ẽr). A member of a powerful and intelligent native race of South Africa.

ka·lei'do·scope (kȧ·lī'dȯ·skōp), *n.* A many-colored changing pattern, scene, or the like.

Kat·rin' (Kȧ·trēn'; Kȧ·trĭn').

Ket'tel·er, von (kĕt'ĕl·ẽr, fôn), **William Emmanuel.** A German baron and Catholic Bishop of Mainz. He championed social and economic reforms.

Ki·be'ti (kē·bā'tē).

Ki'ev (kē'yĕf). A city of Ukraine, a republic of Russia.

kins'folk' (kĭnz'fōk'), *n. pl.* Persons closely related; relatives.

Knut (k'no͞ot).

kon·go'ni (kŏng·gō'nĭ), *n.* A large African antelope, grayish-brown in color with yellow patches on the back.

Kon'-Ti'ki (kôn' tē'kē).

ko'sher (kō'shẽr), *adj.* Sanctioned by Jewish law; especially, indicating food that has been prepared in accordance with Jewish ritual.

Kra'ków (krä'ko͞of). Also pronounced krä'kō for English spelling, *Cracow.* A city in southwestern Poland.

lam·poon' (lăm·po͞on'), *n.* A personal attack in writing or drawing, usually abusive.

Lang'ton (lăng'tŭn), **Stephen.** Archbishop of Canterbury in the thirteenth century, defender of the rights of individuals, and first signer of the Magna Charta.

La·oc'o·ön (lā·ŏk'ȯ·ŏn). In Greek legend, a priest of one of the gods, who, together with his two sons, was put to death by serpents at the command of another god, whom he had offended. A famous piece of sculpture represents this scene.

Lau·da'te Do'mi·num, om'nes gen'tes (lou·dä'tå dō'mĭ·nŭm ŏm'nås jĕn'tås). Latin words, meaning "Praise the Lord, all ye people."

Laz'a·rist (lăz'ȧ·rĭst). A member of the Congregation of the Priests of Missions, founded by Saint Vincent de Paul at the College of St. Lazare.

La·zear' (lȧ·zēr'), **Jesse Williams.** An American physician who sacrificed his life in the work to combat yellow fever.

League of Nations. An association of states of the world, formed after World War I, to help in adjusting their relations with one another and to lessen the likelihood of war.

Leb'a·nons (lĕb'ȧ·nŏnz). Mountains in Syria.

Lebbe, Vin'cent' (lĕb, văN'säN'). A Belgian Vincentian missionary who became a Chinese citizen and did outstanding work in China.

lee'ward (lē'wẽrd; lū'ẽrd). *n.* The lee side, or the side toward which the wind blows. *adj.* Pertaining to, or in the direction of, the lee part or side.

Les'seps, Fer'di·nand' de (lĕ'sĕps, fẽr'dē·näN' dē). A French diplomat and promoter of the Suez Canal.

Le·vi'a·than (lē·vī'ȧ·thăn), *n.* The name of a large ocean liner. A **leviathan** is a huge water animal mentioned in the Bible; hence, something very large.

Lie'ou (lē'ō), **Joseph.**

lit'ur·gy (lĭt'ẽr·jĭ), *n.* The prayers, acts, and ceremonies used in the public and official worship of the Church.

lore (lōr), *n.* Knowledge; learning.

Lourdes (lōōrd). A town in the southwestern part of France, a place of pilgrimage.

Lu·is' (lōō·ēs'). A Spanish name, meaning *Louis*.

Lyau'tey', Louis Hu'bert' Gon'zalve' (lyō'tā', lwē ū'bâr' gôn'zàlv'). A French soldier who saved Morocco from German control during World War I.

Mc·Clel'lan (má·klĕl'ăn), **George B.** General in chief of the United States Army, 1861–1862.

Ma·der'no (mä·dĕr'nô), **Carlo.** An Italian architect. Also known as Maderni or Maderna.

Ma'dre de Dios' (mä'drà dā dyōs'). Spanish words, meaning "Mother of God."

main (mān), *n.* A broad stretch of land, sea, or space.

mal'a·dy (măl'á·dĭ), *n.* Any disease of the body or mind; sickness.

Mar·seilles' (mär·sā'). An important seaport city of France. Sailors and fishermen place themselves under the care of the Mother of God, whose image stands atop one of the churches of the city.

mart (märt), *n.* A market; a trading place.

Mar'tha's Vine'yard (mär'thàz vĭn'yêrd). An island in the Atlantic Ocean, off the southwestern coast of Cape Cod. It is a well-known summer resort.

Mas'si, E·u·ge'nio (mäs'sē, à·ōō·jâ'nyô). Italian bishop of Hankow.

mat'ins (măt'ĭnz), *n. pl.* Early-morning prayers.

mead (mēd), *n.* In poetic use, a meadow.

mean'er (mēn'êr), *adj.* Of less value or poorer quality.

mec'ca (mĕk'á), *n.* Any place sought by many people as a very desirable place, or goal.

Me·di·a'tor De'i (mā·dē·à'tôr dā'ē). The first two words of any encyclical written by a Pope give it its title. *Mediator Dei* was written by Pope Pius XII. It means "mediator between God (and man)."

Mel'chi·or (mĕl'kĭ·ôr). One of the three magi who brought gifts to Jesus at Bethlehem.

me·lee' (mà·lā'), *n.* A confused fight; a skirmish; an affray.

men'tor (mĕn'têr), *n.* A faithful advisor; a wise counselor.

merg'er (mûr'jêr), *n.* A combining or uniting of persons or things for some purpose.

me'sa (mā'sà), *n.* A flat-topped, rocky hill with steeply sloping sides.

Mi'chel·an'ge·lo (mĭ'kĕl·ăn'jĕ·lō). An Italian painter, sculptor, architect, and poet.

mid'land (mĭd'lànd), *n.* The inland or central region of a country.

Mi·guel' (mê·gĕl'). A Spanish name, meaning *Michael*.

Mills (mĭlz), **Clark.** An American sculptor. His equestrian statue of Andrew Jackson was the first large bronze statue cast in the United States.

mi·mo'sa (mĭ·mō'sà), *n.* Any of a group of tropical plants, bushes, or trees, with ball-like heads of small flowers and often prickly leaves.

min'a·ret' (mĭn'á·rĕt'), *n.* A tall, slender tower from which a crier summons the Mohammedans to prayer.

Mo'dlin (mō'dlēn). A village in Poland.

mo·gul' (mô·gŭl'), *n.* A person, especially a ruler, who has complete power; a great personage.

Mo'lo·ka'i (mō'lô·kä'ê). One of the islands of Hawaii on which is a leper colony.

Mon'a·co (mŏn'á kō). An independent principality near southeastern France and the Italian border.

Mon·go'li·a (mŏng·gō'lĭ·à). A vast territory in Central Asia, composed of Outer Mongolia, north of the Gobi desert, and Inner Mongolia, to the south of the desert.

Mont'mar'tre (môN'màr'tr'). A northern section of Paris, located on a hill above the Seine River.

Mo'ra, Mar'ce·li'no (mō'rä, mär'sà·lē'nô).

Mor'gan (môr'găn) **horse.** One of a celebrated American breed of light horses which originated in Vermont.

Mo·roc'can (mô·rŏk'ăn), *adj. and n.* Of, from, or pertaining to Morocco.

mo·sa'ic (mô·zā'ĭk), *n.* A surface decoration made by setting small pieces of glass, stone, etc., into some other material in such a way as to form a picture or design.

motion study. A study of the motions made by a person or persons doing some kind of work to see whether or not time or effort could be saved by doing the work in some other way.

Mu·cher'i (mōō·chĕr'ê).

muk'luk (mŭk'lŭk), *n.* A kind of sealskin boot worn by Eskimos.

mun·dane' (mŭn·dān'), *adj.* Pertaining to the world; earthly.

Mus'so·li'ni, Be·ni'to (mōōs'sô·lē'nê, bà·nē'tô). Italian dictator who became an ally of Germany in World War II.

myr'i·ad (mĭr'ĭ·àd), *adj.* An indefinitely large number.

myr'tle-wreath (mûr't'l·rēth), *n.* A garland of evergreen leaves; in the U.S. a trailing evergreen herb with solitary blue or white flowers (periwinkle).

---

lāte, alwàys, ăm, ăppear, ärm, àsk, câre, sofà, hē, ênough, nĕt, silĕnt, makêr, hēre, rīde, ĭn, possĭble, ōld, ôbey, nŏt, cŏnnect, sŏft, hôrse, ūse, ûnite, ŭs, circŭs, bûrn, mōōn, tŏŏk, oil, out, that, thin, natûre, boN.

Nantes (nănts). A city in the northwestern part of France, on the Loire River.

Nar'ra·gan'sett (năr'a·găn'sĕt) **Bay.** An inlet of the Atlantic Ocean at Rhode Island.

Ne·nan'a (nê·năn'a). A city in Alaska, situated on the south bank of the Tanana River.

Ne·ve·rí'a (nā·vä·rē'ä).

news packet. *See* packet.

nil (nĭl), *n.* Nothing.

non'cha·lant·ly (nŏn'sha·lănt·lĭ), *adv.* In any easy and unconcerned manner or way; casually.

non'com·mit'tal (nŏn'kŏ·mĭt'ăl), *adj.* Not telling or showing what one thinks or has decided to do.

northern lights. Streamers of light, thought to be of electrical origin, sometimes visible in the night sky of northern countries.

north'west'er (nôrth'wĕs'tẽr), *n.* Strong wind or a storm from the northwest.

No'tre Dame' (nô'tr' dàm'). French words, meaning "Our Lady"—a name given to many cathedrals and churches of Europe.

nu'cle·ar (nū'klê·ẽr), *adj.* Designating the central portion of an atom.

oa'kum (ō'kŭm), *n.* Fiber from old ropes, used to stuff in seams of boats to prevent leaking.

ob'late (ŏb'lāt), *n.* One offered or devoted to the monastic life or to some special religious service or work.

ob·lit'er·ate (ŏb·lĭt'ẽr·āt), *v.* To blot out; to remove completely or destroy.

ob·ses'sion (ŏb·sĕsh'ŭn), *n.* A continued and unreasonable idea or desire.

od'ys·sey (ŏd'ĭ·sĭ), *n.* A long wandering or series of travels.

O·lym'pics (ō·lĭm'pĭks), *n.* Short for Olympic Games, which are athletic contests held every four years.

om'i·nous (ŏm'ĭ·nŭs), *adj.* Foretelling evil; like an evil omen.

on'yx (ŏn'ĭks; ō'nĭks), *n.* A quartz stone showing parallel layers of different shades of color.

O'ra et La·bo'ra (ō'rà ĕt lăb·ō'rà). Latin words, meaning "Pray and Work."

or'der·ly (ôr'dẽr·lĭ), *n.* A soldier who attends a superior officer and carries his orders.

Ou·ang' (ou·yăng'), **Paul.**

pack'et (păk'ĕt), *n.* A vessel carrying passengers, mails, dispatches, and goods, with fixed sailing days.

Pa'dre (pä'drĭ; Sp. pä'drà), *n.* A Spanish word, meaning "father," and used to address a priest.

pae'an (pē'an), *n.* A hymn of praise, joy, or triumph.

Pal'o·mar (păl'ô·mär), **Mount.** A peak in southern California, on which is an astronomical observatory.

pam'pas (păm'paz), *n. pl.* Vast, treeless plains, especially in Argentina.

pa·pa'ya (pä·pä'yä), *n.* A large, oblong, yellow fruit of a tropical American tree; also, the tree.

Par'the·non (pär'thê·nŏn), *n.* A famous temple of Athena, built on the Acropolis at Athens in the fifth century B.C.

Pe'dro (pē'drō). A Spanish name, meaning *Peter.*

Pei'ping' (bā'pĭng'). Former capital of China.

pe'nal (pē'năl), *adj.* Having to do with punishment or penalties.

pen·tath'lon (pĕn·tăth'lŏn), *n.* An athletic contest in which each contestant takes part in five events.

pent'house' (pĕnt'hous'), *n.* An apartment built on the roof of a building.

per'go·la (pûr'gô·là), *n.* An arbor or bower, especially one treated architecturally.

per·vade' (pẽr·vād'), *v.* To spread through; to pass through all parts of anything.

pe·tec'ca (pĭ·tĕk'à), *n.* A game popular in Brazil.

phe·nom'e·non (fê·nŏm'ê·nŏn), *n.* A fact or event that is rare or has unique significance.

phil'o·mel (fĭl'ô·mĕl), *n.* In poetic use, the nightingale.

phil'ter (fĭl'tẽr), *n.* A drink or charm supposed to produce a magic effect.

pi·az'za (pĭ·ăz'à; It. pyät'tsä), *n.* An open square in an Italian town.

Pic'card', Au'guste' (pē'kàr', ou'gŭst'). A Swiss physicist.

Pie·tà' (pyä·tä'). A statue of the Blessed Virgin sorrowing over the dead Body of her Divine Son.

pin'to (pĭn'tō), *n.* A piebald horse or pony.

pit (pĭt), *v.* To match against another.

pitch'blende' (pĭch'blĕnd'), *n.* A brownish-black mineral, a source of radium and uranium.

plac'id (plăs'ĭd), *adj.* Peaceful; calm.

plague (plāg), *n.* A serious contagious disease which occurs in several forms and causes many deaths; also, anything that grievously troubles or afflicts.

plumb (plŭm) **line.** A line having a weight or bob at one end, used to find out whether a thing is straight or to measure the depth of water.

point lace. Lace made with a needle on a parchment or paper pattern; needlepoint lace.

Pol'y·ne'si·a (pŏl'ĭ·nē'shĭ·à). The islands of the central Pacific Ocean.

por'tent (pōr'tĕnt), *n.* An event or situation which foretells something, especially something evil; a forewarning.

post'hu·mous (pŏs'tụ·mŭs), *adj.* Occurring after one's death.

Pot'a·wat'o·mi (pŏt'a·wŏt'ŏ·mĭ). An Indian of an Algonquian tribe formerly dwelling on the western shores of Lake Michigan.

po·ten'ti·al'i·ty (pō·tĕn'shĭ·ăl'ĭ·tĭ), *n.* A possibility; something that may exist or occur.

pot'tage (pŏt'ĭj), *n.* An old-fashioned term for a dish of cooked vegetables and meat, a stew.

Prague (präg). The capital of Czechoslovakia.

pre·car'i·ous·ly (prē·kâr'ĭ·ŭs·lĭ), *adv.* In an insecure way; uncertainly.

pred'e·ces'sor (prĕd'ē·sĕs'ēr), *n.* One who has preceded another in a position, office, etc.

pre'ma·ture' (prē'ma·tūr'), *adj.* Happening before the usual or proper time.

pres·tige' (prĕs·tēzh', prĕs'tĭj), *n.* Influence derived from general admiration or esteem; power to command admiration or esteem.

Pré'vot' (prā'vō'). A companion of the famed aviator Saint-Exupéry.

pro·fi'cien·cy (prō·fĭsh'ĕn·sĭ), *n.* Skill; expertness.

pro'té·gé (prō'tĕ·zhā), *n.* A person who is under the care and protection of another person.

Pro'ven·çal' (prō'vän·säl'), *adj.* Of or pertaining to Provence, France, its inhabitants or language.

Pro'vence' (prō'väNs'). An old province in southeastern France.

pyre (pīr), *n.* A heap of wood or other burnable material on which a dead body is burned as a funeral rite; hence any pile to be burned.

quad·ren'ni·al (kwŏd·rĕn'ĭ·ăl), *adj.* Occurring once in four years; also, lasting through four years.

Queens (kwēnz). A borough of New York City.

quirk (kwûrk), *n.* A peculiar trait, habit, or characteristic of a person; an individual peculiarity.

Rac·caud' (rà·kō').

Ra'fa·el (răf'a·ĕl).

ran'cho (răn'chō), *n.* In Spanish America, a farm as distinguished from a large estate.

rank and file. The ordinary people of a community or nation.

Ra'pha·el (răf'ā·ĕl). A great Italian artist.

rat'i·fi·ca'tion (răt'ĭ·fĭ·kā'shŭn), *n.* Act of being ratified; confirmation; sanction.

rav'age (răv'ĭj), *v.* To lay waste; to plunder; to ruin.

re'af·firm' (rē'a·fûrm'), *v.* To say again definitely; to repeat with emphasis.

re·ju've·nant (rē·jōō'vē·nănt), *adj.* Rendered young or youthful again.

re·lin'quish (rē·lĭng'kwĭsh), *v.* To give up; to withdraw from.

re·luc'tant (rē·lŭk'tănt), *adj.* Not eager to act; unwilling.

rent (rĕnt), *v.* Torn apart; split.

re·plete' (rē·plēt'), *adj.* Supplied in abundance; filled to capacity.

Re'yes, Ma·nuel' (rā'yās, mä·nwäl').

rick'sha (rĭk'shä), *n.* Short, colloquial term for *jinrikisha*, a small, two-wheeled vehicle, drawn by one or more men.

Ri'o de Ja·nei'ro (rē'ō dä zha·nä'rō). The capital of Brazil.

Ro·ga'tion (rō·gā'shŭn) **Day.** One of the three days before Ascension Thursday, when special prayers are offered for plentiful crops.

Rom'a·ny (rŏm'a·nĭ). The language of the gypsies.

Ros·com'mon (rŏs·kŏm'ŭn). A county of Ireland.

ro·tun'da (rō·tŭn'da), *n.* A large round room in a public building.

ru'mi·nate (rōō'mĭ·nāt), *v.* To bring to mind and consider again and again.

Sa·cré' Cœur' (sà·krä' kûr'). The Church of the Sacred Heart on Montmartre's hill in Paris.

sa·fa'ri (sa·fä'rĭ), *n.* A journey or expedition; a caravan, with carriers, carts, etc.; especially, a hunting expedition. *v.* To travel in a safari.

sage (sāj), *n.* A very wise man; a profound philosopher.

Saint'-Ex'u'pé'ry', An'toine' de (săN'-tāg'zū'-pä'rē', äN'twàn' dē). French aviator and writer.

St. Stephen's gate. The east portal of the wall that surrounds the city of Jerusalem. *See also* Damascus gate.

St. Stephen's tower. The lofty Gothic spire of St. Stephen's Cathedral in Vienna, Austria.

San Car'los (sän kär'lōs).

San·gal'lo, Giu·lia'no da (säng·gäl'lô, jōō·lyä'nô dä). Italian architect, sculptor, and military engineer.

San Ma·ri'no (sän mä·rē'nô). A small republic in east-central Italy.

Sa·pay·sa' Lu (sä·pä·sä' rōt).

sa·van'nah (sa·văn'a), *n.* A treeless plain; an open level region.

Sax'on (săk'sŭn). One of the race that migrated from northwestern Germany to England in the fifth and sixth centuries.

schoon'er (skōōn'ēr), *n.* A fore-and-aft rigged vessel, typically having only two masts.

sec'u·lar (sĕk'ū·lēr), *n.* As applied to priests and seminarians, one who belongs to the diocesan clergy and not to a religious community.

---

lāte, alwâys, ăm, *a*ppear, ärm, àsk, câre, sof*a*, hē, ênough, nĕt, silĕnt, makēr, hēre, ride, ĭn, possĭble, ōld, ôbey, nŏt, cônnect, sôft, hôrse, ūse, ûnite, ŭs, circŭs, bûrn, mōōn, tŏŏk, oil, out, that, thin, nat*ū*re, boN.

Sep·pa'la (sā·pä'lȧ), **Leonard.**

sex'tant (sĕks'tănt), *n.* An instrument for measuring angular distances, used at sea to observe altitudes in order to determine latitude and longitude.

sheer (shēr), *adj.* Very steep, without break; as, a *sheer* cliff rose from the sea.

ship (shĭp), *v.* To take in over the side; to have a wave come in over the side of a boat.

si (sē), *adv.* A Spanish word, meaning "yes."

Si'mon of Cy·re'ne (sī'mŭn ŏv sī rē'nê). A resident of Cyrene in Libya, who was forced to carry the Cross of Our Saviour for part of the journey to Calvary (Matthew 27; Mark 15).

si'mon-pur'ist (sī'mŭn pūr'ĭst), *n.* A person who is very particular, or oversolicitous, about purity or nicety. *Simon-pure* has its origin in the plight of a Quaker, in fiction, who has been impersonated and has to prove his identity.

Si'ren (sī'rĕn), *n.* In Greek mythology, one of a group of minor deities who lured sailors to destruction by their singing.

Sis'tine (sĭs'tēn) **Chapel.** The Pope's chapel and the principal chapel of the Vatican Palace.

slew (slōō), *v.* To slue; to turn or twist.

sloop (slōōp), *n.* A sailing vessel with one mast, a fore-and-aft rig, and a single jib.

So·bies'ki (sŏ·byĕs'kê). John III, king of Poland, who defeated the Turks at Vienna and saved Christendom in Europe.

sod hut, *n.* A shelter with walls built of sod or turf.

sol'je (sŏl'yĕ), *n.* A Norwegian word for *brooch.*

som·nam'bu·list (sŏm·năm'bŭ·lĭst), *n.* A person who walks in his sleep.

so'nar (sō'när), *n.* A supersonic detector used to detect the location of a submarine. It can receive sound waves above the range of human hearing.

sons of Abraham, *n. pl.* The chosen people of God.

Southern Cross. Four bright stars visible in the Southern Hemisphere and appearing to be the ends of a Latin cross.

Sperry compass. A gyrocompass for ships invented in 1911, by Elmer Sperry; a compass more reliable than a magnetic compass.

spher'i·cal (sfĕr'ĭ·kăl), *adj.* Shaped like a sphere, or globe.

spindle and shuttle. On a spinning wheel or loom, the *spindle* is a round, tapering rod or pin on which the threads are twisted and wound. The *shuttle* carries the thread back and forth from side to side between the threads that run lengthwise.

spud wrench. A type of wrench that fits into a socket. It is used especially in putting together fittings having an outside thread which might be broken by an ordinary wrench.

stew'ard (stū'ĕrd), *n.* A manager or supervisor; a person employed to manage domestic concerns, collect rents, keep accounts, etc.; thus, one who acts as a caretaker.

sto'ic (stō'ĭk), *adj.* Not moved by pain or pleasure; strong and patient through suffering.

sub'si·dize (sŭb'sĭ·dīz), *v.* To aid or support with money, especially money from the government.

sub'tle·ty (sŭt'l·tĭ), *n.* Something subtle; a delicate distinction.

suf'fer·ance (sŭf'ĕr·ăns), *n.* Patient endurance; power or ability to endure.

su'per·nat'u·ral (sū'pĕr·năt'ŭ·răl), *adj.* Having to do with an existence beyond nature; belonging to an invisible world.

su'per·struc'ture (sū'pĕr·strŭk'tŭr), *n.* A structure or edifice built on, or as a vertical extension of, something else; that which is raised on a foundation.

surge (sûrj), *v.* To rise in waves or billows; to move like waves.

sut·tee' pyre (sŭ·tē' pīr), *n.* The funeral pile on which a Hindu widow cremates herself, or is cremated, with her husband's body.

tac'tile (tăk'tĭl), *adj.* Of or relating to the sense of touch; capable of being felt or touched; tangible.

Tam·pi'co (tăm·pē'kō). A seaport on the eastern coast of Mexico.

tar'ry (tăr'ĭ), *v.* To delay; to be slow in acting; to linger or loiter.

Tch·ang'-Ping (chĭ·ăng'pĭng), **Timothy.**

ten'sion (tĕn'shŭn), *n.* Mental or nervous strain; anxiety; worry.

ten'ta·tive (tĕn'tȧ·tĭv), *adj.* Temporary; experimental; not fully worked out or thought out.

ten'u·ous (tĕn'ŭ·ŭs), *adj.* Rare or light; not dense; also, unsubstantial; flimsy.

Teu'ton (tū'tŏn). One of the race inhabiting northwestern Europe—German, Dane, Hollander, Swede, or Norwegian.

the·ol'o·gy (thē·ŏl'ŏ·jĭ), *n.* The science which treats of God and the things of God.

till'er (tĭl'ĕr), *n.* A lever used to turn a vessel's rudder from side to side.

tout'ed (tōōt'ĕd), *v.* Loudly proclaimed.

traf'fick·er (trăf'ĭk·ĕr), *n.* One who transports or does business in goods; one who engages in illicit sales or purchases.

tran'sient (trăn'shĕnt), *adj.* Short-lived; passing quickly from existence.

trap'pings (trăp'ĭngz), *n. pl.* Ornaments; decorations; showy dress.

Trap'pist (trăp'ĭst). A monk of an austere religious order established at the monastery of La Trappe, in Normandy.

Tri'ton (trī'tŏn), *n.* In Greek mythology, a sea demigod who raised or lowered the waves by blowing on a trumpet.

Trum'bull (trŭm'bŭl), **Lyman.** Senator from Illinois, 1855–1873. In 1864 he introduced the resolution which became the basis of the Thirteenth Amendment to the Constitution abolishing slavery.

Tsao (tō), **Emmanuel.** A Chinese bishop.

turn'coat' (tûrn'kōt'), *n.* A person who changes his beliefs; one who forsakes his party or his principles.

U·kraine' (û·krān'). A republic of the Soviet Socialist Republics, just north of the Black Sea.

un·al'·ien·a·ble (ŭn·āl'yĕn·à·b'l), *adj.* Not capable of being taken away, surrendered, or transferred.

u'sur·pa'tion (ū'zẽr·pā'shŭn; ū'sẽr·pā'shŭn), *n.* The illegal seizure of power, position, or privileges.

Va·le'ri·o (và·lẽr'ĭ·ō).

ve'he·mence (vē'ê·mĕns), *n.* Force; violence; great ardor.

veld, vĕldt (vĕlt; fĕlt), *n.* A South African tract of grassland, in which there may also be scattered shrubs or trees.

ven'er·a·ble (vĕn'ẽr·à·b'l), *adj.* Deserving of honor or respect because of virtures, great age, importance, etc.

ven'om·ous (vĕn'ŭm·ŭs), *adj.* Full of spite, malice, etc.

ver'ti·go (vûr'tĭ·gō), *n.* Dizziness.

Vi'a del'la Con·ci'li·a·zi·o'ne (vē'ä dĕl'lä kŏn·chē'lê·ä·tsê·ō'nä). Italian words, meaning "Street of the Conciliation."

Vi'a di Por'ta An·gel'i·ca (vē'ä dê pŏr'tä än·jĕl'ĭ·kä). Italian words, meaning "Street of the Angel Gate."

vi·car'i·ate (vi·kâr'ĭ·åt), *n.* In a missionary country, an area or territory similar to a diocese of a nonmission country.

Vi·cen'te, Ni'ta (vê·sĕn'tå, nē'tä).

Vic·to'ri·an e'ra (vĭk·tō'rĭ·ăn ē'rà). The time during which Queen Victoria reigned in England.

vil'la·nelle' (vĭl'à·nĕl'), *n.* A fixed form of verse, chiefly French.

Vine'yard (vĭn'yẽrd) **Haven.** A town on the northern coast of Martha's Vineyard.

Vineyard Sound. A body of water northwest of Martha's Vineyard, which connects with Nantucket Sound on the northeast and the Atlantic Ocean on the southwest.

vi'ol (vī'ŭl), *n.* A medieval stringed instrument from which the violin, viola, violoncello, and contrabass were developed.

void (void), *adj.* Empty; vacant. *n.* An empty or unfilled space.

War'saw (wôr'sô). Capital of Poland.

West Chop. A small town on the western side of the harbor of Vineyard Haven.

wil'de·beest' (wĭl'dĕ·bēst'; vĭl'dĕ·bäst'), *n.* A South African name for a wild beast; the gnu or African antelope.

wind'ward (wĭnd'wẽrd), *adj.* On the side toward the point from which the wind blows.

with'ers (wĭth'ẽrz), *n. pl.* The ridge between the shoulder bones of a horse.

wiz'ened (wĭz''nd), *adj.* Shriveled up; withered; dried and wrinkled.

wont (wŭnt), *adj.* In the habit of doing; accustomed.

Yang'tze' (yäng'tsē'). The principal river in China.

Ying·shang' (yĭng·shĭ·ăng'). A city of China.

Za'ko·pa'ne (zä·kô·pä'nĕ). A town in the southern part of Poland. It is the chief summer resort and winter sports center.

za'ny (zā'nĭ), *adj.* Being clownish or silly.

Zan'zi·bar' (zăn'zĭ·bär'). A territory of East Africa; also, an island and town in this territory.

zeph'yr (zĕf'ẽr), *n.* A soft, gentle wind.

Zik'a·wei (sĭk'à·wän). A suburb of Shanghai.

Zi'ta (zē'tä).

---

lāte, alwâys, ăm, ăppear, ärm, àsk, câre, sofà, hē, ênough, nĕt, silĕnt, makẽr, hẽre, rīde, ĭn, possĭble, ōld, ôbey, nŏt, cŏnnect, sôft, hôrse, ūse, ûnite, ŭs, circŭs, bûrn, mōōn, tŏŏk, oil, out, that, thin, natûre, boɴ.

Reading 8 - These Are Our Horizons
ANSWER KEY

Page 25
1. C	7. C
2. NT	8. I
3. C	9. NT
4. C	10. C
5. I	11. NT
6. C	12. NT

Page 34
WHAT IS YOUR OPINION?
Student answers.

Page 46
1. Madeline	5. Christine
2. Katrin	6. Nels
3. Papa	7. Mama
4. Madeline	

Page 52
CONTRASTING AND COMPARING
1. Suggested contrasts:
   Jewish, Catholic
   cobbler, priest
   uneducated, educated
   obscure, famous
2. Student answer.

DRAWING CONCLUSIONS
   b.

KNOWING HOMONYMS
   grate; kneads; pare; alter; reed; deer;
   weigh; hear; tolled; isle; reel; herd; sun;
   seen; daze

Page 56
1. Suggested answer: nostalgic, prayerful
2. The central part prayer had in the
   children's lives showed them how
   important it was.
3. That it is also good to fulfill the
   obligations of one's state of life.
4. By showing how the author's father
   accomplished it.

Page 65
SKIMMING TO PROVE POINTS
1. page 61, paragraph 2, The...self-
   forgetful.
2. page 61, paragraph 2, "We"...brother.
3. page 61, paragraph 3, Although...feats.
4. page 61, paragraph 4, My...murmur.
5. page 62, paragraph 1, At...himself.
6. page 62, paragraph 2, Her...course.
7. page 62, paragraph 2, This...much.

Page 88
ORGANIZING MATERIAL
1. (2)The state committee holds a public
   hearing.
   (3)The state issues a certificate.
   (4)District supervisors are chosen, two
   appointed by the state and three elected
   by the first two.
   (5)The five supervisors, together with
   government experts, study the land and
   work out a plan to prevent erosion.
2. Student answer.

Page 98
EVALUATING STATEMENTS
1. F	6. O
2. F	7. F
3. O	8. F
4. F	9. O
5. O	10. F

Page 114
SENSING EMOTIONS
1. The doctor was sympathetic; Cress was
   disappointed.
2. Cress was frustrated.
3. Cress was lonely.
4. Cress was afraid.
5. Cress was amused.
6. Cress was startled.
7. Cress was worried.

8. Cress was in pain.
9. Cress was relieved.
10. Cress was apprehensive.
11. Cress was relieved.
12. Cress was concerned.
13. Cress was horrified.
14. Cress was worried.
15. Scott was feeling the weight of responsibility.
16. Cress was relieved.

Page 118
USING REFERENCE MATERIAL
1. Look up this answer in the dictionary. (a papal letter to the bishops of the church as a whole or to those in one country)
2. at Baptism
3. The liturgy is the official worship of God by the Church.
4. It begins with Advent.
5. It is the movement aimed at achieving active, intelligent, and fruitful participation of the people in the liturgy of the Church.

INTERPRETING A PSALM
1. All of creation should praise God. (It was believed at the time that there was water above the sky.)
2. God created the world simply by willing it to be created.
3. Everything in creation has a purpose and shall fulfill that purpose until the end of time.
4. Man by his free choice can will to praise God. All other creatures do not *choose* to praise God; just by existing and following their natural instincts they praise God. Man's praise is superior because it is freely willed.

USING THE DICTIONARY
Student should look up the words in the dictionary.

Page 124
Student answers.

Page 138
1. NC. Nine states must ratify the Constitution if it is to become the basic law of the Union.
2. NC. He wanted it to include a Bill of Rights and a clause forbidding the importation of slaves.
3. NC. He was a former governor of Virginia.
4. C.
5. NC. It was due to his logical arguments.
6. C.
7. C.
8. NC. The resolution was carried by a margin of only 4 votes.

Page 152
WRITING A CHARACTER SKETCH
Student answers.

Page 170
NOTING CONTRASTS
Suggested answers:

Rise: Jim is noticed by Newman; He joins the scrub team; he is invited to join the track team; he makes the Olympic team; he wins the pentathlon and decathlon; he is awarded his prizes and lauded when he returns home.

Fall: A reporter discovers Thorpe had played semi-pro ball; the AAU declares him guilty of violating the amateur rules; he returns the trophies and his records are stripped.

NOTING THE AUTHOR'S VIEWPOINT
Student answers.

Page 177
READING CRITICALLY
1. Barnaby tries to remember the quotation, Barnaby tries to open the car door with the ignition key, Julie starts to cry when she thinks the horse will bite her. (Answers will vary.)
2. She is thinking of her own wants, not her father's. (Answers will vary.)

3. Nell comforts Julie when she starts to cry, but also disciplines her. (Answers will vary.)
4. No; his comments show that he really wanted to see the horse himself.
5. Student answer.
6. Student answer.

Page 186

SUMMARIZING
Student answers.

FINDING SYNONYMS

1. h	9. g
2. n	10. c
3. l	11. b
4. j	12. d
5. a	13. o
6. i	14. k
7. m	15. f
8. e	

Page 191

FOLLOWING THE SEQUENCE OF EVENTS
1. The architect conceives a plan for the building as a whole.
2. Draftsmen elaborate on the plans.
3. A building contractor makes detailed sketches of each floor, room, and beam in the structure.
4. Iron ore is dug from Lake Superior mines.
5. Beams are trimmed and shaped into columns, girders, and trusses.
6. Two steel cables are dropped to the pavement from the upper end of the boom, and a beam is locked onto it.
7. The beam ascends to the thirty-fifth floor.
8. A man gives the signal, the engineer on the pavement stops the engine, and the girder hangs motionless.
9. Another signal is given, the girder comes forward, and a man takes hold of the cable and swings out.
10. The worker takes his wrench and rivets the girder into its place.

USING SUFFIXES
1. dangerous
2. careless
3. vigilant
4. massive
5. laborious
6. motionless
7. successive

Page 197

RECOGNIZING MULTIPLE MEANINGS OF WORDS

1. a	5. a
2. e	6. b
3. d	7. h
4. g	8. f

RECOGNIZING SEQUENCE
1. The Associated Press, 1900
2. The Havas Agency, 1835
3. The Reuter News Agency, 1849
4. The Wolff Bureau, 1917

Page 207

MAKING A CHART
Student answers.

NOTING CONTRASTS
Suggested answers:
awakening—asleep
laughter—sorrow
static—motion
smiles—suffering
happiness—misery

EXPLAINING PASSAGES
Student answers.

Page 214

DETERMINING THE AUTHOR'S VIEWPOINT
Suggested answer: b.

MAKING COMPARISONS
1. The story.
2. It tells the threat of the disease, the cause of it, and the names of the doctors who discovered a cure.
3. The story.
4. The story.
5. Student answer.

BUILDING ADJECTIVES
1. dangerous
2. feverish
3. dramatic
4. conditional
5. risky
6. thoughtful

Page 233
JUSTIFYING THE TITLE
Student answers.
APPRECIATING DESCRIPTIVE PHRASES
Student answers.

Page 244
1. Lazarists (Vincentians), Little Brothers of St. John the Baptist, Jesuits, Franciscans.
2. France, Belgium, Italy
3. Shanghai, Hankow, Yingshang
4. The Little Brothers of St. John the Baptist.
5. Rice, noodles, meat, fish, vegetables, bean curd.
6. Shanghai and Hankow.
7. The Society for the Propagation of the Faith.

Page 249
RECALLING DETAILS
1. Hawaiian
2. Belgium
3. Vermont
4. 1887
5. 44
6. Theodore Roosevelt
PROVING STATEMENTS
1. "...a place where lepers might hastily and conveniently be hidden from the sight of healthy men."
2. "About the uneasy years before this man Dutton sailed for Molokai we have much scattered information...after the wreck of his disastrous marriage, he took his troubled heart to the Church of Rome...even after months of meditation in the Trappist monastery...he had found no peace."

3. "The vast litter of letters and diaries left behind him bear witness to his love of his country."
4. "Theodore Roosevelt read that letter... in another moment he had the Navy Department on the telephone, and in an hour the cable was catching the admiral in Honolulu with a change of sailing orders."

Page 255
1. e	6. g
2. a	7. d
3. j	8. i
4. b	9. f
5. c	10. h

Page 267
THINKING IT OUT
1. Being a native of Finland, he is more accustomed to cold weather.
2. Because it is rich in natural resources.
3. Tar, salt, bitumen.
4. Radium and uranium.
5. It is important for the building of nuclear weapons.
6. They can be shared by many different countries.
7. It is used for X-rays.

Page 276
ILLUSTRATING THE STORY
A few suggested answers:
air that vibrated to the drone of bees
a thousand springs . . . fed the edge of the ever thirsty plain
The savannahs rolled on and on in changeless succession.
IDENTIFYING LOCAL COLOR WORDS
safaris, mimosa, veldt, zebra, wildebeest, kongoni, eland, impala, savannah, Zanzibar, hyenas
ENJOYING SUSPENSE
Student answers.

Page 285

1. reproduce
2. savory
3. occasionally
4. perpendicular
5. die
6. crevice, avalanche
7. occasionally
8. void
9. crevice
10. enraptured

Page 298

1. c
2. f
3. d
4. h
5. b
6. a
7. g
8. e

Page 306

Student answers.

Page 308

Student answers.

Page 319

IDENTIFYING DEFINITE AND INDEFINITE IDEAS

eighty days - d
60,000 miles - d
in the 1880's - I
few wonders - I
age of eleven - d
six-weeks tour - d
half-century - d
years ahead of Doyle - I
fifteen publishers - d
large sum of money - I
only minutes to spare - I
a hundred years ago - d
thousands of words - I
death in 1905 -d.

EVALUATING MATERIAL

1. F. The island was near Nantes.
2. F. He lived for 77 years; he spent less than one traveling.
3. F. He inspired many scientists through his writings.
4. F. His father was a lawyer.
5. T.
6. F. His first book was Five Weeks in a Balloon.
7. T.
8. F. He received the Legion of Honor.
9. T.
10. T.

Page 334

EXPRESSING OPINIONS

Student answers.

DRAWING INFERENCES

1. p. 323. "When the sea...sunstroke, perhaps."
2. pp. 323-4. "It was ourselves...urge to laughter."
3. p. 328. "To get hold...sausage machine."
4. p. 332. "He realized...had none."
5. p. 332. "The we suddenly...the two men."
6. p. 333. "But otherwise...on board."

Page 358

USING THE GLOSSARY

Student should look up these words in a dictionary.

ANSWERING SPECIFIC QUESTIONS

1. The young nun to whom the letter is addressed.
2. The Benedictines.
3. Bethlehem, Connecticut.
4. The receiver selecting the Host he will receive in Holy Communion after its consecration.
5. The nuns of the cloistered community.

Page 366

1. entirely within Rome
2. less than one square mile
3. a magnificent church in Vatican City
4. the second
5. Vatican Palace
6. the Pope's cathedral and the Mother Church of Christendom
7. the Holy Father's summer residence near Rome
8. the Vatican Palace